THE RACE FOR THE
ATOM BOMB

'All anti-Nazis knew that we were the only hope of destroying the fascist regime.'

Pavel Sudoplatov. *Special Tasks*

THE RACE FOR THE
ATOM BOMB

How Soviet Russia Stole the
Secrets of the Manhattan Project

JOHN HARTE

Pen & Sword
MILITARY

AN IMPRINT OF PEN & SWORD BOOKS LTD.
YORKSHIRE – PHILADELPHIA

First published in Great Britain in 2023 by
PEN AND SWORD MILITARY
An imprint of
Pen & Sword Books Limited
Yorkshire – Philadelphia

Typeset in Times New Roman 10/12 by
SJmagic DESIGN SERVICES, India.
Printed and bound in the UK by CPI Group (UK) Ltd.

Pen & Sword Books Limited incorporates the imprints of Atlas, Archaeology, Aviation, Discovery, Family History, Fiction, History, Maritime, Military, Military Classics, Politics, Select, Transport, True Crime, Air World, Frontline Publishing, Leo Cooper, Remember When, Seaforth Publishing, The Praetorian Press, Wharncliffe Local History, Wharncliffe Transport, Wharncliffe True Crime and White Owl.

For a complete list of Pen & Sword titles please contact
PEN & SWORD BOOKS LIMITED
47 Church Street, Barnsley, South Yorkshire S70 2AS, United Kingdom
E-mail: enquiries@pen-and-sword.co.uk
Website: www.pen-and-sword.co.uk

Or
PEN AND SWORD BOOKS
1950 Lawrence Rd, Havertown, PA 19083, USA
E-mail: Uspen-and-sword@casematepublishers.com
Website: www.penandswordbooks.com

Contents

WORLD CRISIS

Introduction   2

Chapter 1   Modern Times   8
Chapter 2   An Awkward Undergraduate   12
Chapter 3   A Tortured Adolescence   17
Chapter 4   The Magical Spell of Physics   22
Chapter 5   Different Strokes for Different Folks   26
Chapter 6   The World Beckons   30
Chapter 7   Oppie   34

REDS

Chapter 8   The Red Scare   40
Chapter 9   We the Living   44
Chapter 10   Political Activists   48
Chapter 11   The Atomic Bomb Project   52
Chapter 12   Who Was Kitty Harris?   56
Chapter 13   The Nuclear Programme   64
Chapter 14   Germany's Secret Weapons   70
Chapter 15   The Intellectual and the Militarist   73

DESTROYER OF WORLDS

Chapter 16   Merchants of Death   80
Chapter 17   The Pied Piper of Los Alamos   85
Chapter 18   Achieving Critical Mass   90
Chapter 19   A Magical Place   95
Chapter 20   Dangerous Associations   100
Chapter 21   Problem Number One   106
Chapter 22   The Race for the Atom Bomb   113
Chapter 23   The Future of the Human Race   119

SOVIET SECRET AGENTS

Chapter 24   Soviet Spies Saving the World   124
Chapter 25   The Experimental Atomic Test   129
Chapter 26   A Japanese Target   135
Chapter 27   Japan   139

Chapter 28   Unconditional Surrender   142
Chapter 29   Back to Normal   146
Chapter 30   A World Transformed   151
Chapter 31   American Genius   155

WITCH-HUNT

Chapter 32   Enemies in Waiting   162
Chapter 33   Soviet Russia's Atom Bomb   166
Chapter 34   Conspiracy Theories   171
Chapter 35   The Venona Revelations   176
Chapter 36   Witch-hunt   183
Chapter 37   The Problem of Survival   187
Chapter 38   The Hidden Struggle for the H-bomb   192

HUMILIATION

Chapter 39   Trial by Hysteria   198
Chapter 40   A Letter of Indictment   202
Chapter 41   One Thing is Certain   207

Timeline   213
About the Author   215
Notes   217
Index   232

WORLD CRISIS

Introduction

After observing with awe the first ever explosion of a nuclear bomb on 16 July 1945, the physicist Robert Oppenheimer, who was responsible for making it, famously quoted the most significant words from the Hindu *Bhagavad-Gita*: 'Now I am become Death, the destroyer of worlds.'

He was a haunted man.

To encapsulate who and what J. Robert Oppenheimer was behind his public image as an American genius, to a new generation of readers unaccustomed to analysing and assessing history with a cool sense of proportion, is no easy task with so much false news nowadays. Digital technologies and social media have distracted us from our extraordinary achievements into an artificial world that separates us from our past as if it no longer influences us today or tomorrow. And yet, Oppenheimer was a national hero in America in 1945, even known as the 'Father of the Atom Bomb'. But he was publicly humiliated in 1954 by the head of the Atomic Energy Commission and President Eisenhower, who accused him of being a national security risk. In only nine years he had leapt from triumph and fame to tragedy and distrust.[1]

Robert Oppenheimer was a passionate supporter of social justice, and a man who felt personally responsible for everyone. The most disturbing fact about him at the time was that he had apparently joined the Communist Party in 1937. But nobody knew for sure. Mixing with communists certainly appeared to give him a sense of purpose. It established most of his personal relationships, and comforted his conscience that he was doing something to help victims of injustice. But the mere suspicion of disloyalty to the United States of America would result in his downfall.

Marxist doctrine was a paradox that had overwhelmed Russia after a bloody revolution against Tsarist tyranny in October 1917. All sorts of people in the West reached out hopefully for communism in the early 1930s, when the capitalist system appeared to have collapsed with the New York Stock Exchange, and millions were unemployed and even pauperised.

Most communists had learned to conceal their beliefs by 1937, because communism was viewed as a threat to a decent society with family values. Few are left in the West since Marxism was discredited by the end of the Soviet Socialist regime, so that the atmosphere of the times and its most significant political nuances are almost entirely lost to us. Anyone alive who witnessed the phenomenon, and watched the tragedy of that critical period unfold, would have been as close as we

2

can be to an era of wishful thinking, when romantic Party members chose delusions because they could not handle the reality of what appeared to be a doomed world. The 1920s and 1930s were part of a confusing and depressing era, ambiguous and paradoxical, when no one knew how to galvanise the failing economy. There were only personal opinions and untried theories about how to create an ideal society.

I am one of the few people left who experienced that situation at first-hand and observed history unfold tragically as I grew up. Unlike most authors writing about the world crisis in retrospect, I watched the results of a post-First World War Depression play out around me in England – far too young to be keenly aware of what I was witnessing, because I did not always understand its significance. I had to catch up with it later on.

The mood of the times when Britain was virtually leaderless and close to collapse, and of so many subtle nuances in its pre-war and wartime culture, gradually became etched in my mind, so that I can still retrieve them for further examination, reflection and analysis. So perhaps it was inevitable that I should become an investigative journalist after the Second World War, since the nightmare of the rise in power of Nazi Germany, and the communist delusions, still hovered in my mind.

England was still the centre of the world when I grew up in London. Students were not condemned for their ideals and aspirations, even if empire builders or communist destroyers of empires were thought by some to be misplaced. That was all politics, which was considered to be a dirty business that pre-war society chose to reject. Oppenheimer's experience, on the other hand, was an American tragedy, in which the Red Scare sounded an alarm that sent committed communists scuttling underground for safety.

Hoodwinked

Despite our bland middle-class morality, few young people in Britain were immune from approaches by fascists and communists when I reached my teenage years and took an interest in such oddities. Some of them apparently thought I might be persuaded to join the Communist Party. Fortunately I was too young even to recognise that they thought I might be useful in their alleged crusades, and recruiters gave up at my political innocence. When I finally realised their aims, I found it useful to continue to profess ignorance in order to discourage their approaches.

I could not imagine how any reasonably educated individual with common sense could believe in such a doctrine as Marxism or communism, except for those who saw it as a way to achieve power. And there was the rank and file of so-called 'blind instruments' encouraged to support them – gullible activists now described as 'useful idiots', eager to follow a rallying cry. If that seems like over-simplification of events seen through the eyes of an adolescent, it was because I had not yet discovered the key motive for their dedication to a theory that was no more than wishful thinking.

The most famous exposure of communism at the time came from a former starry-eyed Communist Party member in *Darkness at Noon*.[2]

I was born in London in the same year that Hitler wrote *Mein Kampf* while incarcerated in Landsberg Prison for treason, after his failed rebellion against the Weimar Republic. The year 1925 was a crucial one, almost halfway between the end of the First World War and the outbreak of the next. It was not the best of times to be born in. I sensed its ominous atmosphere when I was only eight years old and absentmindedly turned on the knob of a small radio on my father's desk while reading a book in the library. An explosion of sound came from the loudspeaker, which was tuned far too loudly for the intimacy of the quiet room, and filled it instantly with alarm. I appeared to have caught part of Hitler's 1933 'Enabling Act' of 23 March, which allowed the Reich Government to issue laws without the consent of Germany's parliament. It was the keystone of Hitler's dictatorship of Germany. I hurriedly turned off the noise.

Despite not understanding a word of German, I had recognised anger and hatred in that historic speech to the Reichstag, which told parliament how he had been humiliated by the laughter, the scorn and derision in the Ullstein press at his claim to one day lead the German people. This was the time to sweep aside his humiliation and have his revenge by a determined effort 'to get rid of these people'.[3]

Every dictator has his little list of categories of opponents to destroy in revenge for not supporting him. What is most significant to this story is that it was when the wealthy Robert Oppenheimer in the United States decided he must contribute money to fund the American Communist Party.

The rise to world power of the German Nazis was a critical step in an equation that drove millions of political activists to join the Communist Party in order to prevent Hitler and the Nazis from winning the Second World War. Whether Oppenheimer was a member of the Communist Party or not is a mystery, since much of the information at the time is apparently still classified in the Kremlin as top secret.[4]

What we know with certainty is that in 1939, a group of American scientists led by Leo Szilard and supported by Einstein, warned President Roosevelt that German scientists were working on a secret new and devastating atomic bomb to win the war. We also know for sure that on 24 September 1941, Moscow Centre received a confidential report from a British diplomat named Donald Maclean, who was one of the Kremlin's top NKVD agents within the British Government. He advised Moscow that the United Kingdom had decided to build a plant to manufacture uranium bombs.

As first secretary at the British embassy in Washington DC, Maclean knew everything that had been discussed, decided on, and officially put into action by the government and its atomic section, because he was the secretary on the Combined Policy Committee and possessed the minutes of all its meetings.

Although the idea of making an atomic bomb was inconceivable and more like science fiction at that time, copies of the official documents that Maclean passed on to the Kremlin showed that Britain's War Cabinet had given the go-ahead to 'development of a method for the utilisation of nuclear energy of uranium for the production of explosive substances'.[5]

On 10 March the following year, Stalin's director of NKVD intelligence, Lavrentiy Beria, had informed the Soviet Russian dictator that work was already under way by German scientists to use the nuclear energy of uranium for military purposes.

In May 1942, a professor of physics named George Florev wrote directly to warn Stalin that German scientists might be the first to develop an atom bomb, conceivably during the war.

When the British sabotaged the heavy water installation at Vemork in Norway in February 1943, Stalin knew for certain that an atomic bomb project was not just a wishful theory, but a realistic possibility, since heavy water was essential to turn uranium into plutonium to fuel a nuclear bomb. Stalin realised that no time must be lost in order to prevent British or German scientists from developing the first atomic bomb.[6]

Until the outbreak of world war in September 1939, the Russian effort in atomic physics had been relatively modest; it could not compare with the work done by the two nations then leading in research work, England and Germany. However, Soviet scientists were well aware of the war-making potential of an atom bomb. In 1939, when German scientists first split the atom, A. J. Brodsky, a Soviet scientist, published an article on the separation of uranium isotopes.

It demonstrated that the Soviet Union had already made some theoretical and practical progress. Soviet physicist Igor Tamm told his students that 'a bomb can be built that will destroy a city out to a radius of maybe ten kilometres'.[7]

Nevertheless, it was still only a theory that a uranium or plutonium bomb would actually work. That was when top secret scientific information, taken from the British and Americans, tipped the scales in favour of Soviet Russia targeting the secret Manhattan Project managed in the New Mexico desert by J. Robert Oppenheimer.

The Looming War

I was barely aware of the world outside of my home at the age of eight, when I had heard Hitler's ranting voice on the waves emanating from Radio Luxembourg. So I had not understood the significance of several important clues. They failed to illuminate me until six years later on 1 September 1939, when Prime Minister Neville Chamberlain announced on the radio that we were now at war with Germany.

If I had been bewildered by events that occurred when I was thirteen in 1938, I watched with mystification the following year when my three older brothers volunteered for combat duties in the armed forces and appeared for a brief moment in uniform, before vanishing with other airmen into 'Bomber' Harris's hazardous RAF suicide squadrons. The suddenness of the transformation from peacetime to war was nightmarish for most people in England; particularly since many were politically ignorant at the time.

European politics were also generally unknown in the United States, since America had deliberately isolated itself from European affairs for years.

The communist experience in America was very different from the way it developed in Britain. Most Americans had reacted with fear and panic to the Bolshevik Revolution and civil war that ended in 1923 with the establishment in power of the Soviet Union. Americans visualised a real possibility of losing all they had worked for, including the confiscation of their savings, their home, their livelihood, and family life.

The English Professor Ernest Dobb, on the other hand, was the first academic in Britain to proclaim proudly that he had become a card-carrying member of the Communist Party as early as 1920. He taught at Trinity College in Cambridge. His rebellion against The Establishment came during the rise of Adolf Hitler and his cronies who became the first members of Germany's Nazi Party. Dobb boasted that he was not one of the idealists who became communists in order to help the Soviet Union defeat Nazi Germany. He was a dedicated ideologue who was convinced that capitalism had failed and must be replaced by Marxism:

> Few Western social theorists foresaw just how feeble the economic framework of communist nations in fact was. It had been assumed by millions that planned economies could somehow put an end to the depredations associated with capitalism and could open the way to a more just and fair distribution of wealth and, while it might require temporary sacrifice and hardship, would in the end result in a better world.[8]

Never before had one man mesmerised and manipulated an entire nation to believe so many lies as Hitler did. They, and his murderous intentions on a massive scale, triggered the Second World War.

Dobb lived in a fictional dream world of his own from his introverted teenage years, in which Marxism was a kind of science fiction and the Soviet Union a daydream of 'things to come.' He and millions of others were mesmerised by the science fiction predictions in novels by H. G. Wells and Jules Verne, of machines that would destroy from the air and from beneath the sea.[9]

Viewing fascists and communists in London with curiosity and amazement, I had the rare opportunity to observe and wonder at their fantastic delusions. While still a prep school boy, I watched the Battle of Britain from a rooftop in London. Older and wiser, I shared the experience with others of being bombarded night and day in London by Hitler's secret weapons, the V1 and V2 pilotless aircraft and rocket projectiles. I watched Anglo-American troops training inland from the south-east coast with General Eisenhower, to embark for the cross-Channel invasion of Normandy in Europe, until Nazi Germany was defeated and the Second World War ended.

In the post-war period of confusion and misapprehension, when most people in the West imagined the war was over, I observed the Cold War between Soviet Russia and the West, when Stalin replaced Hitler as public enemy number one. It was followed by the crisis when nuclear missiles were assembled in communist Cuba to threaten the United States with extinction. Several incidents would bring a Third World War very close to erupting against the Soviet Union and Communist China. Finally, there came the moment when the Soviet Union and communism collapsed and vanished like an illusory mirage evaporating in an empty desert.

Hitler's Secret Weapons

The threat of a German nuclear bomb destroying everyone before the Anglo-American Allies could build their own atom bomb had hovered over us like a grim cloud of radiation in the 1940s. German scientists had been working on a number of secret weapons during the Nazi period and beginning of the Second World War, including rocket projectiles, pilotless aircraft, and bacterial warfare. They were already building a nuclear reactor in the hope of producing the first atomic bomb.

The race to avoid annihilation by Nazi Germany depended on the support of Communist Russia, which was our ally. However, a handful of brilliant young students and scientists decided they must pass on nuclear secrets to Stalin's Moscow Centre in order to ensure the defeat of Nazi Germany before Hitler could use an atomic bomb to put an end to Western democracy.

The following story describes how British and American scientists overtook Nazi Germany and Soviet Russia in a race against extinction.

1

Modern Times

The modern world, as we know it, began when the theoretical physicist Albert Einstein published his theory of special relativity in 1905. The theory of relativity is considered to be one of the two pillars of modern physics; the other being quantum mechanics.[1] He would be awarded the Nobel Prize in physics in 1921. Worldwide admiration for Professor Einstein's brilliant mind and his benign and quirky nature also established scientists as popular heroes of the twentieth century.

Another leading theoretical physicist who would someday win a Nobel Prize for his theoretical model of atomic structure, and who charmed Einstein through his warm and gentle personality, was the Danish theoretical physicist Niels Bohr. Both would influence the young Robert Oppenheimer when he went to Cambridge University and worked on his first major paper in theoretical physics.

Oppenheimer was conscious throughout his life of having been born into a privileged position in world affairs as a consequence of his family, who were educated, wealthy, cultured, and well established in American society when he was born – as was Bohr in Denmark in 1885.

If we Google Robert Oppenheimer, we are told he was born on 22 April 1904, in New York City, and that he grew up in a Manhattan apartment adorned with paintings by van Gogh, Cézanne and Gauguin. He was educated at Harvard University, and became a physicist, finally earning the prestigious Enrico Fermi Award. All of it is true. But it is only a tiny fragment of what is needed to understand who and what he was, and his considerable contributions, not only to the United States, but to the entire world.

His personality was a curious one – strong-willed and yet uncertain of himself. Modern and scientific, and yet drawn to the natural world rather than popular urban society. Shy by nature and yet determined, he revealed a high level of intellect at an early age. One of its characteristics was to keep lifting the bar to achieve perfection. He 'was painfully aware of the costs of knowing so much more than his classmates'.

'It's no fun,' he once told a friend, 'to turn the pages of a book and say, "Yes, yes of course, I know that."'[2]

He was preoccupied with his studies almost to a point of being obsessive, and always excelled, finding the symmetry and harmony of ideas as 'perfectly beautiful'. According to his own assessment of himself in retrospect, he was an anxious-to-please little goody-goody whose privileged childhood upbringing left him vulnerable to the onslaughts of 'cruel and bitter things' in the world outside his own milieu.

Justice for All

Americans have always been a nation of immigrants. It is their strength that America has provided extraordinary careers for newcomers from whom the country has benefited. The Oppenheimers were no exception to that experience. Robert's father, Julius, had been born in the German town of Hanau, near Frankfurt, and, according to Robert, his grandfather was 'an untutored peasant and grain trader who had been raised in a hovel in 'an almost medieval German village'.[3]

The sophisticated Robert possessed mixed feelings about his Jewish origins and the tragic yet triumphant history of his race, but – as with many Jewish immigrants who became successful – their reflections on their past tended to be somewhat exaggerated. In fact, in most cases, Jews who lived in tiny rural hamlets or villages in Middle Europe possessed an advantage over their peasant neighbours in that they were often guided by the intellect of an erudite rabbi who maintained moral, ethical, and educational standards that drove their flock to succeed in the hardiest environments. What the best of those learned rabbis managed to do was inculcate a spirit of inquiry. It was based very largely on the Jewish Ten Commandments, or the Golden Rule in which they were encapsulated to 'do unto others what they would like to have done to themselves'.

They established a moral conscience and a code to live by, centred on an aspiration for justice for all.

A trend over centuries was for Jews educated in that way to progress from villages and towns to cities where universities were established, like Budapest, Vienna, Berlin, and Moscow. But, rather than being integrated in a Jewish religious community in New York, the Oppenheimers chose a more American Ethical Culture Society, which was secular and progressive. Evidently, more contemporary society did not feel a need to follow the older traditions of an institutionalised or ritualistic religion in order to follow the guidance of the Golden Rule.[4]

Julius Oppenheimer had arrived in New York in 1888. He had followed in the footsteps of his older brother, Emil, who worked in a warehouse sorting bundles of cloth. It seemed that he too had inherited, or acquired, a drive to improve himself and even excel others. 'Emil and Julius rode out the recession of 1893, and by the turn of the century Julius was a full partner in the firm of Rothfeld, Stern & Company. He dressed to fit the part, always adorned in a white high-collared shirt, a conservative tie and a dark business suit. His manners were as immaculate as his dress.'[5]

As well as his intelligence and skills, Julius was helped in his progress to succeed by his likeability as a cheerful young man. And, like many ambitious young immigrants at that time, despite having no formal academic education, he was a keen reader of the classics, a lover of art and music, and a learner of history. Julius married Ella Friedman in March 1903. They lived in a steeply gabled stone house at 250 West 94th Street, New York City. Robert was born a year later.

An Intellectual Household

Robert's childhood years were influenced by his parents' move to a large apartment that overlooked the Hudson River from the eleventh floor at 155 Riverside Drive. It could be described as luxurious, since it occupied an entire level and was filled with elegant European furniture, and decorated with original post-Impressionist and Fauve paintings. One of their van Goghs alone would sell today for about a hundred million dollars. A young man who grew up in such sublime and sophisticated surroundings could have been forgiven for feeling somewhat patronising towards his family's more crude relatives on the continent of Europe.

The process of assimilation comes easily to mind in considering the comfortable lives of Julius, Ella, and the adolescent Robert Oppenheimer, because it had become fairly typical of poor but successful immigrant families in the United States. An even more meaningful word might be the evolutionary one applied to the Schiffs, the Loebs, the Warburgs, the Guggenheims and the Lewisohns, who were gifted with 'adaptation' or Americanisation – since it was a historic time for 'our crowd' in New York society and Manhattan's bustling economy.

'These German–Jewish families are more than a collective American success story. At the point in time when they were a cohesive, knit, and recognisably distinct part of New York society, they were also the closest thing to Aristocracy – Aristocracy in the best sense – that the city, and perhaps the country, has seen.'[6]

Immigrants who wished to improve their circumstances by finding opportunities in which they could excel were always drawn to countries with higher living standards. And New York was no different in having a mixed population that arrived at different times of upheaval in the old countries. Whereas 'our crowd' came from the more sophisticated and scientific German Empire, most Jewish immigrants came from more backward agricultural countries, including Tsarist Russia (which then included Poland) and the Austro-Hungarian Empire. Those with a German background, who worked in banking and finance, tended to patronise cruder types who came from Poland or Ukraine and earned their living in warehouses or tailoring or shirt-making sweatshops.

Young Robert was brought up with the coaxing voice of his mother ringing in his ears to aim at 'excellence and purpose'. Since German was never spoken now they were Americans, Robert had to learn modern and classical foreign languages at school.

By the time the First World War erupted in Europe in 1914, Julius was a wealthy businessman, and his marriage was a loving partnership. He was a jolly man with a good-natured laugh; an extrovert who loved music, and might burst out with a cheerful song at the dinner table.

Automobiles had only recently replaced horses and carriages, and required a chauffeur to maintain them, and deal with parking problems. So the Oppenheimers drove into the countryside on weekends, seated behind a uniformed chauffeur in their Packard. They owned a luxury summer home on 7 acres at Bay Shore, where Robert learnt to sail as a teenager.

Their loving family home relationship was dominated by Ella's protectiveness towards Robert after her second son died young. Robert was equally devoted to his mother, caught as he was between her refinement and the more natural and expressive nature of his father. She was more adapted to New York society than Julius's friends, whom she found coarse. Her instinctive reaction against their crudeness resulted in Robert's occasional embarrassment at being Jewish among Ella's more refined and fastidious friends, who looked down on those who worked in trade or commerce, whereas their social ambitions favoured banking or the professions.

Ella's instinctive snobbery was no more than the typical friction between first- and second-generation immigrants from backward Europe at the time. So that what occasionally irritated Robert also often produced sparks of brilliance in him and others in the more modern environment of Manhattan.

Tradition

By the time Robert was enrolled in a private school in 1911, his parents were convinced he would be a genius. It was partly his sharp intelligence and his preoccupation with rocks and minerals. The school was run by Felix Adler along several streams of thought that criss-crossed contemporary Europe and North America, and influenced by a feeling for social justice for the oppressed working classes, the poor, and Jews who were victimised by others. Anti-Semitism arose out of envy at their success, and was particularly virulent during economic recessions, when more people lost their jobs and listened discontentedly to the conspiracy theories of popular rabble-rousers.

Most Jews wanted to integrate and look like other Americans, whereas Zionism took a different direction by offering separation for Jews seeking a national homeland where they could live in peace with their own people. Adler's answer to anti-Semitism was education – to become more American than Americans. And yet, such an attempt to outwit anti-Semitism in Hungary, Austria and Germany had not worked. On the contrary, success created greater visibility and envy.[7]

In the summer of 1877, 'the Jewish community was scandalised when Joseph Seligman, the wealthiest and most prominent Jew of German origin in New York, was rudely turned away, as a Jew, from the Grand Union Hotel in Saratoga, New York. Over the next few years, the doors of other elite institutions, not only hotels but social clubs and preparatory private schools, suddenly slammed shut against Jewish membership.'[8]

Even with hard work and material success, it was not easy to be a Jew in the United States at the beginning of the twentieth century. Adler's 'ethical culture' encouraged Robert to develop a powerful conscience towards people less privileged than him. At the same time, the aim of the school was to teach pupils to leave 'Jewishness' behind; that undivided allegiance to the United States was more important.

2

An Awkward Undergraduate

John Lovejoy Elliott taught ethical studies at Robert's school. He was described as a 'witty saint' who threw questions at pupils in the Socratic style: Would they prefer to be a teacher, or rather accept a higher-paid job with Wrigley's chewing gum? There were questions on war and peace, on the 'Negro question' in America, economic inequality and sex relations. There was the role of the State, political ethics, and the ethics of loyalty and treason. Elliott planted a moral equation to social relations and world affairs in Robert's conscience.

Ironically, as he developed an even greater conscience, it was at the same time as the rise of the Nazis in Germany, who would banish conscience altogether in the minds and hearts of the German people to turn them into senseless robots or terrorists.

The first time that the adolescent Robert discovered that other people were not like him was when his father enrolled him in a summer camp in the mountains when he was fourteen. He found two strikes against him, since he was an introvert and a highbrow – whereas the other kids were extroverts and jocks.

'He read Plato and Homer in Greek, and Caesar, Virgil and Horace in Latin.' He was a goody-goody, while they were cruel and evil.

He was kidnapped one night and taken off to the camp icehouse, stripped naked and manhandled; then finally humiliated by boys who spread green paint on his buttocks and genitals. They left him naked and locked up inside the icehouse for the night.[1] His one friend later said of this incident that Robert had been 'tortured'. He suffered the degradation in stoic silence, refusing to complain or leave the camp afterwards.[2]

Robert's awkward and prolonged adolescence would continue in other forms. As an introvert, he was often preoccupied in thinking, which separated him from others who were more gregarious. He did not know how to get along with other people. His awareness of his superior mind did not help, because, as an over-achiever, he was always searching for subjects in which he might excel. He was primarily interested in science, but was encouraged by a teacher in the English department to take an interest in literature.

He was fortunate that his school was largely for privileged and intelligent scholars who were keen to study. So, still shy and blushing easily, he was largely protected from distractions, and was good at every subject he tackled. According to his friend Ferguson, he still took straight As in English literature, history, maths and physics. He also took Greek, Latin, French and German when he was sixteen or seventeen.[3]

He was fortunate in the protection of brilliant teachers, and the brilliance of his peers, which ensured they at least understood him. It would not be so after he graduated and left that sheltered academic environment for the real world. Among the problems of being an intellectual was that he possessed a very large vocabulary of long and complicated words that most people did not understand. Although he did not flaunt his erudition affectedly, he spoke precisely and accurately with a sense of responsibility not to misinform others. He knew the correct words to express himself clearly and unambiguously, while most others used common clichés that they heard around them from day to day and had lost their meaning.

The words he used in the letters he wrote to his friends and relatives at that time, and for years to come, seem strangely precious and affected now.

Added to his knowledge of physics, he might talk to another scientist for half an hour without the other individual having any idea what he was talking about. It was not unusual for others to leave the room in a daze afterwards. In short, he was over-educated by comparison with most other people.

He still went hiking and rock collecting, and sailed his 28ft sloop, sometimes with his younger brother, Frank. Ferguson accompanied him on several occasions, and claimed he was 'a pretty skilled sailor'.

After a summer holiday in Germany with his parents upon graduating in 1921, Robert undertook a field trip among several old mines not far from Berlin, where the Germans would mine uranium for their atom bomb project twenty years later in the Second World War.

He enrolled at Harvard, but he could not attend classes until September 1922 because he fell seriously ill from the field trip and had to recuperate. It was described as 'a near fatal case of trench dysentery'. He was brought back home on a stretcher and was bedridden for some time. A case of colitis that followed would reappear from time to time and for the rest of his life.

Harvard University

Robert continued to react against what he evidently thought of as the privileges he had acquired at birth. He had gradually edged away from the 'aristocracy' that his wealthy New York upbringing had represented. Now he refused to accept a scholarship to Harvard on the grounds that he could afford to pay the fees. It was a sign of his independent nature not to want to owe anything to anyone else, but to achieve it by his own merit. Harvard University in Cambridge, Massachusetts, was the oldest and most prestigious research institution of higher education in the United States. It had been founded in 1636. Its motto is *Veritas*, or Truth.

Harvard's alumni include eight Presidents of the United States, thirty-two heads of state, 188 living billionaires, 369 Rhodes Scholars, 252 Marshall Scholars, and eleven Mitchell Scholars; forty-nine Nobel Laureates, eighteen Field Medal winners, and fourteen Turing Award Laureates. Harvard students have also founded numerous prestigious companies all over the world, won ten Academy Awards, forty-eight Pulitzer Prizes, and 108 Olympic medals, including forty-six gold.

As far as Robert Oppenheimer was concerned, the opportunity to study at Harvard was something he had earned by his own merit, which was demonstrated by his academic record to date. Competition with other applicants required an impressive array of straight As. His obsessively hard work deserved nothing less than the best in higher education.[4]

Robert was nineteen years old and a freshman at Harvard in September 1922, where he had acquired a single room in Standish Hall, overlooking the Charles River. Still an awkward teenager whose body had grown somewhat disproportionately, he was considered to be a handsome young man with pale blue eyes and black bushy hair and eyebrows. Photos show him with a narrow triangular face and high cheekbones. Although not much above average height, he looked taller because of his lithe frame, and appeared to be lean and hungry for learning.[5]

'He spoke in fully grammatical sentences with the kind of ornate European politeness his mother had taught him.' His long, thin hands made his gestures seem somehow contorted as he talked. 'His appearance was mesmerizing, and slightly bizarre ... His behaviour in Cambridge over the next three years did nothing to soften the impression his appearance gave of a studious, socially inept and immature young man.'[6]

Although his field trips to New Mexico and Europe had opened up his mind, the studious atmosphere of the university caused him to retreat into the challenges of academic and scientific books of learning, which tended to isolate him in a dazzling world of *Dynamical Theory of Gases* and *Electricity and Magnetism*, and his own introversion.[7]

He was often drawn into bouts of deep melancholy, and read appropriately some of the darker Russian and English classics, likening himself to Shakespeare's Hamlet. He found it difficult in such a self-absorbed state to communicate with other students for days at a time. He was more like an adolescent Dostoevsky than a typical American undergraduate.

Although his teenage years as an introverted highbrow appeared to be unusually extreme in its emotional flights, even the so-called normal development of teenagers is full of potential hormonal dangers until the brain cells grow more fully and the mind matures. According to Erikson's famous theory of socio-emotional development, a search for identity occurs from the age of ten to twenty. Intimacy versus isolation comes sometime afterwards from twenty to thirty. It is perfectly normal to feel identity confusion in early adulthood when individuals search to discover who they are, what their potential might be, and where they are likely to go. Those who think deeply in order to know themselves better, explore alternative solutions and scenarios, which include exploration of possible careers.[8]

So it was with young Robert. The greatest despair, wrote the philosopher Kierkegaard is in 'not knowing who you are'.

The 'melancholy Dane' characteristics of Hamlet would have been entirely appropriate for Oppenheimer, since he was a man who could not yet make up his mind what to be, or do. [9]

He had already reached a stage of individuality, and social morality was important to him. In spite of his awkward adolescence, a sense of individual rights and universal ethics had already developed naturally. At the core of his growing problems was the same source that affects all biological and gender development, which is always the effects of hormones, from which youth is always at risk. Despite the chaos they might have caused, Robert Oppenheimer was still in the course of developing a positive identity.

Academic Paths

True to his carefully responsible thought and teenage indecisiveness, he had not yet decided what career path to follow. The academic courses he took appeared to be unrelated, as if he were floundering: philosophy, French and English literature, history, calculus, and three different chemistry courses; gas analysis, organic chemistry, and qualitative analysis. He found them all intellectually challenging. Since he loved Greek and Latin authors, he even considered specialising in the classics, or architecture, even poetry or painting. But his immaturity had not yet enabled him to settle decisively on any one major subject.[10]

It took him months to eliminate most of the random subjects and settle on his first choice of chemistry as his major study. He chose six subjects, which was the maximum number of courses to enable him to graduate in three years. Since he had no social life to distract him from his intended career, he was able to study during most of his waking hours. It was a matter of pride for him to conceal his studious efforts in order to make his success appear to be effortless.[11]

The modern poetry of T.S. Eliot's *The Waste Land* was published in that year, and influenced his own efforts with a modern poem that was published in *Harvard Crimson*. Evidently he was inspired by the older poet's theme of fading wistfulness overtaken by the sadness of loss. His own imitative attempt was considered promising. But he still felt insecure, and continued to sink into occasional periods of depression.

> Soon after Robert's arrival, the university imposed a quota to restrict the number of Jewish students. (By 1922, the Jewish student population had risen to twenty-one percent.) In 1924, the *Harvard Crimson* reported on its front page that the university's former president Charles W. Eliot had publicly declared it 'unfortunate' that growing numbers of the 'Jewish race' were intermarrying with Christians. Few such marriages, he said, turned out well, and because biologists had determined that Jews are 'prepotent' the children of such marriages, 'will look like Jews only.' While Harvard

accepted a few Negroes, President A. Lawrence Lowell staunchly refused
to allow them to reside in the freshman dormitories with whites.[12]

Despite his family's position and wealth, Oppenheimer's experiences of others had
made him feel like an outsider in the United States. He would have been well aware
of what might have seemed like an ominous circle of walls closing in on him, as it
was already doing to Jews and Christians in Europe and elsewhere, however, much
he might have felt he could rise above them.

He felt lost when the Student Liberal Club took a formal stand against the
university's racial discrimination, describing it as 'asinine pomposity'. He had not
yet become accustomed to organised political activism with its double agendas. He
had more important things on his mind.

He had discovered that what he liked about science was not so much chemistry
as physics. He had encountered thermodynamical and statistical mechanical ideas,
and wanted to find out more about them. He petitioned the Physics Department
for graduate standing in order to take upper-level physics courses. He found
a 'wonderful teacher' in Percy Bridgeman, who would later win a Nobel Prize.
Bridgeman described Oppenheimer as an intelligent student who 'knew enough to
ask questions'.

It is likely that the pathway to the right career – certainly to the right
specialisation – emerged more sharply for Oppenheimer after he attended two
lectures by the famous Danish physicist and Nobel Prize winner Niels Bohr in
October 1923. Bohr had won the Nobel Prize for his 'investigation of the structure
of atoms and of the radiation emanating from them'.

Oppenheimer was deeply impressed by this introduction to Bohr, whom he
venerated. He was not the only one who fell under Bohr's spell. Albert Einstein was
completely charmed by him. And Professor Bridgeman noted of Bohr that 'he is
now idolized as a scientific god through most of Europe'.[13]

3

A Tortured Adolescence

The breadth and variety of subjects that interested the young Robert Oppenheimer were unusual. They now included mathematics under the tuition of Alfred North Whitehead, who had written the best-selling *Principia Mathematica* with Bertrand Russell, with whom Robert was already studying philosophy. But it seemed that much of what he studied was only consigned to an empty hole of discontent.[1]

It is often generalised by psychologists that men are mainly interested in things and abstract ideas, whereas women are much more interested in people. Robert now became more aware of his lack of sensitivity to the society of human beings, whereas ideas thrilled him.[2] As for inviting girls out for an evening, one of his friends recalled they were far too much in love with intellectual life ever to think about girls. Robert's love affairs were with ideas.[3]

The closest he got to girls was contemplating 'a most beautiful and lovely lady writing a thesis on Spinoza' in the university library, whom he wrote about in a poem in the winter of 1923–24. But it seems he never spoke to her, partly because he had no idea how to pick up girls. And, with his insecurity, no doubt he feared rejection. He showed himself as aloof in his poem, hoping that she would make the first move, while admitting to a friend that the desire for a girl was not a need; it was simply a part of the romance that teenagers create in their head, in which they are the hero of their own imagined dramas.[4]

He graduated with a bachelor's degree in chemistry in June 1925. He had taken no more than the three years he had set for himself. But, as he admitted ruefully, much later, he had spread himself too thinly over too many subjects.

Robert was offered a graduate fellowship at Harvard, but decided he had higher aims. He had been drawn to the magic of physics, and decided that the best place to study it was at Cambridge in England. He hoped to learn from the great English physicist Sir Ernest Rutherford, who was famous as the first man to develop the model of the nuclear atom in 1911.

He took a vacation in New Mexico during the month of August, after persuading Percy Bridgman to write a letter recommending him to Rutherford. Eagerly opening his mail as soon as he returned to New York, he found that Rutherford had rejected him. It might have been because he had graduated in chemistry instead of physics. On the other hand, he was not pleased at the tone of the letter of recommendation, which was ambiguous and even indicated that Robert might not be suitable for the job.[5]

Rutherford had passed the recommendation on to the director of Cavendish Laboratory. He was J. J. Thomson, who had been awarded the 1906 Nobel Prize in physics for detecting the electron. Thomson spent little time at the laboratory nowadays, and agreed to supervise the young man's studies. Robert was now twenty-one.[6]

Identity Crisis

It seemed at first that young Oppenheimer was in luck with his timing, as considerable excitement had developed in the sphere of physics in 1920s Europe, particularly in scientists like Niels Bohr from Denmark and Werner Heisenberg from Germany, who were working on a theory known as quantum physics, or quantum mechanics. They investigated what laws applied in the behaviour of molecules and atoms. It dealt with sub-atomic phenomena like electrons orbiting a nucleus of an atomic bomb. Quantum mechanics was still apparently unknown in America, but was at the forefront of scientific studies in Europe.

He found himself living in depressing rooms in Cambridge while working in the corner of a basement laboratory under Thomson's guidance, and took all his meals at Christ's College. After attempting to make thin beryllium films for the study of electrons, he soon discovered he was clumsy with chemical processes, and avoided the laboratory as much as possible to spend his time at seminars and reading the most recent publications about physics instead. But the laboratory did provide him with opportunities to meet prominent physicists, like Rutherford, Chadwick, Powell, and Patrick Blackett, whom he liked, and who would eventually win a Nobel Prize for physics in 1948. Blackett would become one of his tutors.[7]

'I have been to all sorts of meetings,' he wrote to his closest friend, Ferguson; 'High Maths at Trinity, a secret pacifist meeting, a Zionist club, and several rather pallid science clubs.' But, he admitted, he was bad at the lab work, which he found a terrible bore, the lectures were vile, and he felt he was learning nothing.

With aspiration for success on one hand, and hormonal restlessness on the other, Robert found he was caught in the risky web that threatens adolescents of both genders with a sense of unreality, causing them to ask; 'Who am I? Why am I here? What must I do? How can I escape from a feeling of emptiness and dissociation into social consciousness?'

Robert was different from most people because of his very high level of intelligence and the broad variety of his interests and studies. They too were a web that sought to trap him if he made the wrong move. Perhaps it was the difficulty of choice that caused a nervous breakdown, as his fertile mind struggled against the biological limitations that adolescence imposed on him. He seemed to have overreached himself.

The nature of his emotional crisis and the accounts he gave of it to his friends were bizarre.[8]

Perhaps it was a case of an anxiety disorder brought on by overwork. Very likely he was a burnt out case. Or were the fantasies he described a sign of a form of autism? Otherwise they might have been caused by a recurrence of a previous illness. They could even have been the result of an infection caught on one of his field trips. A fertile imagination can be fired by long periods of self-isolation. The main ingredients, which appeared many years later in reflections on the incidents by several of his friends, featured his head tutor Patrick Blackett, whom he had claimed to like, but – according to his own account – had given an apple laced with poison.

His close friends at the time of his prolonged emotional breakdown were Jeffries Wyman, who found Robert lying on the floor groaning and rolling from side to side in distress; Francis Ferguson, who attributed Robert's weird episode to bouts of depression; Fred Bernheim, who was considering marriage that would break up their previously close friendship; former classmate Jane Didisheim, whom he liked but then discovered had decided to marry early; and Rutherford, who saw Robert collapse in a heap on the floor of the laboratory in front of him.

There was also a conflict between Robert and his mother. Ferguson wrote his account of Robert's youthful tragedy in February, 1926.[9]

> But clearly many of the details that Ferguson recorded [in his diary] could only have come from Robert – and it is quite possible, indeed it is almost certain, that in recounting his experiences, Robert allowed his vivid imagination to colour his stories.[10]

Central to Robert's account – like allegedly lacing an apple with poison for his tutor – was another bizarre episode containing sexual implications, which Robert evidently told to Ferguson in more detail. It involved a train journey in which Robert had been intensely studying thermodynamics from a book, when a couple in the same compartment distracted him by making love as if he were not there. Unable to concentrate on his book anymore – even though the man had left – Robert claimed he had kissed the woman in the carriage. According to him, she had not been surprised. But he had been immediately overwhelmed by remorse, and fell to his knees, tearfully begging her pardon. Then he hurriedly left the compartment.

'His reflections were so bitter that, on the way out of the station, when they were going downstairs, and he saw the woman below him, he was inspired to drop his suitcase on her head. Fortunately he missed.'[11]

The Soul and Torment of Man

It was possible that both episodes were fantasies resulting from adolescent emotional confusion from his impetuous hormones. There were other possibilities. Perhaps their significance in Robert's mind had arisen from the transition of his earlier derisive perception of himself as a 'goody-goody', to his later imaginative account of himself as a prolonged adolescent floundering in awkward situations. At any rate, he evidently had no idea how to behave with the opposite sex at that time.

Part of his conflict with his parents had been whether they should visit him as a consequence of their concern for his emotional crisis, or not. When they did visit him, he appeared to have been shocked that they brought with them a young woman undergrad he knew from previous classes; Inez Pollak. Apparently his mother had thought that the undergraduate, who was now studying at Vasser, would have a calming effect on her son. The two students were obliged to go through a courting ritual his mother thought appropriate to the occasion. But it did not work out as either of them had planned, and the whole affair became an embarrassment.[12]

A key to the state of Robert's mind was almost lost among several incomplete accounts of what happened. He was a great admirer of Russian novelists, and gave Inez a book as a parting gift. It was a famous novel by Dostoevsky, entitled *The Possessed*. Robert would have chosen it with care in order to tell her something he thought significant.

The novel describes a young man named Nikolai Stavrogen, who is out of control of his emotions, possibly even possessed by the Devil; for the alternative titles of the Russian classic are *Demons,* and *The Devils*, according to the time of translation and publication in different countries. Dostoevsky's dramatic story was likely also to have been the very first influence on Robert about the role of the revolutionary in society. It describes the troubled mind and antisocial nature of an actual dedicated revolutionary named Sergei Nechaev, whom Dostoevsky had examined very carefully when he had attended Nechaev's trial for murder. The fictional Stavrogin was clearly based on Nechaev, whose bizarre behaviour he had noted in court. The novelist's descriptions of a social misfit are so vivid and accurate that Robert was bound to have recognised some of the symptoms of his odd behaviour.

The Possessed

The classic novel also describes the grotesque behaviour of a revolutionary group of terrorists whom the Nechaev character leads. It became popular about five or six years after the Bolshevik Revolution in Russia. It left an indelible mark in Robert's mind. Some literary critics describe Dostoevsky as the greatest novelist of all time. He had been part of an intellectual circle that met secretly to plan to free the serfs in Imperial Russia, and had been arrested with the other members for treason. They were all tried in court and sentenced to execution by a firing squad. Only at the very last moment when they were tied to posts facing the barrels of the raised guns of their executioners were they unexpectedly reprieved and sent to prison instead.

Dostoevsky was scandalised by young men being recruited by terrorist organisations, and sought to warn them by describing the cold-hearted ruthlessness and irrational mindsets of all revolutionaries as enemies of society.

Robert was now persuaded to undertake analysis by a psychiatrist to correct his impetuous bouts of unreasonable behaviour.[13] The treatment was not a success. Psychiatry was undergoing a transition after the diagnoses of mental conditions in a guidebook by the famous Emil Kraepelin, in which he described symptoms like Robert's as *dementia praecox*. It was not a term that the new Freudian school of psychoanalysis would use. It left Robert protesting, like many other patients, that he knew his condition better than the analysts did.[14]

It seems that Robert was relieved of his emotional confusion in the end by falling under the spell of Marcel Proust's great novel – recognising that the thoughts and emotions of its hero were similar to his own – that his was a normal state of mind and a very human condition, rather than a morbid disorder.

When Robert left Cambridge in the middle of March 1926, three of his friends invited him to join them for a walking holiday in Corsica. They were Wyman, Bernheim, and John Edsall. All of them noticed that as Robert enjoyed hiking through the trails of the craggy landscape, he seemed to be shedding his more gloomy thoughts with each step. He had continued to enjoy reading French and Russian literature, and now discussed the merits of several classical authors as they hiked through the pathways together. He particularly enjoyed the works of Tolstoy and Dostoevsky. After being soaked by a sudden rainstorm in the mountains one evening, they had found an inn, where they dried their wet clothes in front of a fire in their room and wrapped themselves in blankets, while Edsall continued their previous conversation by maintaining he enjoyed Tolstoy best of all. Oppenheimer argued in favour of Dostoevsky as the superior novelist because, 'He gets to the soul and torment of man.'[15]

Robert Oppenheimer's prolonged adolescence seemed to have finally come to an end.

4

The Magical Spell of Physics

Robert Oppenheimer returned to Cambridge University with a more light-hearted view of life, and ended his analysis by June 1926. The historic English countryside with its glittering waterways and lush green meadows engendered a mood of tranquility and ease. The Cambridge that welcomed him then was still a paradise of ruling-class privilege, where everything in this fortunate county of physical beauty appeared to be maintained with care so that future leaders of the nation could amuse themselves in its watery splendour among ancient and confident church spires while they grew up. 'It was a Cambridge of punts and parties, late night conversations and strawberry teas.'[1]

Christ's College might be more modest than the older and more splendid Trinity, which was the biggest and richest college, although probably the most conservative at that time. But in spite of most academics refusing to change by clinging hopefully to the past, he was certain that modern scientific history was in the making right here and now. And, as he would recall when looking back, years later, 'I could now relate to others …'[2]

He had already read enough theoretical physics to understand that the whole sphere was in a stage of vigorous inquiry, investigation, wonder, and open to all sorts of theories to explain the unusual behaviour of tiny particles that contributed to the whole amazing outburst of nature, of time and space.

> One day in a Cavendish seminar, Robert watched as James Chadwick, the discoverer of the neutron, opened a copy of *Physical Review* to a new paper by Robert Millikan and quipped, 'Another cackle. Will there ever be an egg?'[3]

After reading a paper by Werner Heisenberg, Oppenheimer understood that what was developing in this field was a new way of perceiving the way that electrons acted and reacted. Then Erwin Shrödinger published a new theory on the structure of the atom. The two German theoretical physicists had unexpectedly come up with two different but similar eggs. Whereas Shrödinger wrote of a wave curving around the nucleus of an atom, Heisenberg's 1927 Uncertainty Principle theorised that the position and the velocity of an object cannot both be measured exactly, at the same time, even in theory. Were they two versions of the same theory?

'The complete rule stipulates that the product of the uncertainties in position and velocity is equal to or greater than a tiny physical quantity … Ordinary experience provides no clue of this principle. It is easy to measure both the position and the velocity of, say, an automobile, because the uncertainties implied by this principle for ordinary objects are too small to be observed.[4]

Quantum mechanics was now a mysterious and hot topic involving a wave theory and a particle theory. It challenged the intellect and imagination of Robert Oppenheimer to the point where, as he would recall later, 'I began to get pretty interested.'

His subsequent meetings with young English physicists named Paul Dirac at Cambridge, and Niels Bohr, whose lectures he had already attended, revealed an interesting contrast between them on a subject not easy to understand. Nor could it be described simply, since words seemed inadequate. Dirac said he avoided reading because he claimed it interfered with his thinking.

Bohr had grown up in a similar upper middle-class environment as Oppenheimer, in which he had been influenced by a multitude of books, by music and art. He was nearly twenty years older than Oppenheimer, well established and internationally famous in his sphere. Bohr and Dirac had already undertaken the type of groundbreaking work necessary to understand physics that Robert had not.[5]

In essence, quantum theory had developed after Einstein's General Theory of Relativity in 1915. That had involved the universal realm of physics, whereas quantum theory proposed that energy exists as discrete packets (or 'quantum'). Einstein's first reaction to quantum theory was that although it was used as a means to describe nature on an atomic level, he doubted if it upheld 'a useful basis for the whole of physics'. He believed that a theory required firm predictions proved by direct observations, whereas Bohr claimed that quantum predictions based on probability accurately described reality.

Bohr and Max Planck were the two founding fathers of quantum theory, and each was awarded a Nobel Prize in physics. Einstein was considered to be the third, in spite of his scepticism.

His First Important Paper

One of the reasons why Oppenheimer admired Bohr was the same one that had enchanted Einstein when he had met the Danish physicist for the first time – it was Bohr's continual groping with uncertainty for the truth, and never like someone who possessed it. Oppenheimer became acutely aware that it was an unusually fertile time for science and that 'great things were afoot'.

As his mental condition improved, he began working on his first important paper on theoretical physics, knowing that he was competing with three giants in the realm of atomic physics who were well ahead of him and also mature, not only in their years of experience in science but also in experience of the world they all shared. It was an intoxicating moment that caused Robert to describe Bohr as his god. Einstein was viewed with awe by everyone.

Oppenheimer's more positive attitude was elevated by having moved from dismal rooms in Cambridge to new and brighter quarters close to the River Cam, not far from the picturesque village of Grantchester, which had been immortalised in Rupert Brooke's romantic poetry. In that refreshed state of mind in the spring, Robert abandoned his trifling laboratory work in the gloomy basement of the Cavendish to learn the new trade of theoretical physics. He worked on the problems of 'collision' or 'continuous spectrum'.[6]

Bohr would long remember the moment when Rutherford had introduced him to young Oppenheimer. In answer to Bohr's question, Robert had candidly admitted he was already out of his depth and did not know if his difficulties were in the mathematics or the physics. His rueful confession was triggered by Bohr's remark that some physicists worked very largely with mathematics to describe how Nature works. Words are 'only a concession to intelligibility'. Dirac, for example, resorted to algebra instead. Einstein famously reduced the world to an equation on the back of an envelope. And yet, he had sent the thoughts of other physicists on their way in September 1905 with his famous equation, which revealed that energy equals mass multiplied by the speed of light squared; shown simply as $E=mc^2$. It proposed that small amounts of mass could be converted into a large amount of energy.

Bohr used words instead, and it would be Oppenheimer's style, too – whereas the American physicist Richard Feynman would use diagrams that triggered a new way of thinking.

When Robert met the German physicist Max Born, soon afterwards, Born showed interest in Oppenheimer's work. It involved the same problems that had been shown in recent papers by Heisenberg and Shrödinger. Born became impressed with this gifted young man, and invited him to study at Göttingen in Germany.

Born turned out to be a suitable teacher for someone of Oppenheimer's nervous disposition. It probably helped that they were both acquainted with Jewish rabbinic teaching methods that always asked why and continually tackled problems from different perspectives.[7]

An Atmosphere of Neurosis

Robert found rooms this time in a private villa owned by a former physicist who had fallen from grace through medical malpractice and had to cover the costs of his huge house and grounds. Even though the war had been over for eight years, Oppenheimer was conscious of a pervasive atmosphere of loss and mediocrity in Germany, together with bitterness and neurosis, despite the fact that the Weimar Republic had managed to cope with enormous post-war problems. Criminality and violence were in the air. It did not pay to look too successful, or you might invite trouble from the discontented and rebellious, or neurotic stream of fascists and other rebels and subversives.

On the other hand, his colleagues were so helpful at first that, instead of continuing to withdraw into his own room in isolation, as he had done when arriving in Cambridge, Robert found a convivial atmosphere at Göttingen in which he could learn from others. One of his fellow lodgers was a professor of physics named Arthur Compton, who otherwise taught at Princeton University. Scientific specialisation appeared to be the rule among the American expatriates, instead of the broader and more varied type of education he had enjoyed with philosophy, history, literature, or politics.

In spite of his recovery, Robert still suffered from occasional lapses, like sudden fainting, when he collapsed onto the floor. His behaviour could still seem neurotic to others and to himself. But quirkiness was not unusual in creative circles and among scientists. Different personalities seemed to be essential for innovative thinking. Each scientist had his own eccentricity, which enabled him to imagine and think in new and different ways to understand what others did not.

But the damp weather in the bucolic atmosphere in which they worked was not conducive to the best of health for Robert, who was often seen striding and coughing or sneezing, and drawing deeply, even neurotically, on one of his inevitable cigarettes.[8]

He had written two papers for the Cambridge Philosophical Society that had been published before leaving England for Germany, so that now he had something to boast about in open discussions with other scientists in Göttingen. Much aware of his own exceptional intelligence, he annoyed some of his new colleagues by patronising them with his broad knowledge of social sciences, which the other Americans lacked and found him embarrassing.

He would also interrupt other speakers to have his own say in a seminar; sometimes even striding to the blackboard with a piece of chalk to illustrate how things could be done better. He was entirely unaware of his brash behaviour, until his mentor, Max Born, found a way to discourage him without openly confronting him. Born invited Oppenheimer into his office, and then walked out of the room for a moment, leaving a written petition clearly in view on his desk. It had been written by a female colleague and signed by most members of the seminar, stating that they would boycott the class unless the 'child prodigy' was reined in.[9]

What saved him from being snubbed, despite his exceptional brilliance and charm, was that most scientists with a high level of intelligence suffered from a similar problem of either talking over other people's heads or patronising them. They were all impatient and intolerant of having their time wasted by people who could not understand what they were saying. So it was not easy for young Oppenheimer to restrain from acting like an excited schoolboy in class who knows all the answers, and can't resist shouting them out to the teacher, or claiming the floor ahead of everyone else.

'But Robert's lack of tact made others leery. He could be engaging and considerate one moment and in the next rudely cut someone off.'[10]

Born discouraged him from interrupting others, but it was not easy to domesticate a free-thinking mind that flitted in all sorts of different directions in search of the right answers. Nor did anyone want to. Born's patience and admiration for Oppenheimer's personality soon drew him into collaborating with him.

'I have been working for some time on the quantum theory of aperiodic phenomena,' Robert wrote to one of his Harvard physics professors, adding that he and Professor Born were also working on the law of deflection of particles … 'I think we shall soon have it.'

He wrote to his former tutor Percy Bridgman in February 1927 about his thoughts on electrons, that – in accordance with Professor Bohr's suggestion – 'when an electron jumps from one atom to another the two atoms may exchange momentum …' It may have reminded him of Einstein's prior proposal, 'that small amounts of mass could be converted into a large amount of energy'.

5

Different Strokes for Different Folks

Although the question of what was normal behaviour had evidently been on the adolescent Oppenheimer's mind before he discovered Proust, it was generally recognised that different codes of behaviour were followed at different levels of society, whether in America or in other countries. His own code inevitably belonged to the wealthy caste into which he had been born and grew up. There were plenty of other rich people in the United States at that time. It was a situation that had prompted a supposed dialogue between the two novelist rivals and friends, Scott Fitzgerald and Ernest Hemmingway, with Fitzgerald remarking, 'The rich are different from you and me.' At which Hemingway was supposed to have retorted wittingly, 'Yes, they have more money.'[1]

In fact, there was more to wealth than that, depending on whether they were new-rich, or wealthy second-generation immigrants, or recipients of old money. Young Robert had no concerns about money, because he had grown up with it and was accustomed to being able to buy the best of everything without a second thought. The problem with money was that other people admired and envied it, whereas Oppenheimer felt no great need for material possessions. He was perfectly happy to make a present of something that someone openly admired. The reason why the rich were different was that wealth required a sense of proportions and a genuine understanding of the evil eyes of envy that would follow Robert Oppenheimer throughout his life.

For example, when a German physics student named Charlotte Riefenstahl admired Robert's beautiful pigskin travelling luggage on the train to Göttingen, he was surprised that anyone should be interested in such a trivial possession. But there was more to it than that, as there always is between men and women. Charlotte had deliberately asked where Oppenheimer would be sitting on the train, and had sat down beside him while he was quietly reading one of André Gide's novels. Gide was interested in the individual's moral responsibility for others. And Robert was pleasantly surprised to discover that Charlotte had read Gide and could discuss and criticise his ideas. So, of course, he became interested in her, as she had intended.

When she remarked on meeting Oppenheimer on the train to another student afterwards, he remarked on how Robert would now feel obliged to give her his pigskin luggage. She was not the only one who recognised Robert's eccentricity: so did a student in his class named Fritz Houtermans, who was also passionate about literature. Both Robert and Fritz would work on developing an atom bomb in future, but separately, since Fritz would work on a German one for the Nazis.

Robert was delighted when his friend Paul Dirac turned up in Göttingen and rented accommodation at the same private villa. Dirac showed him the proofs of his paper on the quantum theory of radiation. He was so different from Robert that he could not understand Oppenheimer's compulsion towards reading the literature of France, Russia, or anywhere else, since he had not been brought up with books and considered that literature and other social sciences were simply a waste of valuable time.

Dirac's eccentricity was much like Robert's, or any other theoretical physicist's – a lack of understanding how anyone could work on anything else than physics. Robert could only chuckle, as his current reading included Paul Claudel, Scott Fitzgerald, Chekhov, Hölderlin, and Stefan Zweig. He enjoyed a rich intellectual life and could only wonder, in turn, at Dirac's more limited worldview, which was confined solely to physics.

'Why do you waste time on such trash?' Dirac would often say.

Oppenheimer would have liked him for his eccentricities alone, since he enjoyed the company of original people. Dirac was a very private individual who felt more comfortable in retreat from the limelight into the shadows of anonymity where he could focus obsessively on the wonders of physics.

Dramatic Breakthroughs

Quantum theory had existed very largely only by name for about twenty-five years. Only now did it begin to look less like a bunch of purely academic and unproven theories and more like science. But its theories still had to be digested before it could begin to be truly meaningful as theoretical science. Most of the papers were being written at Göttingen, Copenhagen and Cavendish.

Oppenheimer wrote seven original papers at Göttingen when he was only twenty-three. Heisenberg and Dirac were a year older than him. Einstein wrote that he didn't believe in Heisenberg's 1925 paper, even if Göttingen did. His doubts increased on reading Heisenberg's 1927 paper on the critical role of *uncertainty* in the quantum sphere. The uncertainty applied to the precise position and momentum of an entity. It made for imaginative conjectures that Einstein probably regarded with dismay, as he took the world very seriously, even religiously.

Max Born agreed that it was impossible to know with certainty, since it depended on chance. At which Einstein famously declared to Born in a Biblical reference in 1927 that, 'this is not the true Jacob ... it does not bring us any closer to the Old One. In any case, I am convinced that he does not play dice.'

Young physicists felt emboldened to interpret his remark as stubbornness at being left behind by a new young generation of physicists, but they still hoped to recruit him to their side. Oppenheimer, on the other hand, was unimpressed when he met Einstein many years later, even deciding he was 'cuckoo'.

Max Born was a professor at the University of Frankfurt am Main. He supervised several physicists at Göttingen who would become famous, like Wolfgang Pauli, Werner Heisenberg, Pascual Jordan, Enrico Fermi, Fritz London,

P.A.M. Dirac, Victor Weiskopf, Walter Heitler, and Maria Goeppert-Mayer, as well as Oppenheimer.[2]

Born was evidently impressed with Oppenheimer's work. Robert was single-mindedly obsessed with whatever he did, which he considered was a miracle, because it explained so much about observable phenomena in a harmonious, consistent, and intelligible way. There appeared to be three young geniuses among the students of physics at Göttingen at that moment in 1927; Dirac, Jordan and Oppenheimer – 'each less intelligible than the other', as one American student remarked wryly.[3]

When Born wrote to the president of MIT about the American physicists at Göttingen, he added, 'One man is quite excellent, Mr. Oppenheimer.'[4]

Oppenheimer's first paper at Göttingen 'demonstrated that quantum theory made it possible to measure the frequencies and intensities of the molecular band spectrum'.

Here in Göttingen, Oppenheimer began to develop a gift for deep friendships, like with Max Born. But he also, unknowingly, created enemies. His natural impulse was to seek out the more brilliant students whose ideas challenged him. But it meant snubbing others who wanted his company or advice. It would lead to resentment and jealousies that would dog his career and contribute to his misfortunes. As Edward Condon would remark years later, Robert spent so much time working with Born that other students who wanted and needed Born's help were annoyed that Oppenheimer took up so much of his time and cut them out.[5]

Werner Heisenberg arrived at Göttingen that year, and Oppenheimer immediately sought him out because he was probably the smartest of the German physicists. He was three years older than Robert, and appeared to be almost as erudite and articulate as Oppenheimer, and at least as brilliant. The cultured and charismatic Heisenberg had already worked with Pauli in Munich, and Bohr and Max Born. The two young men weighed each other up with cautious admiration, since Oppenheimer was working to improve on Heisenberg's scientific discoveries, and there was no shortage of competitiveness in the new sphere of quantum mechanics.

They seemed to sense that they were contenders for some future championship. Even so, neither of them could possibly have been aware that they would end up as intense rivals over the formula and creation of the atom bomb in the Second World War; Robert in America and Werner in Nazi Germany.[6]

Collaboration

Spurred on by a remark uttered by Heisenberg in the spring, Oppenheimer decided to use the latest quantum theory to explain 'why molecules were molecules', and shared his notes with Born. Born was impressed, and agreed to collaborate with him on a paper. But Robert's first draft turned out to be a light-hearted affair on only five pages, whereas Born knew that academic custom required it to be lengthened to fifteen pages with theorems intended to impress.

Their paper was published under the title of *On the Quantum Theory of Molecules,* or *The Born-Oppenheimer Approximation.* It was a breakthrough in understanding the phenomena of nuclear vibrations.

Robert completed his doctoral thesis. It was a complicated paper that he had handled well, and Born recommended it should be accepted with distinction. It 'contained a complicated calculation for the photoelectric effect in hydrogen and X-rays'. According to the Nobel Laureate Hans Bethe, many years later, it was beyond the scope of most quantum mechanics textbooks.[7]

When one of the Harvard physics professors, Edwin Kemble, visited Göttingen, he wrote to a colleague, 'Oppenheimer is turning out to be even more brilliant than we thought when we had him at Harvard. He is turning out new work very rapidly and is able to hold his own with any of the galaxy of young mathematical physicists here.'[8]

6

The World Beckons

Oppenheimer was glad to leave Germany with his doctorate now confirmed and a formidable reputation to carry back home to America. He gave a farewell party for friends, then said goodbye to Charlotte Riefenstahl, giving her his pigskin satchel as a parting present. She would treasure it for the next thirty years. He sailed back to New York, pleased with his first-hand knowledge of the most recent breakthroughs in quantum mechanics.

He would spend another term at Harvard before taking a teaching position at the California Institute of Technology (Caltech) in Pasadena. Before assuming his position, he enjoyed the comforts of his home again at Riverside Drive. It was an opportunity to catch up with his young brother, Frank, who was now fifteen. He took him sailing along the Long Island coast. Having managed to cope with his own emotional struggles through adolescence, Robert took care to help his brother with advice. Frank had found himself in a typical situation of being distracted from his studies by a young woman, and Robert warned him that while it was her job to waste Frank's time, *his* job was to keep clear of her.

'Don't make love to girls,' Robert advised him.[1]

Robert was acutely conscious of the limitations of time. Neither he nor Frank had enough of it to throw away on self-indulgent romances. They must portion out their time with care only to accommodate those whom they felt were worthy of the effort. Aside from family, their worthiness depended on the weight of their contribution to the advancement of science and the furtherance of literary revelations about human nature and the world. Such people were special to Robert, and he was possessive with them and their time, often phoning and writing to them and doing favours for them, or giving them presents. They were his heroes.[2]

Frank had grown as lanky as his older brother, and had the same icy blue eyes and black bushy hair. He was nearly as tall as Robert. But he was more mature than Robert had been as an adolescent. Frank was intelligent, too, but calmer and without Robert's obsessive drive for perfection.

Charlotte Riefenstahl turned up again in September, before taking up a teaching position at Vassar. Robert entertained her and her two travelling companions. As one of them recounted later, although they were all overwhelmed by Oppenheimer's lavish generosity, the show was mainly for Charlotte. They were met by the Oppenheimers' chauffeur in the family limousine and taken to a hotel he had booked for them in Greenwich Village. After introducing Charlotte to his parents, he spent the next two weeks pleasing her by taking her to his favourite places in New York.

Despite his hospitality, he was back on his own turf, where she sensed his independence, and that it was far too soon to hope to domesticate him. She found the Oppenheimer household over-protective of him and stifling; so that the intimacy of their relationship soon lapsed. She decided to return to Germany, and married one of his former classmates at Göttingen.

His Mercurial Temperament

Robert was still drawn to the open deserts and exotic landscape of New Mexico, and was soon visiting Los Pinos, the ranch he loved, which was owned by Katherine Page. He was similarly attracted to the ambiance of Pasadena in California, when he moved there to begin his teaching assignment in the New Year of 1928. He published six papers in that year alone, all on different aspects of quantum theory. But his repetitive coughing continued, and his doctor thought it might be from tuberculosis. So he returned to the dry mountains and atmosphere of New Mexico in June.

He took his younger brother to Los Pinos, where they slept at Katherine's ranch. While they rode side-by-side through the hills together on horseback, Frank would listen to Robert talking enthusiastically about physics and literature. He explained his philosophy of life, which was to prepare for the future whenever you have the time and opportunity, so as not to be caught unprepared at the pinch, as so many people, and even nations, were. He brought with him a book of Baudelaire's poetry, which he read aloud at night by the light from a campfire. He had been reading a novel by E. E. Cummings called *The Enormous Room*, and enjoyed the romantic notion of a self-sufficient frontiersman being completely independent, and needing only the very minimum of comfort and material possessions.[3]

One day that month, Katherine led the two brothers for a ride up into the mountains overlooking Los Pinos, and took them through a pass that led to a meadow on the top of Grass Mountain. They liked the thick clover and the blue and purple alpine flowers. The ranch she showed them was framed by ponderosas and white pine trees. There was a small rustic cabin with two upstairs bedrooms, providing views of the Sangre de Cristo Mountains and the Pecos River. Katherine informed them that 154 acres of pasture containing a brook and the cabin were available for rent.

The Oppenheimer brothers persuaded their father to sign a lease for four years. Robert would purchase it years later for only $10,000. It would be his home for many years. They called it Perro Caliente (Hot Dog).

Robert returned to Pasadena, only to pack his bags and go back to Europe, where he had received ten job offers from several universities. There was also one from Harvard. He decided on a teaching position at the California Institute of Technology. But first he wanted to study in Europe at the University of Leiden in the Netherlands. He knew he needed a year of post-doctoral studies, particularly in mathematics. So Max Born wrote a letter of recommendation for Robert to his colleague, Paul Ehrenfest, in Leiden.[4]

Ehrenfest informed Born that, 'He is doubtless very gifted but completely without mental discipline. He is outwardly very modest, but inwardly very arrogant.' He found Robert's persistence exhausting, and his obsessive-compulsive nature finally got on his nerves.[5]

Oppie, Heisenberg and Pauli

By the time Robert arrived in Leiden and gave his first lecture six weeks later, he had somehow taught himself to speak in Dutch. It impressed his new colleagues and students, who gave him the affectionate nickname of Opje. But evidently he soon felt he was gaining little there and swiftly moved on. Ehrenfest persuaded him he needed the discipline of studying under Wolfgang Pauli in Zurich, and wrote to him about Robert.

But Werner Heisenberg's name kept cropping up. So Robert stopped off at Leipzig on the way, to hear Heisenberg talk on ferromagnetism. When he arrived in Zurich, Pauli informed him about his own work with Heisenberg. He was the outstanding young German scientist who, unbeknown by any of them at that time, would develop the atom bomb – at least in theory – in Hitler's Nazi Germany in the coming war, which was now little more than a decade away.

Heisenberg was a physicist and philosopher; the son of a schoolteacher from Würzburg. He had studied physics and mathematics from 1920 to 1923, when he earned his doctorate at the Ludwig-Maximilian University in Munich and the Georg-August-University in Göttingen. His method to formulate quantum mechanics in terms of matrices would earn him a 1932 Nobel Prize for Physics. He would become one of the most influential nuclear physicists in the sphere of particle physics and quantum field theory. Even then, he ranked with Niels Bohr and Paul Dirac, and would become one of the most important figures in the development of modern quantum mechanics.

The immensely likeable Heisenberg was a formidable physicist, who would write more than 600 original research papers, philosophical essays and explanations for general readers. He was prominent in the so-called uncertainty, or indeterminacy principle of 1927, and for his 1925 suggestion of a unified field theory, the so-called 'world formula'.

He would remain in Germany during Hitler's Nazi regime, during which he would be in charge of Germany's research and development of nuclear fission during and after the Second World War. Werner Heisenberg would be Oppenheimer's main rival, in addition to the Soviet Union, in the Cold War race to be first to formulate and produce the first nuclear bomb.

Oppenheimer got close to collaborating with Heisenberg and Pauli on a paper, but it was finally decided that he had unanswered questions to address in a paper of his own on 'Notes on Theory of Interaction of Field and Matter'.[6]

Pauli had already established a reputation nearly a decade earlier with a long article on Einstein's Special and General Theories of Relativity, which Einstein had praised for its clarity. Now he taught in Zurich at the Swiss Federal Institute of Technology. He possessed a similarly impulsive drive as Oppenheimer, and was always eager to jump up to question a lecturer. His scathing wit, which was the equal of Oppenheimer's, prompted him to say to a student that, 'he was so young and already so unknown'.

Pauli and Oppenheimer became friends. Pauli admired Robert's wealth of ideas and his fertile imagination, but Oppie's inattention to detail irritated him. And he thought Robert lacked perseverance and thoroughness.

Such was the clash of powerful and independent personalities in Zurich at that time that his friend, Isidor Rabi, said he enjoyed the things about Robert that some people disliked. Robert appreciated Rabi's candour. And they revived a neighbourly friendship from their childhood in New York, as if it had never been interrupted. Their close relationship would endure, in spite of the fact that Rabi came from an impoverished Orthodox Jewish family on the East Side. One of the bonds that held them together was their similar sense of self-deprecating humour, and with it, their shared scepticism about the world, which they overcame with their shared interests in philosophy, religion and art.

Rabi would be awarded the 1944 Nobel Prize in atomic and molecular physics. He said of Oppenheimer, 'I never ran into anyone who was brighter than he was.'[7]

University of California

After the Oppenheimer brothers had spent more time together on horseback in the mountains of the Upper Pecos, it was in the middle of August that Robert packed his bags once again and drove to Berkeley, while Frank remained in New Mexico. Robert wrote to him that he had moved in to the Faculty Club of the University of California, which had appointed him to introduce physics to their graduate students by means of a graduate-level class on quantum mechanics.

Robert opened his classes by attempting to explain Heisenberg's uncertainty principle, the Shrödinger equation, Dirac's synthesis, field theory, and Pauli's latest thinking on quantum electrodynamics.[8]

He felt encouraged by his lecturing ability at first, as he commenced with the theory that quantum entities might behave as either particles or waves. It was a paradox that his students found incomprehensible, and he was told he was moving ahead too fast for them. Although he always put up a performance in front of his class to focus their attention on him, he tended to mumble in a monotone, and often stammered. 'The relentless patter of his voice was interrupted only by puffs on his cigarette.'[9]

Between his impatience to get on and his mumbling and chain-smoking, his students could not understand a word he said during most of his first year as a lecturer. He was no better with his equations on the blackboard. He would have to practise a number of different ways of lecturing before he finally got it right. Even when he became skilled at lecturing and his personality became magnetic, he showed the same intellectual impatience and scathing sarcasm with guest speakers.

'Oh, come now!' he said to one. 'We all know that. Let's get on with it.'[10]

While he continued to make new friends at Berkeley, Oppie made more enemies with his scathing quips, even though he took care to reserve them to spur on his intellectual equals. But in this hotly competitive sphere of sub-atomic particles, even the very best scientist needed only one enemy to orchestrate his downfall. Oppie's intolerant and impatient manner would continue to offend those who were not his intellectual equals for years to come.

7

Oppie

Oppie's reputation blossomed suddenly when he managed to improve his lecturing style, so that anyone who aimed at his field knew that Berkeley was the best place in America to learn it. Three of the five students who received National Council Fellowships in physics in 1934 chose to study under Professor Oppenheimer. They also came to learn from Ernest Orlando Lawrence, who was an experimental physicist very different from Oppie.

E. O. Lawrence came from Norseman Lutheran farm stock in South Dakota, and worked his way through colleges by selling pots and pans to local farmers in Minnesota, Chicago, and when at Yale. He had the self-confident gift of a successful salesman when promoting his own skills, too. Unlike Robert, with his troubled introspection that often made him mumble, Lawrence was outgoing and sociable, and a gifted communicator. He had become the most outstanding experimental physicist by 1930. The two physicists would move forward together in their careers.[1]

Lawrence was twenty-eight years old at the time. He was staying at the Faculty Club when Robert arrived at the end of 1929, and they became the best of friends. Both young men were full of energy and in love with life. Robert was a creative theorist full of original new ideas, and Lawrence a practical activist. They rode on horseback together on most days and talked constantly in mutual admiration, and socialised at night. When Lawrence married some years later, he named his son Robert.

Lawrence had decided to build a machine that could penetrate the nucleus of the atom, and had built his first accelerator by 1931. He improved on it a year later. He called it a cyclotron.[2]

They were at the forefront of a race to solve a number of problems, including the possible existence of antimatter, which Oppenheimer had proposed. This was so much like imaginative science fiction that each physicist argued vehemently with the others in case they stepped outside of reality. Oppenheimer had written an important paper on electrons and protons, and considered there must be a positively charged counterpart to the electron, which would possess the same mass as the electron. Dirac proposed it was a 'proton'. Oppenheimer predicted an anti-electron, or 'positron'. Dirac called it an anti-electron, but was uncertain of his hypothesis.

Pauli and Bohr agreed with his doubt, with Pauli saying it was nonsense and Bohr finding it unbelievable. But Oppenheimer pressed Dirac to predict the existence of antimatter. Then in 1932, an experimental physicist named Carl Anderson proved the existence of the positron – the positively charged antimatter counterpart to the electron – only two years after Oppenheimer had theorised that it existed.

Dirac won his Nobel Prize a year later.

Ralph Fowler, who had been one of Robert's former teachers at Cambridge in England, visited Berkeley in 1932 and observed his old student. When Harvard tried to recruit Oppenheimer several months later, Fowler wrote that Oppie's work was apt to be full of mistakes, due to lack of care, but 'it is work of the highest originality and he had an extremely stimulating influence in a theoretical school as I had ample opportunity of learning last fall'. In short, his physics was good but not his maths.[3]

It seemed that Robert's impatience made him careless, and it was said that others advanced ahead of him after he had opened the door for them to enter and achieve success.

The Nobel Prize

Oppenheimer might well have won a Nobel Prize if he had needed the money, or been ambitious for success. Instead, like many highly intelligent people, he would become bored at doing the same things without continual challenges. He still lost patience very quickly, and failed to correct some of his equations when he moved on to other ideas as part of his mercurial nature, often without editing his previous calculations. And he was shielded from a compulsion continually to prove his worth to others to obtain status, since he did not have to. Julius had not only shielded his son from hard times by his wealth, but provided him with a rich intellectual inner life that made him independent and free of vanity.

But there was no financial security for others at the present time, as banks suddenly closed down without reserves to pay their depositors. Deposit accounts evaporated. The insecurity of paper money spread like an epidemic from the financial centre of the United States to the Bank of England and across Europe.

As well as working prolifically on his own papers, Robert would now collaborate with one or other of his students on a joint paper, as he did with Martha Philips, an Indiana farm girl and his first doctoral student. She thought of him as an ideas man who worked out original new ideas with his students. Another student collaborator was George Volkoff. Then came Hartland Snyder. He and Snyder published an important paper that was ahead of its time, on 'Continued Gravitational Contraction' on 1 September 1939, which was largely overlooked because Germany invaded Poland on the same day and triggered the Second World War.

Nevertheless, the publication of their paper was a momentous event, although it would only be recognised several decades later. It dealt with the phenomenon of so-called black holes left by stars that die and disappear. Its fame had to wait until modern astronomical observatory technology caught up with space theories. Only then would it be considered to be 'one of the greatest papers of twenty-first century physics'.

Although deeply wrapped up in his work, Robert still noticed attractive young women. There was the ladylike Natalie Raymond in 1929, who left for New York to become an editor. Helen Campbell was attracted to him, and spent part of the summer with him and a circle of friends at Perro Caliente in 1934, but she was married. Being pleasing to women was understandable, he wrote to his brother, but it was only a manifestation of vanity. Evidently he was still uneasy about the distractions from work of such relationships. He preferred independence and a simple life.

The Depression

When the shocking collapse of the New York Stock Exchange had occurred suddenly in the autumn of 1929, and the financial depression forced banks to close, the inability of farmers and others to pay off mortgages, the unemployment, poverty, and misery, had not touched the Oppenheimers. Fortunately for them, Julius had retired in the previous year and sold his interest in the company. He had also sold the apartment in New York and their summer home before the stock market crash. Ella and Julius had already downsized into a small apartment in Park Avenue when the economic depression took hold.

Robert was twenty-seven, reasonably well-paid in his job and seldom short of money when, in October 1931, Ella became seriously ill and died before the end of the month.[4]

Julius began to visit Robert more frequently in California and they shared a cottage in Pasadena, where Robert was teaching in 1932. There were not many years left of peace, and governments were almost entirely taken up thinking of ways to stem the financial crisis rather than preparing for a possible war. The Governor of the Bank of England was so overwhelmed by pressures and anxiety that he had suffered from a nervous breakdown and fled overseas to rest.

Germany suffered from the worst effects of inflation, in which its paper money became worthless. The ensuing chaos triggered the rise to power of an unbalanced fanatic with a fixation about different races, who had been gradually arming the Nazi Party into a private army with the most advanced war technology in the world, including a modern air force.

Robert, who had spent his life looking for reasons and answers to explain the actions of the world around him, found it a critical time, despite his independent wealth and the security of his scientific skills. He was somehow persuaded to learn Sanskrit and read the Hindu *Bhagavad-Gita,* whose world philosophy he thought marvellous, and felt compelled to give copies to his friends as a gift.

Whether it was the challenge of mastering another subject, or a useful fantasy in which to escape from the confusion of the world, he enjoyed studying 'The Lord's Song', which was a dialogue between the god Krishna and its hero, Prince Arjuna. Krishna tells the prince that it is his duty as a warrior to fight and kill.

His Jewish friend Isidor Rabi quipped: 'Why turn to Hindu literature for answers – why not the Talmud?'

But Robert was always most challenged by the most difficult ideas. Judaism was too easy, because it already possessed most of the answers in the Ten Commandments, which were the only disciplines required for an orderly and meaningful life. All the rest was study and discussion.[5]

He wrote to Frank in spring 1932 in an attempt to explain that discipline was good for the soul, a means to achieve serenity in a troubled world. Not by discipline alone, but by achieving detachment. It was, he thought, the path to happiness. It was necessary to view the world without the 'gross distortion of personal desire', and accept 'our earthly privations and its earthly horror'.

Robert's poetical soul yearned to escape into mysticism. Perhaps it was the untimely death of his mother that had left him bereft, and he was searching for something to stabilise his emotions and his life.

Communism

There was nothing stable about the shifting sands of the capitalist system, which had suddenly collapsed, and the rising military dictatorships in Europe that imposed autocratic rule as a way to achieve order and conquest. The rise of communism and fascism on the Continent of Europe had created uneasy ripples that spread everywhere and caused people to search for political and military answers. According to them, capitalism had turned the world upside down. Others decided its failure showed the entire system was obsolete, and turned to the Soviet Union for answers.

Some of the most brilliant young undergraduates at Trinity College in Cambridge had already decided that the only way forward was to embrace communism and support the Soviet Union against the horrors of Nazi Germany. Its militarism and indifference to individuals had to be prevented from dominating the rest of the world.

Robert had always been aware of the fragility of human nature with all its flaws. Now he felt he could withdraw from it in a state of moral superiority with good intentions and actions. It was Karma.

Until that moment when he was heading for his thirties, Robert had become tired of his continual introspection, from his Ethical School education to Dostoevsky, Tolstoy and Proust. Now Karma appeared to be the only certainty he could imagine as the sands of his life, and others, shifted and formed new shapes with which they would all have to contend. And yet, his elaborate attempts to explain his philosophy to his brother Frank indicated that he was not entirely satisfied at withdrawing into Indian mysticism. While still attempting to convince himself of its validity he had not stopped searching for answers. Not so very long ago, he had been persuaded by reading André Gide of the need to take responsibility for his own actions and the problems of others. He may even have suspected that he was attempting to escape from reality.

Whatever the outcome of this mystical moment, he turned up at the University of Michigan summer school in June 1934, where he lectured on the Dirac equation.

A young post-doctoral fellow named Robert Serber was so impressed with Oppenheimer's lecture that he immediately switched his studies from Princeton to Berkeley. Soon after Serber arrived at Berkeley, Oppenheimer invited him to a movie and initiated a lifelong friendship.

Serber's father was a lawyer in Philadelphia, and his family was well-connected, with a politically left background. They bonded through their cultural similarity, since Serber was Jewish and his father had emigrated from Russia, as Oppie's father had done from Germany. The difference was that Robert Serber's mother had died when he was twelve and been replaced by a stepmother named Frances Leof. According to FBI files, Frances was a member of the Communist Party.

REDS

8

The Red Scare

Robert Serber grew up in a household that was sociable and noisy with discussions by guests who belonged to the intelligentsia, like leftist playwright Clifford Odets, left-wing journalists and poets. He had been attracted to Charlotte, the youngest girl in the Leof family, and married her. Charlotte had graduated from the University of Pennsylvania, and owed her leftist activist politics to her father. Bob Serber's own politics were almost inevitably bound to be left wing.

Serber published a number of papers on theoretical physics under Oppie's direction at Berkeley, seven of them in collaboration with him, on subjects like high-energy protons and nuclear photo-effects. Oppie considered him to be a first-rate physicist.

It was only when Oppie invited the Serbers to Perro Caliente that Robert Serber realised how much his friend was dedicated to a Spartan life in New Mexico. Nothing had changed in the house since they had bought the property. There were no new decorations or improvements of any kind, and still only the original few upright wooden chairs to sit on. The old ranch house was intended merely as a place from which to embark on horseback for hours and days at a time. It represented the ideal sparse life of the self-contained frontiersman that Oppie most enjoyed. It demonstrated his lack of interest in possessions. He felt free and independent there.

'To many of my friends, my indifference to contemporary affairs seemed bizarre,' he would claim many years later about his time there, 'and they often chided me for being too much of a highbrow ... I had no understanding of the relations of man to his society.'

According to Robert Serber, Robert was 'an unworldly, withdrawn un-esthetic person who didn't know what was going on ...'[1]

It was more that he had been indifferent to the critical state of the world beyond his studies, until it penetrated his singular view of the universe and its atomic particles in 1934. Politics had not managed to hold his interest until then, largely because it involved entirely different skills and views and attitudes than his own. Despite his broad interest in philosophy and literature, he was essentially a theorist of the sort who lived in monastic or academic seclusion from the real world outside.

Politics involved the skills necessary to lead and govern a generally unruly nation, or a part of it. It dealt with the swiftly changing moods of an electorate that acted emotionally, and often impulsively, without knowing all the facts that constituted the current situation or the consequences of their actions. Whereas politicians dealt with the unpalatable facts of life, Robert had read of them largely on the pages of novels by French, Russian, or English classical authors. It was only now that he found himself drawn to the present crisis in the United States.

Perhaps, as an academic theorist, he was not even constituted of the right matter to establish a realistic viewpoint to perceive what was happening to people as individual particles or in mass, while they behaved wildly and inaccurately, as they had always done periodically in a spirit of individual self-righteousness or frantic mass hysteria that amounted to madness – 'the madness of crowds', as French social psychologist Gustave Le Bon described it.

Nor was he alone in that regard, since the more normal dullards in governments across Europe had left their countries unprepared and unprotected once again from plundering by powerful warlords.

Oppenheimer had been protected from reality by his family and friends. As he had naively remarked to one of his graduate students, Leo Nedelsky, 'I know three people who are interested in politics. Tell me, what has politics to do with truth, goodness and beauty?'[2]

Despite Robert's unrealistic insularity as a physicist, a Hungarian-born American physicist named Leo Szilard had already conceived the nuclear chain reaction in 1933, It would lead to the discovery of the atomic bomb.

The Master Race

Britain, Europe and the United States had been living in a dream world for two decades. Now they would pay for turning away from facing reality into an abundance of mindless trivialities and fantasies of wish fulfilment.

When Oppie received a circular letter in the spring of 1934, asking for funds to enable German physicists to escape from Nazi Germany, as the effects of Hitler's dictatorship of only a year took hold, he paused to think of distant Europe. He had known it only as a student, and the people he had known were, he thought, much like he was. But Europe had changed. Now, anyone who opposed the Nazis could expect to lose their job, their citizenship and, very likely their life in one of the murder camps that Hitler had already set up, first at Dachau.

One of the refugees was Robert's former professor in Göttingen, Dr James Franck, who had won two Iron Crosses in the First World War. He had managed to keep his job although he was Jewish, but was forced into exile after refusing to dismiss other Jews from their jobs.[3]

Robert instantly agreed to contribute a percentage of his salary towards the cause, and became a political activist. By 1935, Franck was teaching physics at John Hopkins University in Baltimore. Max Born was forced to flee Göttingen in 1933 and ended up teaching in England.

Among those opposing Hitler had been the influential Jewish-owned Ullstein Newspaper Press. In the previous year, Hitler had forced the Jewish family who owned it to resign from the board. He had not forgotten how their newspaper had scorned, ridiculed, and opposed his rise to power. Now, with independent newspapers and truth banned, Nazi propaganda could rule by means of the most outrageous lies that Germans chose to believe, not only against German-Jews, but also about most other races, including Czechs, Poles, and Slavs, as Hitler attempted to prove that his Germans were the 'Master Race'. His purpose at that time was to demonstrate his own supremacy by victimising the opposition in order to justify destroying them.

It had all been meticulously planned and put into effect. There had been 4,700 newspapers in Germany in 1933. They were either banned, or their printing presses were seized by the Nazis, and their owners eliminated; particularly printing presses owned by the Social Democratic Party, or by communists. The Nazi propaganda ministry used radio, press, and newsreels to induce fear of an imminent and imaginary 'Communist Uprising', whereas, in fact, the Communists had received only about 5 per cent of the votes in the past election and were no real threat at all.[4]

Nazi paramilitary thugs of the SS orchestrated the theatre of the streets by violently arresting all known political opponents, who were hustled off to Dachau concentration camp and lost to history.

Hitler had had nearly ten years to organise his revenge on his opponents since he had been arrested and imprisoned for treason in 1925. In the first edition of *Mein Kampf*, which he wrote behind bars, he had remarked, 'The German people have no idea of the extent to which they have to be gulled in order to be led.'[5] He swiftly eliminated the statement from the second edition.

Trade Unions

The chaos caused by unemployment in the United States was just as severe as in Germany. But Roosevelt's administration found ways to alleviate at least some of the economic problems and hardships in America without resorting to an authoritarian dictatorship supported by secret police. Even so, there was similar hysteria among discontented and desperate people attempting to think and act collectively to find answers. Conspiracy theories flourished. People were forbidden to gather in groups in Nazi Germany, and trade unions were banned. Britain still had laws against assembly to commit treason or imperil the lives and homes of others, while Americans thought they saw Reds everywhere, in and out of government.

Worn down and frustrated by nearly five years of the deepest economic depression in America's history, it was those who had jobs who demanded a better deal. The jobless were too demoralised to protest. Three thousand farm workers in the Imperial Valley went on strike at the beginning of 1934. Police arrested hundreds and the strike was quickly broken. But, as had previously happened in England and Wales in the coal mines, workers ended up having to accept lower hourly rates than before. Similar desperate tactics were followed in the same year by 12,000 longshoremen who sought to prevent food from being unloaded and distributed from the docks, by forming picket lines. They succeeded in wrecking the economies of California, Oregon, and Washington. Police threw tear gas bombs at rioters.[6]

It frequently happened that some police, when overwhelmed by immense crowds, panicked and shot at random, killing strikers and wounding others. San Francisco's labour unions called a general strike that brought the city to a standstill for four days. The longshoremen failed to improve their lot, but public sympathy lent them a moral victory and increased the size and strength of activist trade unions. It was the type of politics playing itself out that Oppenheimer would have viewed with sympathy but scepticism, because it created fear that lingered. The problems, after all, had arisen from a failed economy over which no one had any control.

If the workers were the hardest hit, as in Britain, it was the young undergraduates in the universities who were struck by the ambiguity and purposelessness of the chaos. The problems began to be debated by the more brilliant students and lecturers at Berkeley. When opinions were split between supporters of the trade unions and critics, Oppenheimer could no longer ignore local politics, and invited Bob Serber and Melba Phillips to join him at a large longshoremen's rally in San Francisco.

As Serber described the hysteria in the auditorium, they became mesmerised by the enthusiasm and energy of the longshoremen, and were soon shouting out demands in a chorus with them; 'Strike! Strike! Strike! Strike!' Oppie was introduced afterwards to union leader Harry Bridges.

Oppie was still protected from the worst of the Depression because he was gainfully employed and enjoyed his work; even being offered twice his Berkeley salary to move to Harvard. He turned down the offer, as money was not his primary consideration. He also swept aside two competitive offers from Princeton, since he had no wish to leave the work he loved at Berkeley.

Oppie did his best to persuade Berkeley to hire Serber as his research assistant in the physics department. Department chairman Raymond Birge reluctantly agreed. But when Robert lobbied again to have Serber appointed to a position towards tenure as an assistant professor, Birge firmly refused, even writing to a colleague that 'one Jew in the department was enough'.

Had Oppie known Birge's prejudice at the time, he might well have departed for Harvard. But, sensitive as he was to his own problems and the hardships of others, he was remarkably insensitive to prejudices and political manipulations for power in established institutions.

He had reached his thirtieth birthday by the time that so many political catastrophes were taking place around him he felt he had to take note and address them. By his own admission, he finally matured when he met a woman who captivated him in 1936. Her name was Jean Tatlock.

9

We the Living

It was in the spring of that year when Oppie's landlady introduced him to twenty-one-year-old Jean. He rented rooms from the tall and self-possessed Mary Ellen Washburn and her husband at that time. They lived at 2665 Shasta Road, and both loved partying with intellectuals.

Robert already knew Jean was the daughter of Professor Tatlock, the Chaucer scholar at Berkeley. The two men had met over lunch at the Faculty Club, and the professor had been impressed by Oppie's literary knowledge and appreciation.

The professor's daughter possessed an exotic Irish appearance, with almost black curly hair, thick, dark eyelashes, and reddish lips and complexion. She was relatively tall and, although free-spirited, revealed a shy and somewhat melancholy disposition. It was her literary inclination that caught his attention. She was particularly attracted to the poetry of Gerald Manley Hopkins and John Donne. It created a bond. After meeting her that first time, he found he could not get her out of his mind.

It was only discovered later on by the FBI that Mary Ellen Washburn, his landlady, was an 'active member of the Communist Party in Alameda County'.[1]

The swing of the political pendulum towards communism by some students in the United States in 1936 followed a more determined decision taken a few years earlier in Britain, when Hitler became Chancellor in Germany and the Nazi menace was revealed as a global threat. But, whereas many young British undergraduates did so with their eyes open cynically to all the flaws in the Soviet system, American students who placed their faith in communism were generally more romantic, adventurous and naïve.

It was the year an Italian film company plagiarised American novelist Ayn Rand's dystopian *We the Living*, which takes place in communist Russia. Its hero and heroine manage to escape from the Soviet Union at the end, when he says to her, 'Do you know what we're leaving? An immense prison covered with snow and stained with blood.'[2]

Soviet Russia's grotesque political and social situation was largely ignored when the West decided to support Stalin, as the priority now was to ensure the defeat of Nazi Germany, from where even more reports of violent and bizarre behaviour from the secret police, and the forced labour, or so-called concentration camps, leaked out. If there was no longer any hope for freedom in Hitler's Germany, many members of the Communist Party believed there was at least a glimmer of hope in

Soviet Russia. It was not just a matter of wishful thinking for more informed and pragmatic people, since the West needed a powerful military ally to defeat Germany, and there was no one else. Stalin had been mobilising for war at least since Hitler's aggressive plans to destroy the Slavs and colonise Russia with Germans had been revealed in *Mein Kampf*.

Europe was still far enough away from the United States for most other Americans to be indifferent to whatever freedoms were being lost there, and whatever European military powers intended – so that America's isolationist mindset continued for a while longer, while Robert courted Jean Tatlock and, as he wrote, 'we grew closer to each other'.

A Passionate Adolescence

Jean had grown up in Cambridge, Massachusetts, before Berkeley and was only just completing her first year at Stanford University School of Medicine. Before that she had enjoyed a passionate adolescence that had become integral to her unusual nature. She had visited Europe in the early 1930s and become interested in psychology; in Carl Jung in particular, with his principal theory of a collective human psyche. The idea of collectivism, of belonging to a group, possessed considerable appeal to people who felt lonely or different, and even more for those who felt misunderstood.

She was already conscious of Shakespeare and Chaucer from her parents, and had visited Stratford-upon-Avon to watch Shakespeare's plays performed. She had studied English Literature at Vassar, where apparently her attractive appearance and striking intellect intimidated other students.

As Europe's military dictators dominated the news, she took up an anti-fascist attitude with plenty of other naïve romantics who thought wishfully of an ideal society and were gullible enough to believe Soviet propaganda. It was summed up by one of her wistful remarks: 'I just wouldn't want to go on living if I didn't believe that in Russia everything is better.'[3]

She had graduated from Vassar in 1935 with a powerful social conscience. It was at the same time that the contrarian American author Ayn Rand – who had escaped from Soviet Russia – adamantly believed that being responsible for other people turned us into their victims: What about working towards our own happiness instead of other people's?

But the intellectual best-selling novelist who seemed to have an answer for everything in a form of Libertarianism, appeared to have no answer to the Nazi menace. Nor apparently did anyone else, other than communists. So Jean became a member of the Communist Party.

She wrote articles filled with outrage for the *Western Worker*, which was a mouthpiece for the Party. But she was not an ideologue. Like most members, her attachment filled an emotional need to belong to something bigger than her.

A Social Conscience

Jean and Robert's relationship grew deep because they were two opinionated and wilful individuals with problems. While her female friends described Jean sympathetically as passionate, Oppie discovered very soon how independent and tempestuous she could be. Contemporary novelist and poet D. H. Lawrence was drawn to writing about women who had a will of their own at that time of women's emancipation. And no doubt Jean and Oppie argued about women's rights and responsibilities as Lawrence and his wife Frieda did. Both couples possessed a deep social conscience.

Once drawn in to Jean's outrage for social justice for all, Oppie became as passionate about it as her. He was outraged at the Spanish Civil War, with the fascist military dictator Franco taking over Spain with his brutal army. Oppie would listen intently to all her arguments and agree vehemently that something had to be done about it. Freedom had expired in fascist Italy and Nazi Germany, but there was some hope that the tyranny could be stemmed in Spain, where Hitler, Mussolini, and Stalin drilled their troops and air forces in the ruthless arts of warfare. In April 1937, fascists bombed the Basque town of Guernica while rehearsing for the Second World War.

Jean proved to be more extreme in her left-wing sympathies than others in Oppie's circle of friends. There was something dark in her nature, so that Robert preferred to keep her to himself, and rarely socialised with her, since she was too difficult to handle in public with her manic-depressive personality. She not only stimulated his own social conscience but also drew him into a number of Popular Front causes. He did not resist. Not only was he shocked, like others at the callous brutality of the war in Spain, but – as he would admit later – he was also possessed by 'a continuing, smouldering fury about the treatment of Jews in Germany'.[4]

The situation in Europe was even more serious than Oppenheimer thought from that distance in America. The year 1933 had been a critical one as one man had dominated the news by turning the world on its head when no one was paying enough attention to stop him.

He Was Not Alone

According to his friend Serber, Oppie would often be depressed because of the troubles in Europe and the problems he was having in handling Jean. He had become intensely devoted to her as she had become the love of his life. She was not only a distraction from his career, but a troublesome manipulator weaving a political web that could trap him.

Both Oppenheimer and Serber had become acutely conscious of the way that economic forces could produce unemployment and discontent that drew angry people into extremes. Oppie 'began to feel the need to participate more fully in the life of the community'. In 1937–38 he became interested in the plight of the jobless, whether farm labourers or scientists. Some of his communist friends thought he had become a card-carrying member of the Communist Party, like about a quarter of a million other Americans who affiliated themselves to the Communist Party of the Unites States 'for at least a short time', between 1930 and 1938.[5]

> For many New Deal Democrats, no stigma was attached to those who were involved in the CPUSA and its numerous cultural and educational activities. Indeed, in some circles the Popular Front carried a certain cachet. Numerous Intellectuals who never joined the Party nevertheless were willing to attend a writers' congress sponsored by the CP, or volunteer to teach workers at a 'People's Educational Center.' So it was not particularly unusual for a young Berkeley academic like Oppenheimer to savor in this way a bit of the intellectual and political life of Depression era California.[6]

Jean Tatlock's friends were also Communist Party members, and became his friends. They included Bernard Peters and his wife, who had managed to escape from Nazi Germany before it sealed off its borders to prevent other victims from leaving. Having been imprisoned in Dachau, he had written an exposé of the conditions there. What the Nazis had described as a concentration camp was actually Hitler's first camp designed for murdering his opponents methodically in a dis-assembly-line process. Peters described the tortures, inhuman atrocities, and executions, in sickening detail in 1934.

Since Peters was interested in physics, Robert persuaded him to take a course at Berkeley. He was good enough at it to enter a graduate programme. Friend by friend, and step by step, Oppenheimer was drawn further and further into political activism, while Oppie continued to struggle with Jean's temperament for three years, against all the warnings he had given to his younger brother about vanity, and distractions by discontented girls; above all, not to pity them in a false belief that you were in love with them.

It was at this point that Haakon Chevalier came into his life. Chevalier would turn out to be a serpent in Oppie's Garden of Eden.

10

Political Activists

What sparked Chevalier's interest in Robert Oppenheimer was a remark by a mutual friend that Robert had read the complete works of Lenin. Very few, if any, Party members had. Chevalier was from New Jersey, but his parents had come from France and Norway, and he had spent some of his earliest years in Paris and Copenhagen. He had studied at Stanford and Berkeley, where most undergraduates called him by his nickname, which was 'Hoke'. His doctorate was in Romance languages, his major in French literature. Hoke taught French at Berkeley, and was described as a charismatic teacher.

He was tall, with wavy brown hair and pale blue eyes. He had married into money. His first published book was a biography of Anatole France in 1932. He wrote reviews for the *New Republic* and the *Nation* magazine.

Chevalier was gregarious. He loved partying and joining all sorts of organisations, like the Teachers' Union, the American Civil Liberties Union, the Consumer's Union, and the International Professional Association.[1] He was committed to the Communist Party and dedicated to a society based on co-operation instead of competition for money. But, like many communists whom the Party had found more useful when anonymous, he was deliberately vague about his political beliefs. The political left came in all shades from pale pink socialists and gradualist Fabians, to bright red Marxist-Leninists, or Trotskyite adventurers with a list of victims and an urge to shed more blood.

Many young Americans joined the International Brigade to fight in Spain, as they did in England. Some 2,500 American volunteered to fight against General Franco's fascists by joining the communist-supported Abraham Lincoln Brigade. Both Chevalier and Oppenheimer believed that Republican Spain would be victorious over fascism in Europe, and that Roosevelt's New Deal in America would pave the way for social reforms at home. They attended a meeting of the Teachers' Union, took a liking to each other right away, and decided to form a discussion group of half a dozen or more close friends who would meet regularly to exchange views on politics.

According to Chevalier, their friendship arose primarily from other similarities of interest than politics. Oppie became his closest friend, frequently dropping by Chevalier and his wife's home for dinner. Hoke's second wife was Barbara Ethel Lansburgh. They frequently met for a movie, a concert, or a drink. Hoke claimed that Oppie made the best Martinis. Vodka Martinis became an intimate ritual, while inside their minds they were secretly conspiring against all fascists.

The Upper Hand

Oppie's love affair with the wilful Jean continued. There was little doubt who was in charge, or which led the other. She told him about all her communist memberships, which he preferred to believe were merely a result of immature whims that propelled her into protesting from time to time, and leaving her as discontented as before. He attributed her apparent dedication to communism as a feeling for social justice. According to him, 'She loved this country and its people and its life.'

By the end of 1936, her special passion was the crisis in Spain. When he held back reluctantly from her urgings to get involved, he was caught in attempting to placate her, and she said impatiently, 'Oh, for God's sake, don't *settle* for anything.'

He could not refuse her spirited nature, and became involved in raising funds for relief groups. She introduced him to other political activists, like Dr, Thomas Addis. Addis was chairman of the Spanish Refugee Appeal. He had been Jean's mentor at Stanford, and was now a friend. He claimed that his committee had been responsible for thousands of refugees being rescued from concentration camps in France. All that Oppie knew was that Addis was fighting for democracy and against fascism. But the FBI reported later that Addis was a major recruiter of white-collar professionals for the Communist Party.

He urged Oppenheimer to provide him with funds that would go to relief organisations managed by the Communist Party. Robert continued to provide Addis with money regularly to help the forces fighting against the fascists in Spain. He paid Addis, and 'Pop' Folkoff of the San Francisco Communist Party, in cash, because his funds were not only intended for medical aid, but more likely for military equipment. Robert would also continue to make regular payments to farm workers in California for at least a decade, until about 1942.

'Pop' Folkoff was well-respected by communists for his knowledge of Marxist philosophy.

Whether Oppie really read or understood Marx or Lenin is arguable. It never occurred to him for a moment that his financial contributions 'might be directed to other purposes than those I had intended, or that such purposes might be evil. I did not then regard communism as dangerous; and some of their declared objectives seemed to me desirable.'[2]

His name and Chevalier's appeared in the Party's newspaper, the *People's World*, as financial contributors, with other Berkeley professors, of funds to purchase an ambulance for fighters against fascism in Spain. He appeared to be unaware that he was being used by Jean Tatlock and the Communist Party.

Activism and the Unconscious

Ernest Lawrence was one of Oppie's oldest friends. He had watched Robert's situation sceptically. He was far more realistic than Robert, and took him aside to warn him – and Frank separately – that, 'You're too good a physicist to get mixed up in politics and causes.'

But it was already too late.

> That spring, Robert and 197 other Pacific Coast academics signed a petition urging President Roosevelt to lift the arms embargo on the Spanish Republic. Later that year, he joined the Western Council of the Consumer's Union. In January 1939, Robert was appointed to the executive committee of the California chapter of the American Civil Liberties Union. In 1940, he was listed as a sponsor of Friends of the Chinese People, and became a member of the national executive committee of the American Committee for Democracy and Intellectual Freedom, a group that publicized the plight of German intellectuals. With the exception of the ACLU, all of these organisations were labelled 'Communist Front organisations' in 1942 and 1944 by the House Committee on Un-American Activities.[3]

Political activists were unpopular with older and more conservative academics on the faculty council, who kept clear of the union movement, whereas Robert worked at increasing union membership. He and Chevalier volunteered for all sorts of menial tasks, like addressing hundreds of envelopes to union members at night, and giving speeches for unpopular causes to small and tepid audiences. Whatever Chevalier's personal reasons were, it was felt that Oppie was involved out of guilt at his intellectual brilliance, his scientific skills, and his inherited wealth – not to mention his cultural superiority. But he was acutely aware of what was happening in Nazi Germany, and felt frustrated at how little he could help those who were being victimised.

Julius Oppenheimer died of a heart attack in 1937.[4] It was the same year in which distant relatives arrived in New York as refugees from Nazi Germany. Robert sponsored them and paid their bills.

One of Freud's former disciples, Dr Siegfried Bernfeld, was another refugee fleeing from Europe. Bernfeld was an eloquent and convincing speaker, and Oppie was deeply impressed by him – to the extent of buying a pork-pie hat like Bernfeld's. He began to wear it as sign of fellowship.

Robert attended Bernfeld's seminars from 1938 to 1941. They developed into a study group, which would become the San Francisco Psychoanalytical Institute and Society. No doubt Oppie's involvement with Bernfeld was partly due to his intense and troubled relationship with the moody Jean Tatlock. He felt responsible for her. She was still in training to become a psychiatrist, and was duly psychoanalysed by Dr Bernfeld, as a traditional procedure by Freudian psychoanalysts.*

---

* In March 1938, Sigmund Freud was under house arrest by the Austrian Nazis in Vienna, while Ernest Jones did his best to bribe Nazi officials to release him, so that he could be spirited away to England.

Robert continued to spread himself between his lecturing and research papers, his trade unionism, his literary interests, psychiatry, political activism and fund-raising, and the turmoil of his intense relationship with Jean. Ernest Lawrence disapproved strongly of the time he felt his friend wasted on political activism.[5] He warned him again to leave politics to the experts. Politics were a trap and a delusion. So was Jean Tatlock.

11

The Atomic Bomb Project

German armies invaded Soviet Russia in a massive attack by millions of troops and tanks that overwhelmed millions of Russian defenders in a military invasion code-named Project Barbarossa. It had been Hitler's primary target all along, intended to form the foundations of his plan to carve out German colonies across the whole of Russia's territory after destroying the entire population. He intended to deport men and younger women as slave labour in Germany. They had already successfully invaded a huge territory to reach the outer suburbs of Moscow, with its subway system, in October 1941.

Stalin desperately needed military supplies and aid from America and Britain. Fearing that President Roosevelt and Prime Minister Winston Churchill were about to sign a secret agreement with Hitler to avoid bringing the United States into the war, and to allow German and Russian troops to wear each other down in battle, he summoned Major Vasili Zarubin to the Kremlin to brief him on his new assignment as NKVD resident agent in North and South America.[1]

Zarubin and his wife Elizabeth left Vladivostok on 12 October and arrived in San Francisco on 6 December. Elizabeth was a captain in the NKVD and Zarubin's best senior assistant. She had been trained by Felix Dzerzhinsky, the former Chief of Secret Police in charge of the infamous CHEKA.[2] Their first step was to activate the Soviets' well-placed agents, or sleepers, who resided in California under secret cover names until needed.

The NKVD resident agent in San Francisco was Gregory Kheifetz, who had been instructed to 'look into the state of research on the problem of uranium in the United States, particularly at Columbia University and the University of Minnesota'. Uranium was of particular interest to Soviet scientists for making an atomic bomb.[3]

Kheifetz met Major Zarubin on arrival in San Francisco harbour to lay the groundwork for atomic espionage. Soviet scientists had heard rumours of a powerful new weapon being developed in the West. And a state defence committee had advised the Soviet Government to instruct intelligence officers to look out for news of an atomic bomb being created from uranium in scientific publications. Moscow Centre found information in a Shanghai newspaper called the *North China Daily News* of 26 June 1940. The aim of the NKVD was to steal the U.S. technology in order to build a Russian atom bomb.

Kheifetz used the cover name 'Brown', with which he had already made contacts with atomic scientists in the Radiation Laboratory at the University of California. He had managed to befriend Robert Oppenheimer, whom he met at a fund-raising party for Spanish Civil War refugees on 6 December 1941, at the home of the wealthy Louise Brantsen, who was his close friend. He and Oppenheimer chatted easily together, and Brown arranged to meet Robert for lunch next day.[4]

Soviet scientists had already done some work on the nature of uranium, but it had not yet been funded for research. There appeared to be no great urgency, until confidential nuclear information was obtained by Donald Maclean (code name LEAF). He was one of the so-called Cambridge spy ring who were undercover agents for the Soviet Union. Maclean had sent a sixty-page report to the Kremlin from London on 16 September 1941, to warn Moscow Centre that Britain's government was funding the development of a bomb with an extraordinary destructive force using atomic energy. The project to build it was called 'Tube Alloys' (code-named TUBE). It would be undertaken by Imperial Chemical Industries (ICI) within two years.[5]

Apart from teaching, Oppenheimer was doing consultancy work for Arthur H. Compton, who was director of the Metallurgical Laboratory at the University of Chicago. As far as Robert knew, he was about to have a friendly lunch with a Soviet consul named Brown.

When Kheifetz/Brown talked informally with Oppenheimer over lunch, he had casually mentioned he had heard about an atomic bomb project but Moscow had been too slow to recognise its significance. Oppenheimer was able to confirm that the report to Moscow Centre from Maclean was authentic. He might also have conveyed that he had worked with brilliant German physicists before the war in Europe, like Werner Heisenberg, who now headed Hitler's secret weapons programme in Germany. Kheifetz reported back that Oppenheimer was evidently concerned that German scientists might succeed in building atomic weapons ahead of the Allies.

No one knew how powerful they could be when nature's stored-up power and force were unleashed. One bomb might destroy an entire city or the entire world – nobody knew. It had never been done. How could you trust an equation symbolising a theory scribbled on the back of an envelope to be flawless? Anything might happen with a chain reaction. It could mean the end of the world.

Kheifetz added in his report to Moscow that Oppenheimer told him about the excellent work being achieved in a secret combined atomic programme with brilliant German-Jewish physicists who had managed to escape from Nazi Germany to Britain and the United States. They were Nobel prize-winners and scientific geniuses, like Einstein. Oppenheimer also told him about the secret letter to Roosevelt, signed by Einstein in 1939, which had urged the President to support an atomic programme before German scientists could produce an atom bomb. The U.S. planned to spend 20 per cent of its defence budget on atomic research.

Federal Security

The FBI had already opened a file on Oppenheimer in March 1941, several months before he had met Kheifetz under his cover name. FBI agents had picked up Oppenheimer's name by accident from an unauthorised and illegal wire-tapping of a conversation by the California Communist Party's state secretary, who had been talking to a Party treasurer named 'Pop' Folkoff. Folkoff had mentioned a 3 p.m. appointment at Chevalier's home where 'the Big Boys' would meet. The FBI made a note of licence plate numbers on all cars parked outside the house at that time. One of them was Oppenheimer's Chrysler.[6]

> The FBI noted that he served on the Executive Committee of the American Civil Liberties Union – which the Bureau labeled 'a Communist Party front group.' Inevitably, an investigative file was opened on Oppenheimer which would eventually grow to some 7,000 pages. That same month, Oppenheimer's name was put on a list of 'persons to be considered for custodial detention pending investigation in the event of a national emergency.'[7]

According to Chevalier, members of their alleged 'closed unit' paid dues to the Communist Party, except for Oppenheimer, who paid his separately. Chevalier speculated that it was because Robert paid a whole lot more than he was supposed to. Otherwise the group took no 'orders' from the Party and 'functioned simply as a group of academics who met to share ideas about international affairs and politics'.[8]

'The general mood, which included Oppenheimer's mood, was that it would be tragic if the United States, England and France do not form some kind of alliance against Italy …'[9]

America was still neutral. It was not yet at war with Nazi Germany or Soviet Russia; so that none of that could be described as treason, or even illegal behaviour, as it could be if America were at war. According to Chevalier, they thought of themselves as politically committed intellectuals who were free from Party discipline.

In spite of America's official neutrality, the secret work of the FBI was undertaken to protect the United States from sabotage, espionage, or treason. Despite Robert's friendships with several communists, it would turn out that the FBI never found any evidence that Oppenheimer was or ever had been a Communist Party member.

In fact, as far as the Soviet Union was concerned, Oppenheimer was disillusioned with Stalin's internal political terror and his purges and executions of opponents as early as 1938.[10] He was depressed and agitated by it. By 1939, 'Oppenheimer was already very far from the Communist group.'[11]

In an unpublished memoir by one of the group, named Gordon Griffiths, Robert Oppenheimer denied ever having been a member of the Communist Party. Griffiths claimed that whatever they did could have been done by any member of the Liberals or Democrats.[12]

The outbreak of war in Europe changed everything. Chevalier was anxious for discussion among the League of American Writers. Although Oppie was not a member, he helped Chevalier write a pamphlet aimed at explaining the situation. Oppie even paid for it to be printed on handsome paper and distributed to members, dated 20 February 1940:

> In the last month strange things have happened to the New Deal. We have seen it attacked, and *more and more surely* we have seen it abandoned.

There is a growing discouragement of liberals with the movement for a democratic front and red-baiting has grown to a national sport. Reaction is mobilized.

The pamphlet was a defence of President Roosevelt's New Deal, with its domestic and social programme for millions of Americans who were still unemployed, and against a proposed cut in welfare payments. Oppenheimer felt particularly strongly about the degradation of jobless and impoverished American families, because of his own privileged position. He felt he had to do everything possible to restore financial and social equilibrium in America. He was gloomy about the war in Europe.

Without knowing the President's mind, Oppenheimer was caught in the ambiguity of Roosevelt's situation in which he would be obliged, subtly and cleverly, to turn around the opinions and attitudes of the majority of Americans who had been accustomed to isolation from Europe, in order to confront Hitler and Nazi Germany. He did not trust Hitler and knew he would have to be beaten by powerful military forces. Britain was unprepared for war and possessed only a small and out-of-date colonial army to protect the British Isles. Roosevelt also knew that the United States could not act firmly until he won re-election on 5 November 1940.

Pearl Harbor

Oppenheimer was an ardent supporter of Roosevelt and his New Deal. Ernest Lawrence saw his friend bubbling and lobbying enthusiastically prior to the presidential election, so that Lawrence felt encouraged to cast his own vote for a third term in office for Roosevelt. France had already fallen to Germany in the spring, while Britain fought on alone. Germany began its invasion of Soviet Russia from June 1941.

What helped President Roosevelt after he was re-elected for a further term was the unexpected attack on the American fleet at anchor in Pearl Harbor by the Japanese air force in December 1941. With America suddenly propelled into war, the mood in the country changed rapidly.

Its transformation from self-absorption to enthusiasm for war was fortunate, as Britain's suspicion that German scientists would be interested in heavy water from Norway had been confirmed that year. It had 'indicated that they were taking atomic developments seriously... A contract had been awarded to the plant to produce 1,500 kilograms starting only a few months previously in the autumn of 1941, and it seemed that the Germans were on the way to making an atomic pile in which plutonium might be produced ...'[13]

At least one German scientist, Fritz Houtermans, had envisioned the possibility of making plutonium in an atomic pile to develop a nuclear bomb. He had written about it in a memorandum in case he might be accused by the Gestapo of not having told the German government about its possibilities.[14]

12

Who Was Kitty Harris?

By comparison with Oppie's prolonged adolescence in which girls or young women haunted him but did not figure in his schemes, his hectic and troublesome affair with Jean Tatlock lasted for three years. He had wanted to marry her and, at least on two occasions, imagined they had come close to marriage in spite of all their problems. His continually conventional offers of flowers annoyed her beyond reason. The moment she saw them she would tell him to go away. She had felt the same way whenever he offered gifts to his friends. She appeared to think that such gestures were irresponsible when his money was needed to fund more important operations.

Although her idiosyncrasies were harmless in themselves, anyone else but Oppie would surely have treated her hysterical reactions as a symptom of a more serious condition. But Oppie had questioned his own strange behaviour for years and was still uncertain how he or anyone else should behave with the opposite sex. So Jean's self-centred behaviour may have seemed normal to him in their strange and volatile relationship.

Apparently he never received warnings of a possible breakdown by Jean from the psychoanalysts around him who knew her. And yet, his friend Robert Serber noted that she would disappear suddenly for weeks or months, then deliberately taunt him on her return about the possibility that she might have been having affairs with other men or women. She knew how much he was in love with her, and was determined to use him and hurt him. This was a woman who had been at medical school for three years and was studying to become a psychiatrist. It seemed that she was only waiting until she received her medical degree from Stanford to ditch him – which was what she did when she became a resident physician at San Francisco's Mount Zion Hospital.

She had given him a taste for female company. And now he reacted by doing exactly what he had warned his younger brother against – he spent more and more time with young women of Jean's age. There was Chevalier's sister-in-law, Ann. Next came Estelle, who was the sister of another friend. Serber knew of several others. Even so, Oppie was the one Jean called whenever she descended into a deep depression. And he would always rush over to coax her out of it.

He was introduced to Kitty Harrison at a garden party in August 1939. She was a married woman of twenty-nine. She fell in love with him immediately, and did her best to conceal it. Then they appeared together openly at a party in San

Francisco, making others feel uncomfortable at the way he introduced her, since the hostess was his most recent lover, Estelle. According to his friends, Kitty was far too flirtatious, and they worried at the way she manipulated him.[1]

Kitty was petite, with an attractive personality. Although manipulative, she differed from Jean Tatlock in that she was vivacious, whereas Jean was melancholic. She did not linger on the past, but looked forward eagerly to the future. She made a point of wearing exotic flowers, perhaps because she was a brunette and felt she had to find a way to dramatise herself, like the gypsy heroine in the popular opera named *Carmen*.[2]

Kitty's Version

According to one source, Kitty had been born in Westphalia, Germany, and was reputed to be related to several European royals. She had been educated at the University of Munich and the Sorbonne, and had spent time with the café society lot in Paris, where she had married a young musician. She had very soon discovered he was homosexual and a drug addict. An American court annulled the marriage. Then she had met Joe Dullet and married him. Joe was dedicated to the Communist Party and insisted on imposing Party loyalty on her. He patronised her as a spoilt young bourgeois intellectual. Their arguments increased until 1936, when Kitty decided she could no longer share his hectic and insecure vagabond life, surrounded by poverty among the labouring classes.

She stayed in London with her father for a while, but her gypsy life among the poor was not yet over: Dullet reappeared and told her he had decided to fight in a communist brigade in the Spanish Civil War with a friend named Nelson. Kitty and Joe spent some time together in Paris, while Nelson tagged along. She bankrolled them both for their meals and hotel rooms. Kitty was an adventurous young woman and keen to join the two friends at the battlefront in Spain, but the Communist Party would not allow husbands and wives to be together.

Dullet and Nelson left for Spain, where Joe became a political commissar, which suited his doctrinaire zealotry. He loved everything about the idea of fighting fascists. But deserters had to be tried by a commissar, and some were executed with a bullet to the back of the neck. It meant he was disliked, even hated, by everyone. He became lonely. When it came to the first battle in which he was chosen to lead a battalion, he felt he had to gain popularity with his comrades by taking risks. He boasted he would be the first man to leap across the parapet and attack the enemy. When he did so, he was immediately shot in the groin by machine gun fire, making him a hero for the moment, at least. Then a second burst of fire from another machine gun killed him.

Kitty was said to have been deeply upset at his death for some time. Then she met a British doctor named Richard Harrison in the early part of 1938 and, in her usual impetuous and happy-go-lucky way, married him for security in November.

Their marriage was a failure from the start. After she was awarded her Bachelor of Arts degree, she agreed to move to California with him, since he feared that a divorce could ruin his career. She now felt she was finally in charge of her own life, when she met Robert Oppenheimer. His friends soon noticed that she seemed to have succeeded in humanising him.

The Kremlin Source

According to her classified Moscow Centre file, which was kept in the basement of the Kremlin for the NKVD and KGB, Kitty Harris was also known as Katherine Harrison. Her cover names were, variously, AIDA and GYPSY, and ADA or NORMA in the Venona cipher. She was a 'skilled spy'. According to one source, Kitty possessed no fewer than seventeen different cover names she had used for a variety of different projects. Spymaster Elizabeth Zarubin now asked her to work with the NKVD as her protégé.[3]

According to another version by an author who appeared to have carefully researched her background, Kitty did not come from impoverished nobility:

> Harris was the daughter of impoverished Soviet émigrés who came first to London, where she was born, and then to Canada when she was eight years old. Her father, a shoemaker, could not support the family on his earnings, so Kitty worked in a tobacco factory from the age of 13, where she became a trade union activist. There she experienced violent strikes and labor confrontations; the Soviet Union became the symbol of her aspirations. She moved to the United States and became a member of the American Communist Party, where she met Earl Browder. Because of her dark brown eyes she was thought to resemble the heroine of the opera *Carmen*, from which she acquired her first code name, GYPSY.[4]

Browder was the head of the American Communist Party. 'Elizabeth Zarubin trained Kitty Harris in the use of forged passports, ciphers, and how to hide papers and money in her underwear.'[5]

According to a third source, 'Donald Maclean's faith in the Soviet Union was supported ... by a secret female companion.' She was a KGB officer appointed to look after him. Her name was Kitty Harris.[6] Maclean had a passionate affair with her before he met Melinda. Kitty was 'way more experienced in both her political and personal life' than Donald. She was thirteen years older than him and had already worked for the Soviet Union for sixteen years. She acted as his handler and courier, as well as his lover.

> Harris was born in the East End of London, in a working class Jewish family, but grew up in Canada and then Chicago, where the harsh lives of the worker made her receptive to the arguments of communists – including

the man who was to become her husband, a charismatic party organiser called Eric Browder. She spent a couple of years with him in Shanghai, trying to organise the underground Communist party.[7]

Kitty moved to Europe, where she worked for Soviet intelligence. According to this source, she was headstrong – as her actions appear to be in whichever life she assumed – and passionate in her belief in the Communist cause.

The Maclean Episode

One day Donald Maclean went to meet his usual handler and found Kitty.

'You hadn't expected to see a lady, had you?' she said.

'No, but it's a pleasant surprise,' he replied, as previously instructed.[8]

Moscow Centre had told Kitty that Maclean was the most important spy the KGB had, since he was passing them top secret documents about Britain's atomic bomb programme. He was one of the so-called Cambridge Five spy ring.

'Cherish him as the apple of your eye,' she was told by Moscow. She did. Donald visited her in her Bayswater flat in London's West End, not far from Marble Arch, 'twice a week, late in the evening, bringing papers for her to photograph that he had sneaked out of the Foreign Office for the night. From the start, he'd bring flowers and chocolates with those papers, and after a few months they agreed to have a special dinner to celebrate their birthdays, which fell within a few days of each other. One evening in May 1938, Maclean turned up at her flat carrying a huge bunch of roses, a bottle of wine and a box containing a locket on a thin gold chain.

'Harris wore it for the rest of her life; when she died in 1966, it was still among her paltry possessions. He had ordered dinner from a local restaurant, and they sat eating it and listening to Glenn Miller on the radio. That was the first night they made love, and true to her training she reported the event to her controller, Grigoriy Grafpen, next day.'

When Maclean was posted to the British embassy in Paris in 1938, he asked Moscow if Kitty could come, too, and Moscow Centre agreed. They continued to work together until June 1940, when the Germans broke through the Maginot line and invaded France. Her final report on Maclean to Moscow Centre included her profile of him.

'He is politically weak,' she wrote, 'but there is something fundamentally good and strong in him that I value. He understands and hates the rotten capitalist system and has enormous confidence in the Soviet Union and the working class. Bearing in mind his origins and his past he is a good and brave comrade.'

He had apparently become less interested in her sexually by that time, and more interested in the American Melinda Marling. He told Kitty on the very first evening he met Melinda that he saw another side to the prim American from the one his friends saw.

'I was very taken by her views,' he told Kitty. 'She's a liberal; she's in favour of the Popular Front and doesn't mind mixing with communists even though her parents are well off. We found we spoke the same language.'

Robert Oppenheimer's Romance

Although Kitty had a B.A. degree by now, her real academic interest was to take a doctorate in botany. She began her graduate studies in the autumn of 1939, at much the same time as when she met Oppenheimer. They had begun to date, and would frequently be seen in Robert's Chrysler coupé. A physician named Dr Louis Hempelman, who taught at Berkeley, would remember how 'he would ride up near my office with this cute little girl'.

'She was very attractive. She was tiny, skinny as a rail, just like he was. They'd give each other a fond kiss and go their separate ways. Robert always had that pork-pie hat on.'[9]

Kitty was evidently a survivor, a woman who had managed to remain remarkably youthful, seductive, and evidently lovable, while she watched others around her deteriorate; some from alcoholic addiction, others from power, or a rigid adherence to political doctrinaire behaviour, or an assumption of the macho personality so much admired by fascists; or from complacency, corruption, and so on. Clearly she knew how to manipulate men to her advantage and to the benefit of the Communist Party.

This was the remarkably intelligent and able woman who had set her sights on marrying Robert Oppenheimer.

In the spring of 1940, Oppie had invited the Serbers to Perro Caliente for part of the summer. He explained to them that he had also invited Kitty and her husband, but Dr Richard Harrison had said he could not come along, so he expected Kitty to arrive alone. Kitty turned up with the Serbers instead.

She was pregnant by the end of the summer. When Oppie told her husband, they both agreed that a divorce would be best for everyone concerned.

Bob Serber had watched the affair burgeon in New Mexico throughout the summer, but he was astonished when Oppie told him he intended to marry Kitty.

A Fourth Source

A fourth account of Kitty's identity and origin appeared in an official document on the 'Scope of Soviet Activity in the United States'. That report referred to the application for a U.S. passport in the name of Katherine Harrison. 'Her application was executed on 23 November 1927 and passport No. 476407 was issued on November 26, 1927. The applicant stated that she resided at 350 West 21st Street, New York, N.Y.[10]

'The identifying witness was Vivian M. Wilkinson, 35 Charles Street, apartment 6A, New York City.

'The applicant submitted as evidence of her alleged birth in San Francisco, Calif., on 24 May 1899 in an affidavit executed in the name Jack Harrison who stated that he was the applicant's uncle. It was apparently aimed at exploiting the advantage of the 1906 earthquake that destroyed all official records.[11]

'The applicant used that passport to travel to Shanghai, China, where she lived with Earl Browder, who was using a passport in the name of George Morris. In addition to being known as Mrs. George Morris, Kitty was also known as Miss Alice Read, and rented a post office box in that name. She was also associated in Shanghai with a man who had a passport in the name of W.A. Haskell.

'Miss Harrison made a new passport application at the Passport Agency in New York City on April 12, 1932, giving her address as 101 West 11th Street, New York City. An investigation was thereupon conducted but the applicant could not be interviewed although she was said to be residing at the aforementioned address at that time. Previously an unsuccessful attempt had been made to locate her at the address given in the 1927 application and to locate the alleged uncle, Jack Harrison.

'Efforts of the Department to ascertain the true identity and nationality of the alleged Katherine Harrison have been unsuccessful. She is said to be known as Kitty Harris and to have been serving as recently as 2 years ago in the Soviet Military Intelligence Service.

'Vivian Wilkinson, the identifying witness on the passport application, is a niece of Grace Hutchins, the owner of the building in which the Communist headquarters is located.

'The affidavit of birth, signed by Jack Harrison, was written and signed by John W. Johnstone, also known as Jack Johnstone. He is an important Communist leader and is now located in Pittsburgh.

'Mr. X and General Krivitsky can testify regarding Katherine Harrison.'

They were the only entries in an official government document of the inquiry into the 'Scope of Soviet Activity in the United States', which sought to establish the connection between Kitty Harris and Katherine Harrison. Until then, it seemed almost as if each of them had an identical twin living a separate and secret life – one in Shanghai and London, another in the United States. As it turned out, all of the varied personas in constant motion were part of the vivacious and multi-talented Kitty, who was alleged to be, not of impoverished nobility, but the daughter of an impoverished shoemaker in the East End of London.

Kitty's Paper Trail

That was only according to known records. It is not easy to follow Kitty's paper trail because of her instinctive self-serving lies, her cheerful obfuscations, and deliberate misinformation from Moscow Centre to muddy the waters, in which fragments of her personality might otherwise still be found. In Shanghai with Earl Browder in

November 1927, for example, a police report described her as Mrs Alice Read, while they used their cover names of Mr and Mrs Harrison to set up their spy network in the month after they had arrived.[12]

She acted as a courier for the Communist Party in Hong Kong and Harbin. After three days in Harbin she became Mrs Morrison, then Alice Read again. She returned to New York with Browder in February 1929 to visit her aging parents, and left for Canada in March 1931, where she worked as a secretary until April 1932. She had British nationality while living in Canada.[13]

She was restless as usual, and – after quitting her job on 15 April – was soon happily travelling again; this time on the *Queen Mary* to Bremerhaven under her code name of 'Gypsy'. Kitty was starry-eyed that she would be visiting Moscow at last, which had been depicted as a Utopia for romantic and gullible misfits like her.

'Kitty was lucky to get away. The State Department had issued a circular the previous month to American consular officers worldwide expressing doubts about Kitty's status and asking to be informed if she applied for a new US passport. Since they assumed she was still overseas, the circular seems not to have been drawn to the attention of passport-issuing offices in the US itself, and in those far-off pre-computer days it took weeks before her application filtered back to Washington. It had been processed and granted at Manhattan's City Hall on 12 April 1932 (again in the name of Katherine Harrison …)'[14]

Kitty had arrived in Bremen a year before that fatal 30 January, in 1933, when Hitler won 11 million votes. Hindenburg won 18 million, but had aged and become too senile to rule Germany. The hero of the First World War submitted the position as Chancellor to the rising Nazi dictator instead. Kitty was given a new name in Berlin: she was now 'Eleanor Davies, an American born in Chicago'.[15]

It was a particularly traumatic time for many people who observed the rise of the Nazis in Germany. Its impact was felt not only by Kitty, but by others like Donald Maclean of the notorious 'Cambridge Five' students, who would dedicate themselves to defeat the Nazis by joining the KGB as spies and passing on valuable secrets to the Kremlin. It may be at that time in Berlin when Kitty created the myth that she was German and closely related to one of Hitler's generals, which made her despise her origins and fight the Nazis.

She was in Paris in December 1932, where she met Kim Philby, Guy Burgess and Donald Maclean in a safe house that was her flat, where several spymasters met their agents. She also met Kim and Guy elsewhere in 1934. Her movements were erratic while she was constantly on the go. She enjoyed the excitement of a job that gave her purpose; otherwise she easily became bored.

Kitty continued as a safe house keeper in London, and travelled to Paris before she was 'recalled to Moscow' in December 1937, where she applied for Russian citizenship on the 21st. She had described herself on her application form as; 'Harris, Kitty Natanovna born in London 24 May 1899', and a British subject. Although she thought she had been accepted as a Russian citizen, there was a clerical error with the Russian 'H', which translated into a 'G', and the clerk gave the citizenship to someone else. Kitty left for America soon afterwards. And from New York, she left for London in 1938.

She was still known as GYPSY in Moscow Centre, before they changed her code name to NORMA to meet Maclean for the first time.[16]

It was 'decided to send Kitty to the United States and Canada to obtain two real passports and then return her to Britain, where she was to put all her energies into working with Maclean'.[17]

Her spying schedule appears to indicate that the trail of Kitty Harris or Katherine Harrison, 'went cold when she went back to Canada in the 1930s'.[18] She was NORMA by the time of her secret liaisons with Donald Maclean from May 1938.

It was NKVD spymaster Liza Zarubin who arranged to introduce Kitty to Robert Oppenheimer at a garden party in August 1939, immediately after her assignment with Maclean ended in eighteen months. That was when a new life opened up for her in her old persona as Kitty Harris – married name, Harrison.

That was the critical moment when the records appeared to go awry and turn her into two different Kitty Harrises. One of them was evidently a Moscow Centre invention – a fantasy of disinformation to lead followers of the paper trail away from what the real Kitty Harris was doing as a handler and controller of Robert Oppenheimer. She had suddenly become far too valuable an asset to the Kremlin to risk exposure. Her real mission for Moscow had to be kept top secret, to lead MI5 and the CIA off in a false direction that assured them that Kitty had been taken ill, and become so disoriented that Moscow Centre had established her in a sanatorium, drugged and under the close scrutiny of psychiatrists.

13

The Nuclear Programme

In the spring of 1941, Harry Hopkins sent a note to the popular New York Mayor, Fiorello La Guardia, in which he emphasised that the American Communist Party was a potential danger. Hopkins was President Roosevelt's closest and completely trusted advisor.

'It seems to me that we have got to find a way to beat these people. From my point of view they are just as much a potential enemy as the Germans.'[1]

Despite that view, their attitude changed very quickly soon afterwards. When huge German armies invaded Russia in June, Roosevelt realised that the United States must begin to provide aid to the Soviet Union in the hope that Russia would destroy Nazi Germany. America and Soviet Russia were now ideologically and militarily on the same side, regardless of their different political doctrines.

The Allies could now give their undivided attention to defeating the so-called Axis of Germany, Italy and Japan. President Roosevelt chose the same policy that Great Britain had always used when drawn into battle; to ensure that the battlefields were as far away overseas from the British Isles as possible. Like Britain, Roosevelt was also canny enough to use the military forces of other nations whenever he could. Both he and Churchill knew that Russia's fighting forces were vastly bigger and more ruthless than their own, and were accustomed to the hardships of brutal battlefronts clad in the perishing snow and ice of its legendary harsh winters that repeatedly destroyed foreign invaders.

What had previously been a part-time advisory job that Oppenheimer undertook for Arthur Compton now grew into something more vital. Compton – who had won the 1927 Nobel Prize in physics – asked him to take charge of theoretical problems concerning the design of an atom bomb.[2]

All the great physicists of Oppenheimer's generation had watched with interest the imaginative theories of the pioneers of science, before some of those newcomers too had contributed their own ideas that inched the making of the first nuclear bomb closer and closer – certainly since 1905 when Einstein had explained the relationship between energy and mass. It was more than a generation ago. And yet, the romance of nuclear energy had continued to mesmerise them all. But it was still only theory.

The crux of that theory was critical assembly, or having enough fissionable material to sustain a chain of reaction. Critical mass meant using the smallest amount of material to support a self-sustaining chain reaction. Some scientists still feared that a chain reaction might destroy the world.

Since German experimental scientists split the first uranium bomb successfully, in theory, at the Kaiser Wilhelm Institute in Berlin in 1938, they, and the Allies, had considered that a bomb with extraordinary destructive force might be built if enough fissionable material could be produced. That material would have to be either Uranium 235, or plutonium. Plutonium had been newly discovered by British and American scientists.[3]

Oppie was deeply interested in the whole project, and watched thoughtfully through 1941 and in the spring of 1942 how Compton's people had recruited a special team of nuclear scientists at the Metallurgical Laboratory. It began with Enrico Fermi and Leo Szilard, then Eugene Wigner. The Chicago Group was formed in March with a team of forty-five individuals, including secretaries, guards, and elevator operators. They increased to 1,250 by June. The numbers were still growing.[4]

Security and secrecy forced them to undertake the project under one roof and as far away from everyone else as possible. If they could achieve their goal with their scientific discoveries, it would be 'the greatest single achievement of organised human effort in history'.[5]

They received the official U.S. Government go-ahead in the summer of 1942 to build as urgently as possible the first ever nuclear weapon. None of them knew what to expect. All they knew was that they would have to design every component and also apparently design and develop suitable new factories to manufacture them; then assemble them to introduce the fissionable material for an atom bomb, and hope it would work.

The Manhattan Project

So far, they had concentrated on centralising work on 'piles' and plutonium at the University of Chicago lab. A pile soon became known as a nuclear reactor – a device to cause a fission chain reaction. Until now, the principals had comprised Arthur Compton, Vannevar Bush, James Bryant Conant, Ernest Lawrence, and Harold C. Urey. Compton headed the project. He was one of a family of esteemed academic intellectuals, who had been awarded the Nobel Prize in physics with his pioneer work on cosmic rays.

Compton was a fit and energetic man who had been a college football player. He was pleasant to deal with and considerate with everyone. His Presbyterian background had given him deep religious feelings, and he was abstemious. He believed deeply in scientific progress and was a passionate explorer of physics.[6]

He was also a good organiser, co-ordinator, and manager. As far as secrecy and security were concerned, he shared everything with his self-confident and highly responsible wife, to whom he was devoted. Both received security clearance, and Betty became an influential and helpful member of the metallurgical lab.

The scientific problems they faced were awe-inspiring. Fortunately, all the members of the team were the type of people who thrived on the challenges of the almost impossible, and were inspired and galvanised to solve the problems and turn the possibilities into reality.

What they had not anticipated was an official military aim or policy that was contrary to their scientific goal. The first officer chosen to lead the U.S. Army's part in the project was Colonel James C. Marshall (District Engineer of Manhattan District). He and Colonel Kenneth D. Nichols (Deputy Chief) assembled the resources they would need. But Vannevar Bush, who headed the U.S. Office of Scientific Research and Development (OSRD), became dissatisfied with Colonel Marshall's failure to get the project moving forward with sufficient urgency, and the low priority allocated to the project by the army – which should have been Triple A.

Bush felt that the project needed more aggressive leadership, and wanted a more prestigious officer in overall command. Groves was chosen for the position, and promoted to brigadier general. He received his orders to take command of the Manhattan Project on 23 September 1942. Marshall was now Groves's liaison officer, while Groves was directly under the command of Major General Somervell.

The first big problem that confronted General Groves was to find a suitable director for Project Y, the group that would design and build the bomb. It should be a laboratory head, like Urey, Compton, or Lawrence. Compton immediately recommended Robert Oppenheimer, because he was intimately familiar with the bomb design concepts. But Oppenheimer had very little administrative experience. Nor had he won a Nobel Prize like each of the others. Moreover, there was serious concern about his security, since many of his associates were communists – as were his brother Frank, his wife Kitty, and his former girlfriend, Jean Tatlock.

By the time that Oppenheimer was appointed in June 1942, they had reviewed all those personal details with him at length during a train journey the previous October. Groves and Nichols were convinced that Oppenheimer understood all the complexities involved in setting up a laboratory in an isolated area, and were satisfied to confirm his appointment as scientific director. Groves formally and personally issued a security clearance for Oppenheimer on 20 July 1943.

U.S. Military Policy

The scientists had not expected to find themselves watching the project being taken out of their hands by the military. Almost immediately, in June 1942, it emerged that the military policies and aims were very different from what the scientists had believed was their goal. The scientific point of view was that, if the atom bomb worked, only one bomb would be required to end the war because of the threat of its enormous devastation. It should be enough of a warning to the enemy to achieve peace, although they might need a second one in reserve, just in case. Marshall intended to sort out that fundamental problem immediately, since it was not the way the military strategists viewed the situation. However destructive the bomb turned out to be, it was essential to have the ability to continue to deliver the weapon. That was what determined whether it was useful.

'If you folks succeeded in making only one bomb,' Marshall told the scientists, 'I can assure you it will never be used. The only basic principle on which the military can operate is the ability to continue to deliver … What we are talking about is "production capacity" to consider delivering bombs at a given rate.'

The argument from the scientists was that while they would be spending time with considerable delays on creating production capacity, the Germans, who were understood to be working desperately on *their* bomb, would overtake the United States by producing and detonating only one atom bomb. And that would be the end!

Although the scientists now sensed that the army would inevitably win the argument, they were confronted by the fact that no scientific laboratory in the world was big enough and capable enough to provide large-scale and regular production of atom bombs. They feared the job would have to be turned over to industry, whereas they were convinced that *they* were the only ones capable of producing a nuclear bomb.

They were haunted by an uneasy feel that Hitler would be a day ahead of them – so they were determined to get the job done themselves.

On the other hand, Arthur Compton knew very well that most of the physicists had absolutely no experience of industry and had never worked with engineers. Industrial design and plant construction were not part of their culture. Compton, who did have at least some industrial experience himself, knew that the military were right.[7]

Only a few weeks previously, Colonel Groves – as he then was – had been a military engineer and the army's Chief of Construction. He had been eager to go overseas on a combat assignment at the front. He had informed his superior officer, General Somervell, of his intention. The General had replied, 'Sorry, Groves … you can't leave Washington … The Secretary of War has selected you for a very important assignment … Here in Washington.'

When Groves objected that he wanted to serve overseas, Somervell told him, 'If you do this job right, it will win the war. You can do it if anyone can …'

The first scientists from Europe who had brought news of Germany's nuclear project were those who had fled from Nazi Germany. According to them, a new form of energy, nuclear energy, could be achieved by splitting or 'fissioning' the atom. If so, the explosive power would be millions of times greater than any previously known to mankind. They were convinced that German scientists would do everything possible to produce and use an atom bomb on Britain or America, or both.

President Roosevelt had passed the entire United States atomic project over to the army, and Groves was given command. The President relied heavily on the advice of Vannevar Bush, through whose U.S. Office of Scientific Research and Development (OSRD) most wartime military research and development was undertaken.

Bush, in turn, depended on the Atomic Committee for advice. His principal collaborator was Dr James B. Conant, the president of Harvard University. Conant had served as a major in the Chemical Warfare Service in the First World War.

According to Conant, 'If the new weapon is going to be the determining factor in the war, then there is a desperate need for speed. Three months delay might be disastrous.'

It meant that, regardless of which process or method to produce the atomic bomb might be better, success would depend on one factor – which one was fastest.

Collaborating with the British

Britain and America initially exchanged nuclear information, but without combining their efforts. The British even discouraged attempts by Bush and Conant for closer co-operation in 1941 between Britain's Tube Alloys project and the Manhattan Project, because Churchill did not wish to share the British lead in technology, or help the United States develop its own atomic bomb. When Roosevelt offered to pay for all research and development in an Anglo-American project, Churchill had rebuffed him for security reasons. So the United States decided, in April 1942, to work alone.

Britain had made significant contributions early in the war, but lacked the necessary resources to undertake such a research programme while fighting for survival against Nazi Germany. That was why Tube Alloys fell behind the American project. Churchill and Roosevelt came to an informal and unwritten agreement for atomic collaboration, but it was not an equal partnership. The positions of the two countries had changed from late 1941, when America's scientists no longer needed outside help; so that Britain's bargaining position worsened.

American scientists also wanted to prevent Britain from exploiting post-war commercial applications of atomic energy. Hence, by January 1943, Conant was instructed by the President to notify Britain that they would no longer receive atomic information from America, except in certain areas.

Britain stopped sending research and scientists to America at much the same time as the Americans stopped sharing information with them. They considered ending the supply of Canadian uranium and heavy water to force the Americans to share, but Canada needed American supplies to produce them. And Britain finally decided that an independent nuclear programme could not be ready in time to affect the outcome of the war in Europe.

When Conant decided, by March 1943, that British help would benefit some areas of the project, physicist James Chadwick and several other British scientists were invited to help the bomb design team at Los Alamos, in spite of the risk of revealing weapon design secrets.

The Decisive Battle

Four months later, in July 1943, Russian forces fought the greatest massive tank battle in history near Kursk, out on the open steppes, south-west of Moscow. It was their most decisive battle against the German invaders. Fortunately, British code experts at Bletchley Park deciphered German military messages on their Ultra machine, which had the ability to read the German Enigma machine. Secret German directives were passed on to the Red Army by the British KGB spy John Cairncross, who had worked at Bletchley. They prevented Russian troops from being taken by surprise by the German Army, by giving Red Army commanders time to change their order of battle.

As a consequence, the communist Cairncross – who would later be recognised as one of the 'Cambridge Five' spies working for the KGB – could claim to have helped Britain's Soviet ally win the decisive Battle of Kursk against Nazi Germany by his spy craft.

After the Russian victory, the three major Allies could seriously plan post-war strategy and tactics with a sense of optimism about the defeat of Nazi Germany. But Anglo-American policies would only be realistic if an American atomic bomb were to be built ahead of Hitler's so-called secret weapons, with which he intended first to destroy London with German air supremacy, and then invade Britain by sea and land.

What was not known at the time was how far ahead of the United States the German nuclear programme was. The Manhattan Project was built on fear that Nazi Germany already had the atomic bomb and was almost ready to use it. So the race was on in Los Alamos to ensure that America possessed atomic supremacy before Hitler could make his decisive move.

14

Germany's Secret Weapons

The first time the West heard that German scientists were already working on what became known as Hitler's secret weapons, was soon after the war began. It was early one morning on 4 November 1939 when a guard at the British Embassy in Oslo saw, by chance, something small beneath a layer of snow on a ledge near the porter's lodge. On investigation, he found what looked like a block of legal-size paper addressed to the British naval attaché. It was handed to the attaché as soon as he arrived. He found a note inside, signed by 'a well-wishing German scientist'.

The package was despatched to London by diplomatic bag in the usual way, where it was passed to the scientific department of MI6, headed by Dr R. V. Jones. He studied it with interest and curiosity. Reginald Jones was an intelligent and solemn physicist of twenty-eight, described as a natural philosopher and an astronomer. Despite his seriousness, he was fascinated by deceptions, and well aware of the deadly tricks developed by German Intelligence. He was full of purposeful practical jokes himself, which he enjoyed devising in order to beat the Nazis at their own games of deadly mischief. He had been appointed to MI6 only two months previously, when war was declared against Germany, and installed in an office at No. 34 Broadway at the beginning of November.

'The Old Chief of M.I.6, Admiral "Quex" Sinclair, had just died. He was succeeded by Stewart Menzies, who had previously been Head of Section V of M.I.6, but I was not to meet him for another year.'[1]

Dr Jones was responsible for examining Britain's Secret Service files on the latest German weapons, and for providing a report. He already knew they had little information about German weaponry; so he was the most suitable scientist to evaluate the so-called 'Oslo Report'.[2]

According to his own account, 'Just as I was finishing the secret weapons report one evening, Fred Winterbotham came into my room and dumped a small parcel on my desk and said, "Here's a present for you!"

'I can remember gingerly opening the box because it might easily have been a bomb …'[3]

He was surprised to find a great deal of highly technical information about a new torpedo that could apparently home in on its target by sound. There was also a new system that enabled Germany's air force to bomb chosen targets without seeing them. Then he read of the development of two radar systems. One was named 'Würtzburg', the other 'Freya'. He found a great deal more, and was particularly drawn to a fascinating report of a rocket programme with the name of 'Aggregatprogramm'. German scientists were already testing it by firing long-range rockets in an experimental establishment he had never heard of, named Peenemünde, on an island in the Baltic.

Jones realised with amazement that a whole new weapons programme had already begun to be developed by German scientists who were evidently far ahead of any of the Allies. Their ingenuity appeared to be extraordinary, but no one was in a position to validate it.

Whether or not the Oslo Report was authentic, and not a deception by German intelligence, what was perhaps most significant was that there was no mention in it of any work by German scientists on an atomic bomb programme. Either it was too important to be mentioned, for reasons of security, or the Germans were not as far ahead as was supposed. How could anyone know, since the German nuclear programme was bound to be top secret?

The German Uranium Club

Germany had begun a secret programme, called *Uranverein*, or 'uranium club', in April 1939, a few months after German scientists Otto Hahn and Fritz Strassmann inadvertently discovered fission. Germany had a significant head start over the Manhattan Project, as well as some of the best scientists, a strong industrial base, sufficient materials, and the interest of its military officers.[4]

News of their discovery had spread quickly. Leo Szilard read the Hahn-Strassmann paper and wrote to Lewis Strauss on 25 January 1939:

> 'I feel I ought to let you know of a very sensational new development in nuclear physics. In a recent paper ... Hahn reports that he finds when bombarding uranium with neutrons the uranium "breaks up" ... This is entirely unexpected and exciting news for the average physicist. The department of physics at Princeton, where I have spent the last few days, was like a stirred-up ant heap. Apart from the purely scientific interest there may be another aspect of this discovery, which so far does not seem to have caught the attention of those to whom I spoke. First of all it is obvious that the energy released in this new reaction must be very much higher than all previously known cases ... This in itself might make it possible to produce power by means of nuclear energy, but I do not think that this possibility is very exciting, for the cost of investment would probably be too high to make the process worthwhile. I see ... possibilities in another direction. These might lead to large-scale production of energy and radioactive elements, unfortunately also perhaps to atomic bombs ...

Lewis Strauss would become chairman of the Atomic Energy Commission.

It was the firm opinion of General Groves that, without positive evidence to the contrary, the United States government remained equally as afraid as American scientists 'that the most competent German scientists and engineers were working on an atomic programme with the full support of their government and with the full capacity of German industry at their disposal. Any other assumption would have been unsound and dangerous.'[5]

The idea of kidnapping Werner Heisenberg in Switzerland in 1942 had even been considered, as he was the scientist most likely to be in charge of a German nuclear programme. A year later the United States would launch the Alsos Mission, a foreign intelligence project aimed at learning the extent of Germany's nuclear programme.

Under the command of General Leslie Groves, those intelligence-gathering operations would advance with the Allied armies in the spring of 1945, to learn at first-hand how close Germany was to developing an atomic bomb. The top priority would be to capture most of the key German scientists who had developed the V2 rockets, physicists who were working on an atomic bomb, and scientists who worked on the artificial intelligence of advanced communications systems; also to take stores of uranium ore and other nuclear raw materials, and thousands of research documents regarding the development of atomic energy.[6]

Among other findings would be a German experimental reactor at Haigerloch.

Werner Heisenberg headed the Kaiser Wilhelm Institute for Physics in Berlin during the war. Although it was where research into nuclear reactors continued, he either deliberately took a back seat when it came to actually making a German nuclear bomb, or he was overtaken by about half a dozen others physicists whose names were not generally known.

When Hitler became Chancellor of Germany, and the Nazi Party rose to power in 1933, Heisenberg won a Nobel Prize. Numerous other scientists were dismissed or resigned, including Born, Einstein, and Schrödinger, as well as several of Heisenberg's students and colleagues in Leipzig.[7]

It was said afterwards that Heisenberg made quiet interventions within the bureaucracy, 'rather than overt public protest', hoping that the Nazi regime would not last, since his public opposition to Hitler would have resulted in his execution for treason.[8]

Whatever Heisenberg was doing in Germany during the war was top secret. And yet, with his glowing reputation in physics, Hitler would have been certain to press him into working on his secret weapons. Heisenberg was apparently not a Nazi, but he was a German patriot. It was an ambiguous position that would place many such German patriots in a perilous situation in which most considered it more prudent to sit tight and hope they might be invisible to the scrutiny of the Gestapo.

15

The Intellectual and the Militarist

What the personalities of General Groves and Robert Oppenheimer had in common was a sense of perfectionism, since each man knew his own worth, and was determined to get things done. But in appearance and psychological make-up they were entirely different. Whereas Groves was a burly soldier with a military bearing and a fleshy, though handsome, square face, Oppie looked skinny at 6ft tall, and his high cheekbones in a lean face tended to exaggerate his beanpole appearance. While Groves, with his self-discipline, appeared calm, even when he was smouldering with anger inside, Robert was edgy, with his piercing and speculative icy-blue gaze, and an inevitable cigarette in hand for the nicotine he craved.

Oppenheimer was a thinker who flowed with original ideas, whereas Groves was an administrator of other people's plans. President Roosevelt was his Commander-in-Chief. It was Roosevelt who had issued the Executive Order that created the Office of Scientific Research and Development in June 1941.

Arthur Compton meticulously planned a schedule of events and activities according to the traditional PERT chart milestone method, with the possibility of a successful chain reaction being demonstrated by 1 July 1942. Tests would be completed by January 1943; the first production of Plutonium 239 in a nuclear reactor by January 1944; and the completion of an atomic bomb by January 1945.[1]

It was only a strategic forecast of what he hoped would be achieved, but it would be Oppenheimer's responsibility to ensure that those milestones would be reached. Groves's responsibility was to plan and implement what would be required to support Oppenheimer and his team of scientists, like building and managing suitable industrial plants.

Vannevar Bush met with the President on 17 June 1942, and advised that the making of the bomb should be divided between the Office of Scientific Research and Development and the Army Corps of Engineers. The former would continue with the scientific research, while the latter would build the plants. The President agreed that the army would take control of the project, and initialled the proposal that Bush asked him to sign, 'OK. FDR.'[2]

Groves, when young, had achieved his ambition to join West Point military academy, and had reported there in 1916. His father had been a Presbyterian army chaplain who had become disappointed in the army, which he thought from his own experience, 'to be filled with drunks and gamblers'. But his son was impressed with 'the character and devotion to duty of the Army officers I knew …'[3]

He prepared for his career by spending his first two years after leaving West Point at an engineering school. After marriage, came a typical series of army moves – to San Francisco, Honolulu, Galveston in Texas, Delaware, Nicaragua, and Washington D.C., where he had worked with scientists for the first time. His skills were noted in particular after he was made chief of operations and deputy chief of construction in 1940. He could be demanding and blunt with his staff, because he could not tolerate hesitations or delays. Everything had to be done according to schedules. His Presbyterian background and his own efficiency made him deplore mental laziness and frivolous behaviour. He hired and fired impatiently to get the right people for each job. In 1941 he was assigned to oversee the construction of the new War Department building that would become known as the Pentagon. Groves knew what he wanted, and was highly critical, abrasive and sarcastic if he did not get it.

As a practical and methodical manager, Groves was shocked at the science and scientists under his new command, because their outlook and approach was mostly about possibilities instead of probabilities. He had been ordered to build huge and costly factories and assembly lines to develop 'previously unknown substances', and there was no evidence that they would work when it came to using them in the main project, which was to produce and detonate the first ever nuclear bomb. It might not explode as planned.

Oppenheimer found himself in a somewhat different position when he was just as suddenly made responsible for creating an enormous scientific organisation. He was not only involved in employing and managing other scientists and support staff, and understanding the value and skills and problems of a team of physicists. He was confident in his usual capacity for hard work and deep analysis of problems at all hours. They were skills that should enable him to succeed in more normal circumstances. But this was an enterprise that had never come about before, anywhere, in the whole of history. Moreover, his old friend and colleague Ernest Lawrence insisted he wanted Oppie to contribute his own scientific ideas to such critical problems as the amount of uranium 235 required for the bomb.[4]

'In May, when Breit resigned as director of the fast neutron research being done under S-1 Committee auspices, Compton asked Oppenheimer to take his place. So, among all his other responsibilities, Oppenheimer assumed the task of coordinating theoretical calculations on basic nuclear reactions with experimental data, in order to estimate both the critical mass of material needed for fission and the efficiency of the proposed weapon.'[5]

Seeking Consensus

To bridge the gap in thinking and practice between the physicists and the military-minded Groves, Vannevar Bush proposed that a triumvirate military policy committee should work closely with the general. To speed up the process of competing with German scientists, they and Groves decided to centralise the work to solve any problems quickly, instead of continuing with projects scattered across several universities. The old system also left problematic gaps in the security process.[6]

Oppenheimer and Groves had first met at a party on 8 October, at the home of Berkeley's president. Groves was particularly impressed at the candid way Oppenheimer explained scientific processes to him with clarity and unambiguous answers without patronising him. Gone was the old adolescent Robert who had not been able to communicate without using long words that had separated him from non-scientists. The general had found Oppie engaging. It was only a few days later that Oppie had been invited to join Groves, Nichols and Marshall on the train that took them from Chicago to New York, while the military officers made up their minds whether to appoint him.[7]

Groves recognised Oppenheimer's genius and gave him 'major responsibility for planning the new laboratory in November 1942'. It was only then that Oppenheimer's past initiated a more intense and prolonged security investigation of his politics. Arthur Compton had a more intimate discussion with him, and left satisfied that Oppie's interest in communism was purely philosophical, and unlike the devotion accorded to its doctrines by some of his friends.[8]

James Conant's view was that Oppenheimer felt it was the responsibility of American citizens to know what the growing new communist movement might mean to them. Groves considered that Oppie's loyalty was never in question.

The general ordered security investigations of all major participants in the Manhattan Project. Oppenheimer's clearance was postponed for months while he provided all the information he was asked for. His interrogator was Colonel Boris Pash.

Pash had fought the Bolsheviks in Russia when young, and escaped to America. Now he was employed as a senior security officer at Los Alamos. He decided that Oppenheimer was a security risk, but he had no evidence to support his instincts, and his superior officers did not agree with him.[9]

Groves finalised the issue decisively by issuing an order to the G-2 security office.

> In accordance with my verbal direction of July 15, it is desired that clearance be issued for the employment of Julius Robert Oppenheimer without delay, irrespective of the information which you have concerning Mr. Oppenheimer. He is absolutely essential to the project.[10]

Security

FBI agents and Manhattan Project security agents continued their investigations of Oppenheimer, even after he had already been in office for about six months and shown he was completely dedicated, responsible and efficient, and admirably suited for the job. Evidently Groves might even have thought he was irreplaceable.

Nevertheless, the security officers would discover two problematic incidents that would raise questions about Oppenheimer's loyalty in the future.

The first would take place in 1943, and would involve his former university colleague and questionable friend Haakon Chevalier. Robert and Kitty would invite him and his wife to dinner at their home in Los Alamos. When Robert went into the kitchen at one point in the evening, Chevalier contrived to join him, and recounted a confidential conversation he had had with a British scientist named George Eltenton who worked for Shell at Berkeley. Robert knew him, too. Apparently Eltenton had offered to pass on any technical or scientific information to the Soviet Union, and suggested that Chevalier should approach Oppenheimer to invite him to do the same thing.

Although Robert firmly rejected the indirect proposition in the kitchen, what he did not do was report the conversation to security. Nor was it the only time he would show loyalty to his friend Chevalier by protecting him from disclosure as a communist.

The reason for Eltenton's approach was an emotional one, since the Russians were 'battling for their lives and needed help which they were not getting from their allies'. They had no radar – because Britain did not want to reveal their defensive invention to the Germans – nor products of American research they needed, because of disagreements between the Anglo-American Allies.[11]

Instead, Robert mentioned Eltenton's name to the Manhattan Project security officer on 23 August 1943, and recommended that he should be investigated. He did not mention Chevalier's name. His approach to the security service initiated a second meeting the next day. It too involved Pash. And, unbeknown to Robert, it was recorded.

This time Robert revealed he had heard that someone in the Soviet consulate could pass scientific information back to Russia, and that approaches had been made to other people Robert knew. When Pash pressed him for names, Robert replied that there were three, but declined to tell Pash who they were. He did not wish to jeopardise the careers of anyone who might be innocent. Evidently, he felt he must protect Chevalier by attempting to distract attention from his friend. But Pash was alarmed to hear of three possible security risks, and reported the incident to Washington.

Groves and top security officer Lieutenant Colonel Lansdale asked Oppenheimer who the mysterious contact was while travelling together on a train, although Groves did not directly order Robert to reveal a name because he had sufficient confidence in him. But he did ask him again on another occasion when they were driving together, and Robert admitted he had been approached confidentially by Chevalier. But the damage had been done by his suspicious hesitation in not having reported who it was sooner. Robert had failed to clarify Pash's erroneous assumption that there were three security risks involved in the Manhattan Project, instead of only Chevalier, who was not even employed on the project.

Groves and Lansdale had not been alarmed. Both had assumed that Robert was covering up for his brother Frank, whom they already knew was a communist. As

Groves would describe the situation later on, he recognised it as a typical schoolboy reluctance on Robert's part not to sneak on friends to the headmaster.

Another suspicious incident would occur during a trip to Berkeley in the same year. Jean Tatlock had fallen into another deep depression and contacted Robert in some urgency. Robert felt compelled to hurry over and comfort her. Although he knew he was always being followed by security agents because of his responsible position, he took a cab and spent the night with her.

Groves was not unduly disturbed. No doubt he recognised Robert's naivety with young women by that time, as well as his loyalty to friends, and he knew that his colleague in the Manhattan Project was loyal to the United States, even if Oppie sometimes behaved bizarrely, like some of the other scientists. Lieutenant Colonel Boris Pash, on the other hand, suspected that not only was Oppenheimer a security risk, but a possible Soviet agent.

When Jean Tatlock took her life in January 1944, she left a note that indicated she could not handle realities anymore. The two different worlds she lived in were incompatible, and she had finally given up.

Fallout from her suicide was inevitable because of her wild behaviour, her communist sympathies, her intimate link to Oppenheimer, and the fact that she had been under suspicion by agents of several security services who had been watching her antics for some time. Colonel Pash had already spent two months in the autumn of 1943 attempting to find out who had asked Oppenheimer to pass on top secret information to the Soviet consul. He had become so obsessed with Oppenheimer's guilt that Groves had decided Pash was prejudiced for some personal reason and was wasting everybody's time on fruitless investigations.

Jean's father, Professor Tatlock, discovered his daughter's body in her flat. He had found her lying in her partly filled bath against a pillow, and carried her into the living room to lay her on the sofa. He found her unsigned suicide note on the dining room table. Evidently, she had decided she would be a liability all her life, while so many others were fighting for a cause. She had taken Nembutal C, and possibly several other drugs too, like codeine, and had drowned in her bathtub.

Professor Tatlock took several hours to search for any personal correspondence to destroy, and burned a number of papers in the fireplace before the police arrived.[12]

The psychoanalysis that Jean had been obliged to undergo for her own training revealed she had been struggling with latent homosexual tendencies that, before Freud had diagnosed to the contrary, had been categorised as a pathological condition. Suspecting she might be a lesbian, Jean had indulged in a lot of sleeping around with masculine women to discover her gender.[13]

Wiretaps

It had taken too much time for Robert to understand the need for stricter security, or that 'walls have ears'. His first slow perception of the need for free speech to cease when outside the confines of the small community of scientists with whom he worked, evidently came towards the end of 1942. He realised that a number of people at Berkeley already knew that Robert and his students were working on the feasibility of an immensely powerful new weapon associated with splitting the atom.

He had sometimes discussed his work even with strangers when the need for security had not occurred to him. John McTernan was one. He was a lawyer for the National Labor Relations Board. He recalled later on that he had encountered Oppenheimer at a party one evening and Oppenheimer had chatted freely with him about his work, but spoke so rapidly and technically that McTernan had not understood a word of it. Perhaps he had made it unintelligible on purpose, or had been thinking aloud. For when McTernan came across him again and raised the subject, Robert had made it firmly clear that he was no longer free to discuss it.

Except for the close coterie of physicists with whom he worked, Oppie was thought to be working on some mysterious hush-hush project connected with the war effort. All of them were. Then, after a while, it became evident that they were going to build a huge weapon.[14]

Even though Oppenheimer was beginning to learn to hold his tongue, it was no secret. A congressman boasted about what was being achieved at Berkeley, and it even appeared in the newspapers. A number of Oppie's graduate students had mentioned it, innocently or otherwise, to top people in the American Communist Party, including Steve Nelson, who was their liaison with Berkeley students. FBI agents had bugged Nelson's home by the spring of 1943.[15]

According to the conversations the FBI picked up on 30 March, any contact with communist members now made Oppenheimer extremely uncomfortable. He did not wish to talk to them.

'He's changed a lot,' said someone named Joe.

'I know that,' said Nelson.

To which Joe said, 'You won't hardly believe the change that has taken place.'

'He's just not a Marxist,' Nelson remarked.[16]

The transcript of the conversation was passed to Lieutenant Colonel Boris Pash, Chief of G-2 Army Counter-Intelligence in San Francisco, who soon discovered that Joe and two others were Oppie's students. But they could not act legally against them because wiretaps were illegal. In any case, it showed that Oppenheimer had now become more security conscious.

Documents from Soviet archives made available later on indicated that the NKVD knew that Oppenheimer was working on *Enormoz*, which was their code name for the Manhattan Project.[17]

DESTROYER OF WORLDS

16

Merchants of Death

By the end of November 1942, Enrico Fermi had come to the conclusion that a chain reaction could be produced and kept under control. 'Two weeks earlier, at the beginning of November, he had informed Compton that all calculations and theoretical work had been checked and rechecked, and that the danger of an accident or an uncontrollable reaction was practically nil.'

Fermi was considered to be one of the true great geniuses of modern physics. Even so, Compton was faced with an enormous responsibility, since the danger of an accident could not be completely ruled out. Neither Fermi nor Compton could be entirely sure of some unknown phenomenon when the chain reaction was initiated.

Nevertheless, Compton approved the construction of the pile on the university campus.[1]

> All precautions would be taken, of course, and the reaction would be performed very slowly, step by step, with the control rods released an inch at a time. An atomic explosion was not possible – unless all the science, the mathematics and the logic of the best brains in the Chicago group were completely wrong. And yet some unexpected radioactivity, for instance, or some effect that had never been observed before?[2]

Compton updated his team of physicists, who now looked more like coal miners as they formed a group around him in a corner of the Berkeley campus racquets court. Their hands and faces were covered in shiny black graphite from carrying graphite blocks and piling them in layers. The black graphite powder covered their clothes and the ground, which was as slippery as a dance floor.

He told them he had attended a meeting of the S-1 Committee to inform its members of what they had achieved on the campus. Conant had paled at the thought of a possible atomic explosion in the middle of Chicago. And Groves had immediately addressed whether and when other, more isolated accommodation would be ready. They were all caught in a hurry and unable to stop work, however dangerous it might be, with the chances of success completely unknown.

November was a critical month in which they had to decide which method to proceed with from five different possibilities to produce fissionable material. They had already rejected the centrifuge method in favour of the graphite pile and instead of the heavy water reactor. It had left a choice from only three of the original methods – gaseous diffusion, the graphite pile for producing plutonium, and the electromagnetic process.[3]

They had begun to construct the Chicago reactor – known originally as 'the Chicago pile' – at the beginning of the month. The structure had been designed by Enrico Fermi, Walter Zinn, and Herb Anderson, using forty thousand graphite blocks. Holes were bored in about half of them, for pieces of uranium to be inserted. The pile was spherical and approximately 24ft in diameter. Leo Szilard had persuaded the Speer Carbon Company to produce pure graphite, but they could not come up with enough. They might need 5,000 tons. So Groves had approached Union Carbide to supply them. Transportation caused difficulties at the railways. Covered vans had to be used to conceal what was inside for security.

Then the air proved to have a poor effect on the reaction, so that the entire structure had to be built inside a giant balloon, after which the air had to be pumped out when the reactor was ready. The custom-made square balloon was supplied by the Goodyear Tire and Rubber Company in Akron, Ohio.

Building the pile in the racquets court was Fermi's idea. He was the leader of the team and had overall direction of his creation. It was a cold winter, but they could not ask for heating without causing attention. Nevertheless, the increasing number of trucks arriving with various materials soon created curiosity, particularly in the middle of the night.

The scientists estimated the reactor would cost $1.5 million. And still, no one knew with certainty if the reactor would work. Fermi had previously experimented with about thirty smaller piles, which he had tested with uranium, but only up to the point of reaction, and then torn down. A lot of guesswork was involved. But Fermi was confident that the big reactor would work. His team of scientists accepted his word for it. But was he infallible?[4]

Detonation

Word came in the same month from James Chadwick in England that plutonium seemed more likely to produce spontaneous fission than uranium, and that the bomb would demand plutonium in greater purity than had previously been thought. As a consequence, Oppenheimer, Manley, Serber, and Teller, reappraised what discoveries and theories they thought were known about atomic bombs.

They summarised their findings for Groves, Bush and Conant. It involved the materials Uranium 233, U235, and Plutonium 239. According to their new data, they now believed that 'any one of the known possible materials', U233, U235, or Pu239, 'would produce the same energy per gram as any other'. The minimum amount required would probably differ, while the exact amount was uncertain.[5]

The generally considered method of detonation was 'to shoot together with high velocity on a sufficiently low neutron background'.

The Policy Committee undertook its own project-wide review and provided its findings to President Roosevelt on 16 December 1942, with projected delivery dates. The likelihood of a weapon being ready by June 1944 was considered small – more likely by January 1945 – 'and good by mid-1945'.[6]

Conant remarked grimly to Groves, 'It is possible that the Germans are a year ahead of us, or perhaps have even eighteen months head start … I would judge there was an even chance that the Germans would produce a number of effective bombs by the middle of 1945 and a slight chance (perhaps 1 in 10) of their achieving the same result by the summer of 1944 … To my mind, it is this fear that the Germans may be near the goal which is the prime reason for an all-out effort now on this gamble. This being so, it is clear that nothing short of a full-speed, all-out attempt would be worthwhile.'[7]

That fear would torment the minds of Groves the engineer and Oppenheimer the scientist for several years to come. Despite their differences, they were able to collaborate with each other because of their mutual respect and a shared commitment.

The Cyclotron

The four members of the Reviewing Committee arrived in San Francisco on a Saturday morning at the end of November, and met with Ernest Lawrence, who was waiting for them in the Cyclotron Building at the Radiation Laboratory in Berkeley. The giant 184in cyclotron, which was Lawrence's invention, was being adapted to the magnets in his 'calutrons'. So far, his results for the atom-smashing machine, for which he had become a Nobel Laureate in 1939, had been disappointing.

Lawrence's students were informally dressed in checked shirts and dungarees, and looked not at all like nuclear scientists. Among them was Oppie's young brother, Frank. Despite their air of informality, he expected nothing less of them than the best, and was just as demanding of himself. They considered him a genius. Most called him E.O.L. by now.

After Lawrence had given the committee a demonstration, the first question they asked was, 'How much Uranium 235 have you separated?'[8]

They had hoped for pounds and were disappointed when he spoke of micrograms, and impure ones at that. They wondered how such a fantasy as the newly invented cyclotron could be transformed into reality, since the atom bomb was still only a theoretical object of their imagination.

> His explanation was an illuminating exercise in self-confidence and bold imagination. For the realistic, down-to-earth engineers from Stone & Webster, it was an unusual experience. As Lawrence described his vision of gigantic industrial complexes and laboratories, armies of specially trained scientists and arsenals of newly invented tools and instruments, his voice rose with enthusiasm. It was contagious enthusiasm that overwhelmed doubts and drowned all sense of reality in a flood of buoyant optimism. For a moment the mesmerized engineers

felt as though their ties with practical common sense were being cut. Somewhere deep in their minds they knew that all this was too fantastic to be feasible. But while Lawrence was talking, it was impossible not to fall under the almost hypnotic spell of his enthusiasm.[9]

The reality was intimidating, since Stone & Webster had agreed to design huge production plants, the like of which no one else had ever produced before. And they had to start immediately, although no one knew whether the electromagnet process would work, or even what it would look like.

When E.O.L. took Groves to the top of Radiation Hill afterwards, to show him the much larger experimental machine at the summit, Groves was even more dismayed when Lawrence remarked, 'This is all experimental you see …'

Groves had already received a report on obtaining uranium. Instead of being readily obtainable, as he and others had assumed, the report from Colonel Nichols explained that the metal ore was scarce and almost impossible to obtain. Some had been brought out of the Belgian Congo. The world's largest producer of uranium ore was in Katanga. Sengier was president of the Union Miniére du Haute-Katanga, who asked Nichols for his ID when they met in the company's New York office. Then Sengier made it plain that he was only interested in selling it for military purposes, not commercial ones. He seemed to have been holding it in reserve for this moment.

It placed Nichols in a difficult security situation. But, having overcome it, he found that, while he had been searching for the ore all over the world, the Union Miniéres held a stock of 1,200 tons of uranium ore in steel drums in their Staten Island warehouse. Sengier had removed it for safekeeping before Belgium fell to Nazi Germany. The thought of what might have happened if he had left it in the hands of German scientists was too horrible to contemplate.

Saving Thousands of Lives

Although the Boston construction firm of Stone & Webster had been contracted to supply all engineering work for the Manhattan Project, it became clear that they did not have the expertise to produce chemicals. Chemicals had been provided in the First World War by du Pont de Nemours and Company. Now du Pont were brought in for the same purpose, and Groves now realised that this was going to be an even greater industrial enterprise than he had thought, as no single company could possibly carry the entire burden. Others would have to be brought in. The need for secrecy added to the complications.

Stine was du Pont's chief research man and technical adviser. He travelled to Chicago to study the work already done on plutonium. When he met afterwards with Compton, he said bluntly, 'I don't think you have a … chance of getting this done in five years.'

'You don't want to do it?'

'And yet I can't see that the nation can afford *not* to try it. I just think it's too big, too difficult.'

When the president of du Pont met with Groves, the general told him candidly, 'There are three basic military considerations … First, it's very possible that Germany will soon produce some fissionable material. We have no evidence to the contrary. Second, there is no known defense against a nuclear weapon. And third, if we succeed in time, we'll shorten the war and save tens of thousands of American lives.'[10]

The president was impressed by the general's intelligence and bluntness, from which it was clear they had no choice. But manufacturing munitions was a sensitive affair that had placed them in trouble before, in the 1930s, when they had been described as 'merchants of death' by the Nye Committee investigation.

Groves sensed his hesitation and added, 'This opinion is shared by President Roosevelt, Secretary Stimson and General Marshall.'

'And you, General – you personally – do you agree?'

'Absolutely and without question!'

As an American company, du Pont felt they had no alternative.[11]

Big Trouble

General Groves and Colonel Marshall met another possible supplier at Kodak Tower in Rochester, New York. The meeting lasted the whole day. Its purpose was to get Tennessee Eastman to operate the electromagnetic plants that were not yet built in Oak Ridge. But another wartime project did not seem to appeal to them.

Groves had been impressed by the work they were doing at Holston Explosives Plant in Tennessee. 'We're not looking for scientists,' he told them. 'We have so many PhD's now that we can't keep track of them.' What they needed was industrial experience. He assured them that they would need no more than 2,500 people.

Eastman's director of research turned out to be the most conservative on the board. As the only scientist present who had any experience in the field, the British-born Dr Charles Mees bombarded the army officers with masses of pertinent questions. The other directors were undecided, and remained on edge for most of the day. After the two army officers were finally asked to leave the room while the board arrived at a decision, they looked at each other inquiringly in the corridor outside. 'How do you think I did?' Groves asked.

Marshall looked worried and didn't answer. But when they were called back, they were informed that the head of Tennessee Eastman would be in charge of the operation.

One of the members of the team was still evidently hesitant. He added grudgingly, 'You two have just put us in the biggest trouble we've ever been in.'

The Pied Piper of Los Alamos

A possible location for the Manhattan Project was the Jemez Springs Valley that Groves and Oppenheimer had studied in the morning, but it turned out to be too narrow for what they would need. It was a deep and thin canyon cut into the mountains. Oppie had wanted Los Alamos for the site from the beginning. He had an affinity for New Mexico. Groves had invited him to accompany him on a tour of the possible locations for Site Y, as the top secret bomb laboratory was called.

Isolation was vital, not only for secrecy and security, but in case of a possible catastrophe. Making a nuclear bomb was an entirely new venture with no previous experience to rely on or guide them. What they did know was they would need a moderate climate to work year-round. The site required access by road and rail, and a vast area for a testing ground – who knew how vast? They reckoned on at least a 100-mile radius to exclude neighbouring communities.

Oppenheimer wanted some existing facilities so that a think tank of six scientists could move in immediately. Colonel Dudley had already surveyed parts of California, Nevada, Utah, Arizona, and New Mexico. Coastal areas had been excluded because of the possibility of attack by sea. He had quickly shortened the list to five possible sites. Jemez Springs had been the fifth, he figured it was the best. But too many Indian families farmed there.[1]

At Los Alamos, Oppie told Groves, 'If you go on up the canyon, you come out on top of the mesa, and there's a boy's school there which might be a usable site.'

Oppie knew the terrain well from his numerous horse-riding treks of discovery out from Perro Caliente in the Pecos Valley. It was across the other side of the Sangre de Cristo Mountains. He'd had the Otowi site at the back of his mind all along, while he had patiently listened to all the other possibilities before raising it. Now they drove along the dirt roads, kicking up clouds of dust and sand from their vehicles, to the Los Alamos Ranch School. By the time they reached it at the top of the mesa in the late afternoon, light snowflakes had begun to fall. They got out of their trucks and automobiles to stand at the gate and gaze in at the boys and their teachers in shorts, out on a playing field, despite the cold weather.

As soon as Groves saw it, he said, 'This is the place.'

They inspected the site carefully with Ernest Lawrence four days later. It was located only 35 miles from Santa Fe, but was otherwise isolated and almost inaccessible.

Lawrence and Oppie were happy, and immediately began hiring suitable scientists. It took up much of Robert's attention and time, while Groves went about acquiring the school and the land surrounding it.[2]

First off, Oppenheimer flew to Cambridge to persuade Hans Bethe and his wife to join him. They had left Germany as the Nazi threat rose against all people with Jewish ancestry. Oppie viewed the thirty-six-year-old German-American nuclear physicist as an outstanding scientist. Bethe would go on to win the 1967 Nobel Prize in Physics. Robert also attempted to recruit his long-standing friend from New York's East Side, the physicist Isidor Rabi. But Rabi was doing important work on radar at the MIT radiation lab, and thought the project's odds for success were only fifty-fifty. Nuclear physicist Robert Bacher took his place.

The Pied Piper

As a consequence of Groves's command that the new laboratory must be run as a military installation, Oppenheimer had officially become a lieutenant colonel as soon as it opened. But when the scientists objected to militarisation, he orchestrated a compromise that the military would not take charge until later on, and only in a crisis. Rabi agreed to offer his advice, because, as Bethe said, 'Without Rabi's practical advice it would have been a mess.'

Robert had hardly thought of life in the desert as being too Spartan for scientists, but *they* did. He had to persuade Rose Bethe in particular about living conditions with a laundry service, kitchen and canteen facilities, and other comforts in their isolated mountain hideaway. There would even be a small garden, a hospital, and garbage collection.

Throughout that winter, Robert and Kitty were host and hostess to the comings and goings of a continuous stream of scientists to their home, which was a Spanish-style ranch at Number One Eagle Hill Road. It was situated on a steep hill above the city, providing a panoramic view of San Francisco. He entertained guests with his special vodka Martinis. True to his comfortable upbringing, his new home was tasteful and artistically furnished. It tended to establish him as a strong and self-confident leader of a scientific community.

Oppenheimer planned to have around thirty physicists with him in the desert to build the nuclear bomb. Much of the planning took place first in his home as he held forth in front of his fireplace in the evenings. Serber had moved in to Oppie's garage apartment with his wife, so he and Serber discussed who should join the team, and 'whose intellectual powers might have a catalytic effect on the less qualified'. Since there was nothing there, Charlotte Serber, listening in, thought they were out of their minds.[3]

When Groves was asked by a bright young assistant what the new director of the Manhattan Project was like, he admitted; 'He looks right through you. I feel like he can read my mind.'

It seemed that Groves had become mesmerised by the effect of Robert's pale blue gimlet eyes. But, just as when Robert had been a student and a lecturer, he was seen differently by different people. No one doubted his brilliance, nor the capacity he had developed for leadership. But Teller thought that Robert was just a clever politician who understood people and knew how to manipulate them. Some thought him ambitious for power, while others believed he was just a good actor who had taken Groves in. Others believed that Oppie had acquired so many masks to conceal who he really was that there was nothing of him left. The reality was that he had always been a private individual with immense creative and imaginative resources that he had absorbed from romantic and adventurous novelists, like Dostoevsky, Tolstoy and Conrad. But scientific theory had absorbed him from the start, and now he was in his element surrounded by other serious scientists, he enjoyed the role he appeared to have been made for.

Rudolf Peierls, the British-German theoretical physicist who played a major role in the Manhattan Project, said of him, 'Robert is one of those people who take his job, but not himself, seriously.'[4]

According to Bethe, he was very different from the Oppenheimer he had previously known. Robert had been somewhat hesitant before, but now at Los Alamos he had become a decisive manager and leader. Whereas he had previously been focused on exploring the deep secrets of nature, now he was running an industrial enterprise. Whoever may have been right, he had completely changed to suit his new role.[5]

Robert Wilson had been a student of both Ernest Lawrence and Oppenheimer, and been sceptical about the intellectual Robert Oppenheimer leading such an immense and varied project. But now he was amazed that Oppie had become a charismatic and efficient administrator. By the summer of 1943, Wilson realised that when he was with Oppenheimer, he felt like he was a larger person, and idolised his boss. 'Eloquent, inspiring, and elusive, perhaps deliberately so, Robert Oppenheimer became the pied piper of Los Alamos.'[6]

Los Alamos

One of Oppie's appointments was a new assistant named Dorothy McKibbin, who would take charge of the lab's Santa Fe office. Famous scientists and families already weary of travelling would drop in to her tiny office in a courtyard at 109 East Palace Avenue, where they would be informed, comforted, and encouraged, before being sent further on to another mystery tour that finally settled them on the new site at Los Alamos.

Robert and Kitty moved into the laboratory site when the headmaster's log and stone bungalow at the Ranch School was ready for them. It was on a quiet road shielded by bushes and shrubbery. They were followed a few days later by Lawrence's former secretary, Priscilla Green, their two-year-old son Peter, and his nurse. Oppie would be given three assistants to lighten the load of his enormous and complex work.[7]

An impression of the early attempts to create a scientific community in the New Mexico wilderness reads, in memoirs and letters, like an adventure in the early epoch of the North American Wild West, with its frontiersmen and women. 'It began with planes buzzing overhead and bulldozers arriving to build roads, and the arrival of construction workers to create habitations. Hammering and buzzing sounds of saws, all going in a hurry as if they were prospectors erecting a new town and impatient to get to work with pickaxes on the seams of gold. The bulldozers roared as they dug ditches for the foundations of flimsy new houses. Everything was conducted in an element of extreme haste and mystery.'[8]

'One day,' as Peggy Pond Church would write later in her memoir of the project, 'I recognised Dr Ernest Lawrence, whom my husband and I had met one summer in California. He seemed strangely different when I questioned him about mutual friends, and broke away as quickly as possible from my attempts at conversation … Another afternoon I was introduced to a young-looking man by the name of Oppenheimer. Cowboy boots and all, he hurried in the front door and out the back, peering quickly into the kitchen and bedrooms. I was impressed even in that brief meeting, by his nervous energy and by the intensity of the blue eyes that seemed to take in everything at a glance, like a bird flying from branch to branch in a deep forest.'

Three thousand construction engineers had been working to build new laboratory blocks since the middle of December, surrounded by piles of lumber and wallboard and tarpaper, all muffled up against the freezing winter weather, and all hurrying because they were behind schedule. To Priscilla Green, the site was a shambles. There was no time for order, and nothing was finished. It looked as if it would never be ready for everyone to move in.

Edward Teller was one of the first scientists to arrive in April 1943. He helped Oppenheimer recruit others, and organise the project.

Niels Bohr and his wife arrived at Los Alamos for the first time in December. By agreement with Groves, he would be referred to in correspondence between them by the cover name of Dr Baker. All mail to and from Los Alamos was censored. He would be permitted to visit all parts of the Manhattan project, despite his close connections to the British.[9]

The Bohrs left on 17 January 1944. Oppenheimer kept Groves scrupulously informed on his visit.

> On the technical side Dr Baker concerned himself primarily with the correlation and interpretation on the many new data on nuclear fission and related topics which have been obtained by this project. He left with us a brief report on the theoretical understanding of these data. It has been the point of view of this laboratory that in matters of such great importance, and where theories were involved which were new and unproven, all important quantities would have to be determined by experimental measurement, and I believe this policy was and is sound. Nevertheless, the advantage of some theoretical insight into

the phenomena is very great indeed in that it enables us to evaluate experiments critically, to determine the relative priority of experiments, and in general to reduce the amount of futile discussion and waste motion. For all these reasons the work that Baker did for us should prove of very great value in the months to come. Baker concerned himself very little with the engineering problems of our program although he is of course aware of their importance and their difficulty.[10]

It had previously been arranged with Dr Chadwick that Niels Bohr was on Britain's payroll, and his expenses were covered by the British. Oppenheimer emphasised that he hoped the collaboration would continue: 'I should like to make it quite clear that the effect of his presence on the morale of those with whom he came in contact was always positive and always helpful, and that I see every reason to anticipate that this will be true in the future.'

British scientists worked primarily on the implosion method of assembling the bomb at Los Alamos. Explosives experts and theoretical physicists 'preferred to push work on the gun device'.

Oppenheimer's concern about hydrodynamics was relieved by the arrival of another British consultant in May 1944. G. I. Taylor's new theory of interface instability turned out to be useful in several areas. As usual, British and American scientists had different views according to their own research results. Whereas the Americans tended to 'obtain as many and as detailed results as possible with rather questionable methods, the British had erred in the opposite direction, obtaining too few results by fairly reliable methods.'[11]

When they compared their separate progress in September 1943, they found that each complemented the other.[12]

Rudolf Peierls became deputy head of the British group working in Los Alamos, while Chadwick in Washington supervised all British scientists working on the project in the United States. He and Oppenheimer had first worked together in 1929.

Many years after the war was over and the American-Hungarian theoretical physicist Edward Teller was an old man, respected as 'the father of the hydrogen bomb', he would sound bewildered in a television interview at the fact that he had managed to escape from Nazi Germany, and that 'Hitler could have taken over the world'.

He was traumatised by the feeling of desperate panic at the probability that Nazi Germany would win. The fear never left him. Most others who were fortunate to escape from German-occupied Europe were left with similar anxieties, because what happened had surely been impossible. Their minds were stressed out by the thought. What particularly confused Teller in the years just before he died was the realisation that a new generation of young people had no idea of their extraordinary good fortune at having being born.[13]

18

Achieving Critical Mass

Critical mass is the smallest amount of fissionable material required to support a self-sustaining chain reaction. Oppenheimer had often considered and discussed the problems of critical assemblies, in what he described as 'a romantic way', but he 'had not learned the secret until September 1941'. And that was only because of the indiscretion of a British scientist while talking to his friend Ernest Lawrence. Now achieving critical mass had become his goal.[1]

Edward Tolman had drafted a memorandum for Groves and the review committee regarding the Los Alamos project as of March 1943. It summarised 'the physics behind fission, the primary materials to be used, and the current thinking on how to detonate such a device'.

It included a number of questions to establish the purpose of the project. What was presently known about critical masses? What about the conditions that affect nuclear reactions and detonation? What of the chemistry and metallurgy of uranium and plutonium? Or the possibility of a thermonuclear or hydrogen bomb? What did the project need to know about production and delivery schedules of uranium and plutonium? What about the military's logistical requirements for the bomb itself that, if airborne, would need to fit into the fuselage of an existing or planned aircraft?[2]

The committee's recommendations expanded the work of the lab far beyond what anyone had previously imagined. Oppenheimer was glad to have the guidance. At least the recommendations in the area of critical mass were already under way. Staff would be increased by over four hundred to five hundred, particularly in the field of engineering, engineering-physics and chemistry. The original plan of a hundred scientists in a small laboratory vanished for good.

More bulldozers and construction crews appeared with carpenters to turn the small scientific community into a sizeable government and military institution. Only a few years later there would be five thousand people working at Los Alamos. It would be barely enough – and all to develop and make a bomb.

The Children

The theoretical physicist Richard Feynman was an irrepressible practical joker who seemed to have no control of his actions. It was probably why he was overflowing

Right: Friends or enemies? Arthur Compton and Werner Heisenberg in Chicago (1929). Heisenberg was a German 1932 Nobel prize-winning theoretical physicist, a key pioneers of quantum mechanics, who published his breakthrough paper in 1925, planned the first West German nuclear reactor at Karlsruhe, and was the leading German nuclear scientist in World War 2. Copyright GFHund

Below: Robert Oppenheimer at Heike Kamerlingh Onnes's Laboratory in Leiden, Netherlands in 1926. In middle row, third from left.

Albert Einstein lecturing in Vienna in 1921.

Right: Compton at the University of Chicago in 1933 with his cosmic ray telescope. With graduate student Luis Alvarez.

Below: Soviet secret agent Kitty Harris, now Kitty Oppenheimer after marrying Robert in 1940. Photograph used with permission from Kitty Oppenheimer and the J. Robert Oppenheimer Memorial Committee.

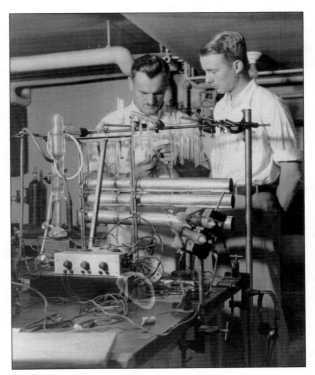

The "Via Panisperna boys." Enrico Fermi on right at Rome University. With Oscar D'Agostino, Emilio Segrè, Edoardo Amaldi, and Franco Rasetti. Photo taken in 1934 by the elusive Bruno Pontecorvo, who spied for the Soviet GRU.

General Groves and Robert Oppenheimer in 1942: The intellectual and the military construction man.

Ernest O. Lawrence, Arthur H. Compton, Vannevar Bush, James B. Conant, Karl T. Compton, and Alfred L. Loomis. March 1940 meeting at Berkeley, California.

Shift change at the Y-12 uranium enrichment facility at Clinton Engineer Works in Oak Ridge, Tennessee, where 82,000 were employed by 11 August 1945.

Hanford workers collect paychecks at Western Union.

Alpha I racetrack at Y-12. Uranium 235 electromagnetic separation plant. (1945).

Young women who monitored calutron control panels at Y-12.

Oak Ridge K-25 plant.

Above: The S-50 plant is the dark building behind the Oak Ridge powerhouse with its smoke stacks.

Left: Workers load uranium slugs into the X-10 Graphite Reactor.

Hanford B-Reactor site, June 1944.

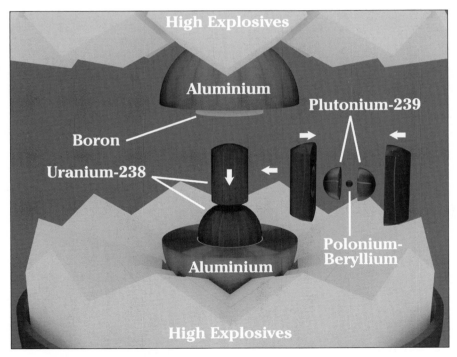

Implosion-type nuclear bomb.

Explosives of "the gadget" being raised to the top of tower for final assembly.

General Leslie R. Groves, Jr., talks to service personnel at Oak Ridge Tennessee in August 1945.

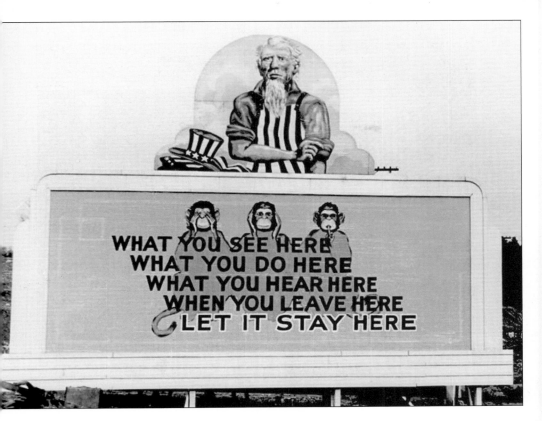

Above: Top security. Oak Ridge billboard.

Right: First nuclear test explosion in July 1945, named the "Trinity" shot, in the New Mexico desert.

MI6 officers dismantling German experimental nuclear reactor in underground lab at Haigerloch in April 1945. Rupert Cecil at bottom. "Bimbo" Norman at extreme right. Eric Welsh standing. American at upper left is Lieutenant-Colonel John Landsdale Jr. From the Manhattan Project.

Silverplate B-29 Straight Flush with false tail identification used on the atomic missions.

Left; "Little Boy" explodes over Hiroshima, Japan on 6 August 1945; "Fat Man" over Nagasaki on 9 August 1945.

President Harry S. Truman signs the Atomic Energy Act of 1946.

Above: Physicists Albert Einstein and Oppenheimer in 1950.

Left: Nuclear physicist J. Robert Oppenheimer in 1946, the first director of Los Alamos National Laboratory.

President Dwight D. Eisenhower receives a report from Lewis L. Strauss, Chairman of the Atomic Energy Commission, who pressed for Oppenheimer's security clearance to be revoked. March 30, 1954.

Oak Ridge K-25 Plant.

Left: Hungarian-American physicist Edward Teller, known as "the father of the hydrogen bomb," testified against J. Robert Oppenheimer's security clearance in 1954.

Below: President Ronald Reagan awarding the National Medal of Science to Edward Teller in 1983.

with new ideas and approaches; he was not confined to traditional disciplines or ways of thinking. Groves would often refer to the group of scientists as his children, and he was not far wrong in the case of Feynman. Although some scientists found Groves to be 'a distasteful regimented militarist', he was remarkably tolerant of their foibles.

Try to satisfy these temperamental people, he urged Captain da Silva, one of his commanders. 'Don't allow living conditions, family problems, or anything else to take their minds off their work.'[3]

Typically, West Point graduate da Silva suffered from a huge failing in the eyes of the scientists in that he could not laugh at himself. They knew from their own experience that laughter opened up the mind to fresh and unconventional ideas. He was so stiff and formal that he could not bear scientists dropping into his office and sitting on the corner of his desk. The military indiscipline was painful for him to see. Oppenheimer had to explain patiently to him that they all sat on each other's desks whenever they felt like it.

On the other hand, the security restrictions annoyed the scientists. When Edward Teller remarked that they were complaining at having their mail opened, Oppenheimer replied that *he* wasn't even allowed to talk to his own brother. Feynman and his wife sent letters to each other in code, not for security's sake, but to baffle the censors, whereas Oppie was becoming more acutely security conscious all the time the Manhattan Project grew.

One example of the irreverent relationships between 'the children' was the continuing banter between the genius refugee Hans Bethe, who was the heavyset German leader of the Theoretical Division, and Dick Feynman, who buzzed around him like an irritating wasp.

When Feynman talked physics, his enthusiasm made him completely distracted from where he was, and indifferent to whom he interrupted. The stolid and imperturbable Bethe confronted problems squarely, analysed them steadily, and ploughed straight on, while pushing all obstacles aside. But Feynman would keep on interrupting him impatiently before he could get as much as a sentence out, either to 'shout his admiration or to express his disagreement by irreverent remarks like, "That's nuts!" or "You're crazy!"' Bethe would quietly and laboriously explain why he was right.[4]

Feynman's approach to everyone was the same, even with the Danish Nobel Prize winner and much-worshipped prophet of nuclear science Niels Bohr (code-named Dr Baker). When Bohr explained his reasoning with an equation on the blackboard, Feynman would shout out, 'No! That's wrong!'

Professor Bohr would listen to what Feynman had to say and then demolish him with evidence. But only a moment later, Feynman could not resist retorting, 'That's crazy! I think I can do it a better way.' Bohr would consider Feynman's contributions as a good rehearsal before making a presentation to the laboratory chiefs.

After MIT, Feynman had lost no time in establishing himself as 'one of the brightest young scientists in the field of theoretical physics'.[5] He was offered an assistant professorship at Cornell University.[6]

The Gadget

Despite Groves's preference for militaristic regulations and security, which Oppenheimer and the other scientists knew would extinguish all imagination, creativity and innovations, and would prevent new discoveries, Robert had convinced Groves to be more flexible by now, and allow a free exchange of ideas among the staff. If there was to be compartmentalisation it would be in other spheres than in the scientific community, where openness and a free flow of thoughts was essential to reach their goals.

Oppenheimer scheduled lectures on specific dates to make sure that everyone knew what everyone else was doing and why. He briefed Robert Serber to start the series of lectures in their small auditorium with a general summary or overview.[7]

Although Serber tended to be shy, and spoke with a slight lisp, he was the ideal lecturer because of his knowledge of engineering physics. Theoretical scientists were often too abstract to communicate meaningfully to experimental scientists. With a cigarette held loosely in one hand and a piece of chalk firmly in the other – like Oppenheimer whom he idolised and emulated – Serber could dart to the blackboard whenever examples of algebraic formulas or diagrams were necessary to illustrate a point. His first lecture needed no equation to emphasise to the scientists, and give comfort to Groves, that their objective was to make a practical military weapon.

There were three possible ways to make a bomb, he told them. There was the *gun* method. It required 'one subcritical mass of fissionable material to be fired rapidly into another'. Its aim was to cause a supercritical or explosive reaction. He illustrated it by drawing a circle with a smaller circle inside it. It represented a sphere with a hole bored into the centre. Another subcritical mass in the shape of a cylinder would be fired into the sphere. Alternatively, there was the autocatalytic or self-assembling process in which 'clusters' of neutron-rich materials embedded into the U235 or Pu239 were compressed or expulsed. He was sceptical about that method, as it would require larger amounts of fissionable material and yield a relatively low explosive force.

The third possibility would be difficult to construct. It was an 'implosion' bomb, for which a sphere of fissionable material is surrounded by high explosives. 'When the explosives are detonated and part of the blast wave flies inward, the subcritical mass is compressed into a supercritical mass and releases extraordinary energy.' He called it the 'gadget'.[8]

The damage from any of those three designs would be huge – if they worked.

> Radioactive materials generated in the explosion would contaminate everything within one thousand yards of the detonation point, and Serber estimated that five kilograms of U235 would produce a destruction radius of two miles.[9]

The one factor that would determine the damage was the energy release; so their aim was to get as much energy from the explosion as they could. 'And since the materials we use are very precious, we are constrained to do this with as high an efficiency as is possible.'[10]

Teller made his own unique impression when he spoke ponderously and convincingly afterwards with his heavy German accent. He emphasised the possibility of a thermonuclear weapon, or super-bomb. It had become almost an obsession with him as essential to defeat Hitler and the Nazis, no doubt because of his lucky escape from Nazi Germany and his knowledge of what German nuclear scientists were working on. Once ignited, it would be five times as explosive, or energy-producing, as U235.

A super-bomb's destructive power would be vastly greater than that of a fission bomb. They could not ignore the possibility at Los Alamos, where the daunting challenge for the scientists would be to turn theory into reality, by producing an effective bomb that could be dropped on Germany and Japan, to end the war as quickly as possible.

Artificial Intelligence

Victor Weisskopf was the oracle of the group and a famous authority on the theory of the atomic nucleus. He appeared to make his calculations like a slide rule, used before modern computers were invented. But his slide rule was in his head. The results appeared through intuition. As an example, when a scientist from another division visited him anxiously to ask, 'What is the plutonium cross section at 2.5 million volts?' Weisskopf would go into a trance, and then say with complete confidence, 'Two point two'.

Weisskopf did not need artificial intelligence, but others did. Some had even more complex problems they needed to solve instantly. Enrico Fermi, who became associate director of the laboratory in September 1944, concentrated largely on the first reactor to be made of enriched, rather than ordinary, uranium. 'This was an important new research tool for determining the critical mass of uranium.' Fermi conducted his experiments at the bottom of a deep wooded canyon.[11]

Although so many of the brilliant scientists whose imaginative and complex brains were essential to achieve the unprecedented goals set at Los Alamos were foreign – mostly from Italy, Germany, Hungary or Denmark – what most had in common was Jewish ancestry. It appeared to place them ahead of most non-Jewish British scientists – an interesting phenomenon that would be questioned with curiosity in years to come.

The British mission of twenty eminent scientists was led, at first, by James Chadwick, then by Rudolf Peierls. Otto Frisch was among them. He had explained atomic fission in 1939. There was also Sir Frederick Taylor, William Penney, and Klaus Fuchs. Seven were experimental physicists, two were electronics experts, five worked on theoretical problems, and five on explosives. The British contribution was 'inestimable'.[12]

Before IBM invented their massive computers, scientists in the Theoretical Division used simple little calculating machines operated by the scientists' wives. But they found they were too slow for complicated calculations. More sophisticated but larger mechanical devices were used in the astronomy department at Columbia University. The group leader of Bethe's division investigated their possibilities and ordered a few of the machines from IBM. They were operated by perforated cards, like ones used in old-fashioned mechanical player pianos. Their great advantage was the rapidity at which the same name or datum could be sorted in seconds from thousands of cards. Feynman and Frankel invented imaginative methods to prepare the mathematical data to suit the punched cards. Now more complicated implosion calculations could be made.[13]

Using the IBM machines soon became an addiction to figure out all kinds of mathematical problems. Mathematical genius John von Neumann saw them when he worked at the Manhattan Project in 1944. He became fascinated by their possibilities and developed theories on which bigger and more modern computers would be based.

19

A Magical Place

In addition to its unique physics laboratory, run by prominent nuclear scientists, Los Alamos engendered a unique character of its own. In the interest of security, everyone's address was described as PO Box 1663. When Kitty gave birth to a daughter she named Katherine, on 7 December 1944, the baby's birthplace was registered as a mailbox.

The average age of the community was unusually low at little more than twenty-five. There was a preponderance of young singles, 'no in-laws, no unemployed, no idle rich and no poor'. Once having entered the project, there was a feeling that a huge door to the outside world had shut behind them, so that it no longer existed.

An extraordinary feature of the Manhattan Project was how many of its leaders were the son of a minister with high ethical standards, like the so-called Protestant work ethic. The independent J. C. Hobbs, General Groves, Vannevar Bush, Arthur Compton, Harold Urey, and Norman Hillberry, who was Compton's top assistant, all held firm ideas of what was morally right and wrong.

'J. C.' differed, first in that he was in his fifties; secondly, he was a builder of power plants. Thirdly he was an independent consultant. He worked on the project as an important part of the unusual new construction companies, and his management style was very different from anyone else's. When appointed to give advice, he would first ask to see the scrap pile, because he could recognise the company's mechanical problems at a glance; whether poor design, inferior materials, poor craftsmanship, wrong operations, or lack of good quality controls.

He distrusted 'theoreticals'; by which he meant intellectuals and academics who spent time on research and came up with theories that were unlikely ever to work – like what he called 'left-wing demagogues and parasites living on public money'. He was a self-righteous moralist, but a practical individual who had no time for doctorates or theses. He was a 'no-nonsense man' who made things work by designing them, and often even by making them himself.

He was hired as an engineering consultant by Kellex – Kellogg with X (for secret) – at a salary far less than he had earned before. He only worked part-time, because he was still required half the time for work in the U.S. Navy, which needed him. He was a stubborn and independent man. What convinced him to work among intellectuals and theorists at Los Alamos was the ominous tone of voice in which he was told, 'When this plant goes into operation, the war ends.'[1]

He already made plenty of money from his own patented inventions. He had a reputation for walking out of a job if he encountered stupidity or incompetence, stubbornness or complacency. Then he would declare, 'I will not work with anyone who does not cooperate on progress.'[2]

Kellex had been contracted to design and build a unique mile-long gaseous diffusion plant in the shape of a 'U' for the Manhattan Project. The Oak Ridge plant was code-named K-25. It was where isotopes of Uranium 235 could be separated from U238 by turning uranium metal into uranium hexafluoride gas and straining it through a barrier material.[3]

'J.C.' began working for Kellex on 8 September 1943. After examining the trash heap, he asked to see the drawings for the entire proposed plant. When he had studied them carefully, he took out a crayon and made several small notations on the plan that deleted about two thirds of the miles of piping on the complicated blueprint. It would reduce the time of work on the project by six months and save $20 million worth of materials.[4]

Lost Horizon

A letter had arrived for Oppenheimer from President Roosevelt on 29 June 1943, requesting that Robert assure the scientists that their efforts were appreciated.[5]

'I am sure we can rely on their continued wholehearted and unselfish labors,' wrote the President. 'Whatever the enemy may be planning, American science will be equal to the challenge. With this thought in mind, I send this note of confidence and appreciation.'[6]

The first winter snowfalls came early and stayed for an unusually long time. Sometimes the temperature fell to below zero, producing a thick fog over the valley below. Some staff skied up to work until May.

Although the project was barely six months old, Oppenheimer believed the Pajarito Plateau was an enchanted environment, and he had managed to convince other people into thinking the same way, despite the work and hardship, and absence of luxuries. Their well-appointed location above the world provided them with beautiful sunsets beyond the mountain peaks. Oppie had hoped from the outset that they would share his love of the terrain and feel mentally uplifted. For, isolated as it was, it presented an atmosphere redolent of the fabled 'Shangri-La' in James Hilton's popular escapist 1933 novel, *Lost Horizon*.

Dorothy McKibbin still ran the office at 109 East Place in Santa Fe. She thought of Los Alamos as a magical place. It was already obvious to her how everyone looked up to Oppie as a remarkable man, and relied on his leadership to get through the uncertain challenges ahead of them.

'Of course,' she told a reporter many years later, 'at first we didn't know what was going on, we didn't know anything, and then it began to unfold like a book just being written ... He commanded the greatest respect and gave us all the ability to do things we didn't think we could do.'[7]

What Dorothy did not know was that Soviet intelligence had already established its own safe house in a pharmacy close by her Santa Fe office. It had been quiescent ever since it had been set up by Pavel Sudoplatov to organise and undertake the assassination of Trotsky in 1940.[8]

It is likely that Kitty met KGB officer Elizabeth Zarubin on some of her trips there, since Elizabeth's main duty at that time was to co-ordinate atomic energy information and other activities for Moscow Centre. Liz also worked with Sam Semyonov in New York and Enrico Fermi's protégé, the physicist and KGB agent Bruno Pontecorvo.

Soviet intelligence arranged for some of the intercepted Venona material, 'to be handled by a separate courier channel that operated through Mexico City, Santa Fe, and the Soviet consulate in San Francisco. The Mexico-based courier line operated out of the drug store on the Plaza in Santa Fe and was run with illegals who do not appear in the decoded VENONA traffic from Mexico City. Manhattan Project atomic secrets passed to couriers such as Harry Gold and Lona Cohen were handled by the *residentura* in New York City.'[9]

When Moscow Centre had first heard from Kheifetz in 1941 that Oppenheimer was working on an American atom bomb project, they had instructed their chief agent in North America, Major Vasili Zarubin, to seek out information on 'chemical and bacteriological weapons, radar and the problem of uranium'; and in particular on 'the importance of the problem of uranium and the construction of bombs with enormous destructive power which are being actively developed in Britain, Germany and the US'.[10]

The Mystery of Life

While Oppenheimer attended to his new duties by meticulously replying to official letters of congratulations and other correspondence, he was having second thoughts about his ability to take on such a heavy task and its stressful responsibilities. It had been exciting to begin with, but now he was not so sure he could handle it.

Although he continued to understand the need to create confidence, he was filled with doubts. He was appalled to find himself trapped behind his desk in an administrative capacity to deal with a variety of pressing military and bureaucratic problems, like accommodation, supplies, and salaries, the security of classified documents, draft deferment, health and safety, plant maintenance, staffing problems, office organisation, and patents. Priscilla Green noted that he looked drawn and haggard, more and more thin, and under considerable strain and anxiety. He became increasingly depressed at the immensity and complexity of the job.[11]

He confided in Robert Bacher that he could not carry on. Bacher told him that no one else could do the job. So Oppenheimer had no choice but to continue holding the forces together in the Manhattan Project.

Unusual instructions from Groves made him feel even more trapped. In his ultra-responsible position, and with his knowledge of ultra-top secrets, he was forbidden to fly in aircraft. Risk had to be considered as a priority over time saved. Nor was he allowed to drive for long distances. He must be safely guarded even for short distances by an able-bodied companion. If he was required to travel, he had to get permission from Groves first. A guard had to be used even for driving about town, particularly at night. All of that safety and security was imposed by official order.[12]

According to John Manley, who was Robert's assistant, despite Oppenheimer's anxiety, he grew with the job. That estimation would be confirmed by Hans Bethe when he looked back on the project after the war was over.[13]

One of the marks of Oppenheimer's superior leadership was that he always left his office door open so that anyone could drop in on him with their problems at any time. It also ensured that he was never excluded from what was going on around him. His secretary's office door was also kept open. Sometimes, when he noticed someone passing by, he would call out to ask if they had a minute to talk to him. Then he would close the door to ensure such discussions were confidential. He might talk about work, but more often it was to communicate by philosophising about the mystery of life.[14]

Oppie also frequently got up from behind his desk to circulate in the premises and outside the buildings, and appear unexpectedly at meetings, often leading them in the right direction with a few significant words when they were floundering.

Even though Los Alamos was an army camp, Robert Oppenheimer forged it into a social community. Despite all sorts of restrictions for security reasons, there was plenty of fun between the younger set, which gave it a unique and even jocular atmosphere. One joker used the new public address system to page Werner Heisenberg at regular intervals for two days, until finally she was cautioned by one of the physicists that Herr Heisenberg represented the enemy while he led the German nuclear bomb project in Berlin.

Housekeeping

The local Native Americans also believed that this was an enchanted community, since housekeeping and grocery shopping for single scientists presented an opportunity for employment for the indigenous population. Most of the young scientists and other staff were of college age, so that romances blossomed from time to time, babies were born and nappies needed washing.

Groves believed that the wives of the scientists should be employed, 'to keep them out of mischief', as he put it. A school was established for the older children of the scientists and a nursery school for infants. There was plenty of talent among wives with graduate degrees to teach English history, social studies, maths and science. Soon enough there was plenty of housekeeping and janitor work to be done, and not enough staff to handle it. They needed domestic help.

Oppenheimer asked Dorothy McKibbin to help them out, and Dorothy roped in Anita Martinez, because her mother-in-law, Maria, was well-known locally for her blackware pottery. She recruited Spanish and Native American women, who reported to Dorothy in Santa Fe. Dorothy screened them carefully for security purposes, and even fingerprinted them; finally issuing the men and women she chose with special passes to serve on The Hill, as the site was known, as maids, waitresses, cooks and janitors. They communicated in English, Spanish, or native Tewa.[15]

The women were dressed in Pueblo shawls and high, white, deerskin boots. Their shiny black hair was knotted in plaids and worn as chignons, as they walked to and from Dorothy's office. Army buses took those who were hired to the housing office in Los Alamos.

Very soon the non-working wives of the scientists demanded more help to relieve them of domestic chores, and requested extra Native American housemaids. At first, they were hired on a priority system for staff who were pregnant or ill, followed by full-time working wives. As for the singles who were working away from home for the first time, they had developed a social scene at the two PX stores on the army camp that provided cigarettes, Coke, hamburgers, and jukeboxes.

Dormitory parties began to flourish in the lounges outside the singles sleeping quarters, with an amateur dance band. Punch laced with alcohol was provided from Santa Fe, using cheap rum and Mexican vodka. Dick Feynman was a formidable solo drummer, and Rabi occasionally performed on his famous comb. There were also bigger and more lavish alcoholic parties with guests dressed in finer clothes and neckties. There were few single women, and always a long stag line at dances. Dorothy was in great demand.

'Oppie always put in an appearance,' said Shirley Barnett. 'We were all young and liked to have fun.'

Mathematician John von Neumann loved parties and his own version of vodka Martinis. A great deal of alcohol served as a handy distraction to blot out the thought of the race against German scientists, not just for nuclear superiority, but for their own survival.

Many of the scientists and their wives looked and acted like college students, and there were secretaries and lab assistants who were even younger. But army officers and non-commissioned military police could not treat them with the same discipline as soldiers; 'there were the inevitable broken curfews, alcoholic binges, fist fights, incidents of "co-mingling" in the single-sex dorms, and outbreaks of the clap'.

At one time, one of the Women's Army Corps shacks was placed off-limits, but the women protested against interference by the MPs. Those smart young men and women scientists were accustomed to leading their own lives. Oppie wrote a mild letter to the army authorities to say that the young were mature enough to know what they were doing and should not be interfered with.[16]

Everyone was gossiping about the love affairs by autumn. Priscilla Green had fallen in love with a young chemist named Robert Duffield. Their wedding took place in the first week of September. They drove off for their honeymoon in Taos. Three weeks later a young secretary from Berkeley named Marjorie Hall married a young physicist named Hugh Bradner. Several more weddings followed very fast.

Groves soon discovered that romances had blossomed between the young single laboratory assistants and chemists with the hired helps. He put a stop to it on security grounds, and many of the maids and waitresses were sent away, not only to the chagrin of the frustrated and bored young men, but in particular to the dismay of the Pueblo Indian maidens who had been making a considerable living from charging for their favours.

20

Dangerous Associations

Kitty Harris was transformed by her new persona as Mrs. J. Robert Oppenheimer. Whether she was still leading multiple lives, or was the same happy-go-lucky young woman who had previously been the lover of the head of the American Communist Party, and a part-time courier, official keeper of KGB safe houses, and controller and mistress for Soviet agent Donald Maclean, was unknown. Anyone who suspected anything suspicious about her would be met by a complicated puzzle, a tangled web, far more impenetrable than the carefully contrived plot of a crime mystery novel, because it had been woven by experts in the craft at Moscow Centre. Even had security officers torn their way through the well-crafted deceptions, they would have found themselves up against a blank wall at the end of a false paper trail.

Oppie was the cook at home, not Kitty. He had already become famous with his student friends for his Indonesian nasi goreng, but his steak dishes proved more popular in Los Alamos. Guests were invariably introduced first to his special cocktails of either a gin sour or his vodka Martinis. To celebrate his thirty-ninth birthday on 22 April 1943, he organised the first big party on The Hill. Everyone danced as a consequence of the potency of his cocktails, even the more sedate Isidor Rabi. Oppie danced the foxtrot formally, holding his partner away from him with stiff arms, while Rabi played his comb like a harmonica.[1]

Kitty was generally independent and bossy, refusing to adopt a secondary role of the project director's wife. She was not given to displaying herself in what she thought of as bourgeois frocks, hairstyles, and jewellery, but – slender and petite – she wore blue jeans and a checked Brooks Brothers shirt. She was now working part-time as a lab technician under the supervision of Dr Hemplemann, and had become a familiar figure in the corridors of the lab, where she was trailed by 'attentive disciples'.[2]

Robert was frequently seen when he left their home early on most mornings and walked to his office. Their current house was now 1967 Peach Street. He no longer wore his frivolous old pork-pie hat. He had exchanged if for a more austere wide-brimmed fedora that made his face look leaner. Sometimes he could be seen taking Peter to the nursery school before arriving for work at 8 a.m.

In spite of the pressures of his job, he and Kitty appeared to be happy with their lives at Los Alamos. He had loved this part of New Mexico ever since he had first discovered it on horseback. Now he and Kitty would go horseback riding whenever they could on weekends, across the Sangre de Cristo Range, and on into Pecos Valley, where they would camp overnight. Anyone watching them leave would see the bizarre sight of a GI following them at a short distance on horseback, according to security regulations by General Groves.

On weekdays, Robert worked in his sparse office on the second floor of what was a typical utilitarian army base. The view from his window extended as far as the distant mountain ranges. His office was modest, but he had everything he needed – his desk and a visitor's chair, a long conference table, and a blackboard. It was big enough for him to pace back and forth while talking and chain-smoking, and often also coughing.

He always maintained his old-fashioned courtesy to the staff and guests.

Groves knew of the unfavourable intelligence reports on Oppenheimer, but thought he understood Oppie well enough to trust him. He sensed that he was always attempting to shield someone he thought worth protecting, either his brother Frank or his communist wife, or someone else, like Haakon Chevalier. Chevalier was fired from his teaching job at Berkeley, and was now watched by the FBI and the Los Alamos security service.

Groves was now under pressure from both security services to terminate Oppenheimer's position as director. The Tatlock case was still not closed. But Groves knew that releasing Oppenheimer would slow down the Manhattan Project, and that must not be allowed to happen. Groves knew his goal and was determined to achieve it. When the security officers pressed him again, Groves told them, 'Oppenheimer stays'.

Mrs Katherine Oppenheimer

Kitty had married Oppie as soon as her divorce from her previous husband was finalised in Nevada in November 1940. Their first child, Peter, had arrived only seven months later. Groves thought of Katherine Oppenheimer as a small and slender woman, not beautiful in his opinion, but pretty, intelligent and witty, with brown eyes and a wide mouth; all of which charmed men, but only when she wanted to.

Once married, the couple had begun to withdraw from their communist friends. He had become sceptical about Soviet Russia ever since the Nazi-Soviet pact and the Russian attacks on Finland and Poland. His brother Frank now denied he was a member of the Party. His friend Lawrence was relieved when Robert told him he had ceased his own political activities.

Whereas Oppenheimer loved his 'Shangri-La', Groves could see that Kitty did not. She had been accustomed to wealth in her previous marriage, and living in a sophisticated city where she had been the centre of attention. Her new husband's world was not hers. The small town of Santa Fe was squalid. The people she now mixed with were different from the ones she had known. Nor was she the primary focus of Robert's life. She acted the role of the gracious hostess whenever he told her it was necessary, but she found it gruelling to be the 'first lady'.

She did not get on with the Bethes or the Serbers, and dropped them socially as soon as she could. Priscilla Green found her unfriendly: she was the boss's wife and she could be mean. She could cause trouble, so you had to be careful. According to Priscilla, several men referred to Kitty in hushed voices, as 'a bitch'. Others found Kitty 'difficult to handle'.

Kitty had begun to drink heavily and became reclusive. She shut herself away at home. One afternoon, she invited Frank's wife Jackie to cocktails with a few other women who were lonely, like her. They drank steadily away and had nothing to say to each other.

Instead of shopping in Santa Fe, Kitty preferred to travel further afield to Albuquerque and California, sometimes staying away for weeks at a time, as Jean Tatlock had done.

'Occasionally, after drinking excessively at parties, she would reveal deeply intimate information about her married life.'[3]

As far as the community was concerned, what she was good at was welcoming new arrivals with baskets of essential items they would need to settle down in their new surroundings. She was solicitous then, and also in greeting visiting VIPs, who found her 'clever, vivacious, and charming'. It was as if those special occasions had been organised by Oppie to present a pleasing face by behaving favourably before newcomers to Los Alamos. It was like a trade-off to let her be freed from other social duties. Otherwise she could be 'difficult and divisive'. She was also imperious. All of Oppenheimer's assistants 'quickly learned to give her a wide berth'.

Emily Morrison was the wife of one of Oppie's protégés, who said of Kitty that 'She could be a bewitching person, but she was someone to be wary of.'[4]

Nevertheless, Kitty was lonely and needed companionship to prevent her from being bored and brooding on her own. She chose Shirley Barnett, a part-time assistant of her husband.

'She would invite me to spend my days off with her, and we'd go for lunch and shopping trips to Santa Fe, or as far as Albuquerque. She always had a bottle or something with her when she was driving, and you could always tell when she was getting drunk because she would talk more freely.'[5]

No one knew what Robert thought of his wife's erratic behaviour, or if they had privately come to terms about how to play their individual roles. It might have been natural for Robert, after his three-year affair with the manic-depressive Jean Tatlock, to become accustomed to such erratic behaviour. He may even have thought it a normal part of marriage. He was a scientist, and most were unconventional. As the famous mathematician and professor of biology Jacob Bronowski would remark, 'if we are so different as to be scientists, you must expect us to be questioning, rebellious, and uncomfortable to be with.' It is 'an adventurous strain – that is what makes progress'.[6]

It is often forgotten that Kitty, too, was a scientist. Records describe her as 'Katherine (Kitty) Vissering Oppenheimer (née Puening), a German-American biologist, botanist; best known as the wife of political activist Joe Dallet, and then physicist J. Robert Oppenheimer.' But some records featuring Kitty must be false, since they show her living two lives in two different countries, and one Kitty still living while the other Kitty died somewhere else. Apart from when she was accompanied to Santa Fe by a friend, like Shirley Barnett, there are no accounts of any clandestine meetings there with Elizabeth Zarubin, or any other communist agent, spy or spymaster, because, if there were any, they were undertaken in secret.

Kitty and Robert felt frustrated and trapped by that time. But they carried on. Robert was held on track by a sense of purpose. But Kitty was restless. She wanted something more than being a lab assistant, and soon quit her job. Robert gave her their five horses to look after instead.[7]

A Complicated Life

The commonly known version of Kitty's life was that she had been born in Germany as Kathryn Puening in 1910, and her parents brought her to the United States when she was three. She became an American citizen when her father, Franz Puening, was naturalised in 1922. He was a mining engineer and they lived comfortably when they settled in Pittsburgh and he worked in the steel industry. Kitty lived a privileged life as a spoiled only child, and soon became a rebellious and wilful young woman with an impetuous nature that bordered on recklessness.

According to that biographer, Kitty was restless and unfocused when she entered the University of Pittsburgh, and left after only a year to head for Paris. 'She drifted through courses at the Sorbonne and then did a stint at the University of Grenoble, but she was by her own admission more interested in the nightlife than in her studies.'[8]

Her European escapade apparently reached an unhappy point in the spring of 1933, when she had an affair and appeared to have married a young musician from Boston named Frank Wells Ramseyer Jnr. Although she had attempted to cast the memory of it into oblivion, she would be pressed to confirm to the FBI that it had been annulled after only a few months. She enrolled in the University of Wisconsin in the autumn. Then she abandoned her studies again, several months afterwards, to run off with another man, Joseph Dullet, whom she described from then on as her first husband.

Joe had been another young rebel; a tall and handsome son of a Boston investment broker who had rejected his family with their wealth and respectability, to dedicate himself to unionising steel workers. He too had dropped out of university in his first year and sought to escape from his conservative family. According to one source, he travelled around Europe attempting to make a living in one business or another before failing and becoming a longshoreman. He would claim it was not because he was a failure, but because he refused to be a parasite on society; intimating that was what his father was. In this, he was typical of Sigmund Freud's claim that rebels against society began by rebelling against the authority of their father.

Joe and Kitty met at a New Year's Eve party. He had already joined the Communist Party by then, and become a steel union organiser in Youngstown, Ohio. Kitty saw him as a romantic and heroic figure. Persuading workers to join a union and leading them in strikes was a tough and continually dangerous occupation that required a special bitter and ruthless attitude towards society. It involved him in fights with sluggers and gunmen.[9]

Evidently, Kitty was in love with Dullet, and impetuously rejected her education to join the Communist Party and involve herself in the drudgery of menial work associated with the trade unions. She was one of many straying young men and women who drifted away from home and conventional middle-class society to the Communist Party. There would be endless case histories of adolescent strays and drifters who abandoned their homes or were rejected by families and took to the streets, in San Francisco's Haight-Ashbury, with Charles Manson's so-called 'family'; exotic cults that took them in, the Baader-Meinhof gang in post-war Germany; Patty Hearst and the 'Stockholm Syndrome'; the Flower Children in 1950s America and the Permissive Society in the UK in the 1960s. They were part of a discontented generation that followed the pattern of wilful individuals searching for an identity soon after the First World War had ended.

Those prolonged adolescents were obliged to prove to committed communist labour leaders that they were not the sons or daughters of privileged middle-class families, but dedicated to being more working class than blue-collar workers. Kitty had typed letters, made copies of pro-communist leaflets, did other jobs around the office to demonstrate her dedication, and distributed copies of the *Daily Worker* and other propaganda, which was expected of her.

She had never known such squalor. Without money, they were forced to share accommodation in slum quarters with members of the commune, and prove their commitment to the 'class struggle'. She coped with a grim life of solemn and bitter Party meetings filled with class hatred for two years, before deciding to give up on it in June 1936, when she told Joe she'd had enough and wanted a separation.

She was welcomed back home by her parents in London, where she brooded morosely on her life and loneliness for a few months at home, before suddenly deciding to rejoin Dullet, and wrote to him. Months passed with no reply, until she discovered that her mother had been hiding his letters from her.

'Her mother was a real dragon,' Anne Wilson recalled; 'a very hard, repressive woman. She disappeared one day over the side of a transatlantic ship, and nobody missed her.'[10]

Kitty re-joined Dullet in Cherbourg, where her ship docked in March 1937. They spent ten days in Paris before he left to join a group of American volunteers fighting for the Loyalist forces in the Spanish Civil War. Wives were not encouraged to join their husbands at the front in Spain, but she was passionately in love with him and eager to be with him; so he managed to get permission. But it was too late. A formal telegram arrived in October that he had been shot at the battlefront, and was dead.

It took her a week to overcome the first stage of shock and defeat in Paris, where Joe's friend, Steve Nelson, comforted her. Both of them viewed Dullet as a hero who had fought against the fascists. But all that was left of his bravery was their love letters.

Kitty remarried a year later, again on impulse; this time to a British medical doctor named Richard Stewart Harrison. She told Shirley Barnett it was 'singularly unsuccessful from the start'. She returned to America that autumn, enrolled at the University of Pennsylvania, where she majored in biology. She met Robert Oppenheimer at a party as soon as she had graduated.

Kitty had trapped Robert into marriage and pregnancy because she fell deeply in love with him, and it was by no means the first time that such a deliberate ruse was used successfully. She knew enough of him by that time to realise that he would always do the gentlemanly thing.

21

Problem Number One

Whichever was the real Kitty among all the alternative versions on record, no one could possibly know – partly because most of the stories of her life were a mixture of second-hand versions of fictionalised ones, purposefully planned as disinformation by Moscow Centre, and only small fragments of those stories were known by anyone. Others were concealed as classified secret material in the filing cabinets of the KGB. Nor could anyone outside of Moscow Centre tell with certainty what was the purpose of all the distortions of the truth and the secrecy surrounding her.

The official Soviet mind worked differently from the open reasoning of the West, because the Soviets thought differently about most subjects. Their approach was oblique and not easy to understand by Westerners, as a consequence of unreasonable and dubious objectives. The Bolshevik attitude veered away from what the outside world took for granted. Communist Russia still preferred to create its own 'false reality', based on a rigid and artificial doctrine founded on a theory and Stalin's preference for weaving escapist fantasies for the Russian people and the world outside. Much of it was intended to distract them from what was really happening.

Whereas such deception was possible in a closed society like Russia, it was not the case in open societies like the United States and the United Kingdom in the 1930s. Those who chose to join the Communist Party in the West viewed it as a reasonable alternative to a capitalist society that had failed with the collapse of the financial system in 1929.

Some of Kitty's reflections on her life arose between her and other women when they drank together and Kitty evidently felt the need to consider her past, and probably seek to justify it, if only to herself. Other thoughts too emerged under the watchful eyes of Colonel Lansdale, a senior security officer with overarching responsibility for the Manhattan Project. Lonsdale had written a report that Groves ruminated on, long and hard. It was a most secret document entitled *Transcript of Interview with Dr Oppenheimer by Lieutenant Colonel Lansdale, September 12, 1943*.

Lansdale was a thirty-one-year-old lawyer from Cleveland who served as head of the security service. It was he, not Groves, who ordered Oppenheimer to be secretly shadowed or followed openly whenever he left The Hill, had his mail opened and his telephone bugged. Everyone in the security service was suspicious of Oppenheimer because he did not conform to what they had expected. He was unique and much misunderstood.

Groves had previously received a separate report on 29 June 1943 from Lieutenant Colonel Boris T. Pash, who was chief of the Counter-Intelligence branch in San Francisco. 'Information available to this office,' it began, 'indicated that subject may still be connected with the Communist Party. Results of surveillances conducted on subject, upon arrival in San Francisco on 12 June 1943, indicate further possible Communist Party connections.' It was a reference to the Jean Tatlock affair, which would not go away.

Later in the summer, Lansdale went to talk with Oppenheimer at Los Alamos about several scientists Oppie had recruited from the West Coast and appointed to the project against the advice of the security service. 'A group in a nearby industrial laboratory in California was suspected of collaborating with Soviet agents.' Oppenheimer had evidently been concerned, and responded firmly with his belief that no member of the Communist Party should be hired for the Manhattan Project. He maintained that loyalty to the Party was incompatible with loyalty to their work.[1]

Oppenheimer had worried about the security situation ever since Lansdale had warned him of what could occur. And he had finally realised the seriousness of what might happen to the project and his own career if nuclear secrets were allowed to leak out.

Key Insights

Lansdale's security interests naturally spread to Kitty, who found she was being politely but skilfully interrogated by him in her own home. He had realised that, as a result of her untidy background, she could provide him with elements of her husband's character that could be the key to his questionable behaviour. Lansdale took as many opportunities as he possibly could to probe into her complicated background and into her husband's complex personality.[2]

Kitty generally served Lansdale a Martini on arrival. As he remarked wryly afterwards, she was not the type of hostess to offer him tea. He decided that Kitty was a powerful woman with strong convictions. When it came to her political sympathies, there was no doubt in his mind that she was a convinced communist, and, 'It requires a very strong person to be a real communist.'

Even so, during the course of their meandering and still civilised conversations, he recognised that her primary loyalty was to her husband. He was also startled to realise during their duel of words that 'she hated me and everything I stood for'.

It seemed appropriate to the exotic New Mexico environment that she was attempting to rope him with her femininity, as he did his best to rope her in with his interrogation skills.

'I felt she'd go to any lengths for what she believed in. The tactic I fell back on was to try to show her I was a person of balance, honestly wanting to evaluate Oppenheimer's position. That's why our talks ran on so long ... I was sure she'd been a communist and not sure her abstract opinions had ever changed much ... She didn't care how much I knew of what she'd done before she met Oppenheimer or how it looked to me. Gradually I began to see that nothing in her past and nothing in her other husband's past meant anything to her compared with her love for Robert Oppenheimer. I became convinced that in him she had an attachment stronger than communism; that his future meant more to her than communism. She was trying to sell me on the idea that he was her life, and she did sell me.'

Lansdale summarised his interview with Kitty by claiming to Groves that, 'Dr. Oppenheimer was the most important thing in her life … her strength of will was a powerful influence in keeping Dr Oppenheimer away from what we would regard as dangerous associations.'

Birth Control

It was no wonder that Kitty felt she was being constantly scrutinised through a microscope in the artificial world of Los Alamos, where she felt trapped by surrounding barbed wire.

General Groves had remarked to Oppie on the added difficulties of all the new babies who kept on appearing at the Manhattan Project. And Robert had retorted jocularly that birth control was not one of his responsibilities. Apparently not, since that was the moment when Kitty, too, was pregnant for the second time. She gave birth in the army hospital to her daughter, Katherine, on 7 December 1944.

Their experience with their first child, Peter, had not been without problems, since Kitty lacked a maternal instinct and had no idea how to deal with the normal stages of contrariness in infants, like the 'terrible twos'. Her son appeared to her to be more difficult than most toddlers. He was frequently cross and fractious.

Four months after Kitty gave birth to her daughter, she felt she needed to escape, and said she wanted to go home to her parents. Her constant scrutiny and the unwanted experience of pregnancy, giving birth, and post-natal depression, had apparently been too much for her, even with the anaesthesia of repeated Martinis. She was on the edge of a nervous breakdown.

'She was drinking a lot,' Pat Sherr would confirm afterwards. And Kitty had become impatient with Peter. Pat, who had been trained as a psychologist, considered that Kitty had no instinctive understanding of children. Kitty's sister-in-law, Jackie, remarked that when Kitty went off for days on her shopping trips to Albuquerque – or even further afield to the West Coast – she would leave the children in the care of a maid. Then she would bring back a gift for Peter, to assuage her guilt.

She took Peter with her when she left for Pittsburgh in April 1945, leaving behind the four-month-old baby Katherine with her friend Pat Sherr, who had just had a miscarriage. They were away for three and a half months. Pat's doctor thought it a good idea for her to have a baby to care for. Robert was far too busy working long hours, and the stress had taken its toll on his health: he was skinny and strained. Although he dropped in on Pat, ostensibly to visit the baby, he didn't ask to see Tyke – which was her nickname – but took the opportunity to unwind.

Finally, Pat said, 'Wouldn't you like to see your daughter, she's growing beautifully?' And he said, 'Yeah, yeah.'

After two months of such visits, Robert remarked, 'You seem to have grown to love Tyke very much.'

'Well, I love children,' Pat said, 'and when you take care of a baby, whether it's yours or someone else's, it becomes a part of your life.'

'Would you like to adopt her?' Robert asked.[3]

'Of course not,' she replied, 'she has two perfectly good parents.'

When she pressed him to explain why he wanted his daughter adopted, Robert admitted, 'Because I can't love her.'

He added that he was not an attached sort of person. He had not mentioned the idea of adoption to Kitty because he'd wanted first to find out if Pat would agree, since she could offer the baby a warm and welcoming home.

Pat decided to view his request as a generous gesture to her as well as to Tyke. Robert was, after all, a man of character with a powerful conscience, and he knew that if Pat adopted his daughter, she would be provided with long-lasting love and care that he could not give her.

Oppie, 'as usual, looked at Death's Door'. He was sleeping for only a few hours a night. His weight had fallen to 114lb. Groves was concerned at his poor condition, and brought Frank to Los Alamos in the hope that he would have a calming effect on his older brother.[4]

Kitty had fallen into a depression after the birth of Tyke and rarely left the house. Shirley Barnett recalled that, 'She was often ill and took various drugs to quiet her nerves … I don't know what Oppie thought. He wasn't in great shape himself at that point, and he had so much to do he couldn't fret too much about it.'[5]

President Roosevelt had died suddenly by the time Kitty returned from her trip home to Pittsburgh in July 1945. She found an atmosphere of tension, with everyone working longer hours to compete with the German scientists in producing the first nuclear bomb. She made up for her absence by inviting groups of women to visit her for daily cocktails. But Pat did not feel it was simply an opportunity for Kitty to avoid drinking on her own. Pat thought she drank no more than anyone else in the project. Dr Hempelmann, who knew Kitty well, agreed; 'everybody got tired,' he said. 'And tense, and irritable, it wasn't so good. Everybody was living in each other's pockets.'

Everyone knew everything about everyone else, and they were tired of seeing the same faces every day. Nevertheless, you'd accept invitations even when you didn't want to go. They had no choice but to put up with their discontents because of the life-or-death situation with the atom bomb.

The Perversion of Knowledge

The truth about who Kitty really was, and might become, was ever more complicated to anyone searching for the difference between what appeared to be two very complicated and remarkable women who had been named Kitty Harris and Mrs Kitty Harrison. The mystery would become clearer only in the far distant future when a book called *Special Tasks* would be published by a Soviet agent named Pavel Sudoplatov in 1994. He was able to reveal that something momentous had happened less than a decade previously in the Soviet Union. Moscow Centre was skilful at ambiguity and duplicity, and rewriting history to conceal the truth. Their special mastery included identity theft, and any other means to ensure that guilty secrets were hidden and the public and overseas news media were kept completely confused about what had taken place, and the real motive for what was really happening right now.

Kitty had been used by the Soviet Union in a highly imaginative way as disinformation to obscure the trails that led to the Kremlin's mass murders, to distract its own population and its outside enemies from what was really happening in Stalin's Russia.[6]

Stalin had ordered a new section of the NKVD to be set up in 1936. It was called AST, or 'Administration of Special Tasks'. It consisted of three hundred of Stalin's trusted supporters, headed by Nicolai Yezhov. 'The AST was used to remove all those who had knowledge of the conspiracy to destroy Stalin's rivals.'[7] It would involve blood, poison, and terrorism.[8]

One of the first victims to be disposed of was Genrikh Yagoda. Since he was director of Soviet Russia's secret police in 1934–36, he would know where all the bodies were buried and who had arranged to have them executed in one way or another; so he had to go.

No nation was more skilled and masterful in inventing false news than the Soviet Union. And they would stop at nothing to rewrite history in their favour. They used the art of disinformation to cover up their crimes and to distract attention from someone to something else. They had done so by inventing a fictional Kitty Harris – in effect by splitting her into two separate personalities, each with her own different past. One of them was complete invention, whereas the other was part-invention based on fact.

It was nothing new. From the earliest days of the CHEKA secret police at the time of the October Revolution in 1917, they had used a multitude of cover names to conceal what was happening from the Russians and from the outside world. Attempts to trace what really happened would lead to a wrong address in a dead end.

According to the entirely fictional Kitty Harris, whose identity was invented by the Russians to distract the FBI or Lansdale's security service at Los Alamos, or anyone else who might make inquiries;

> Kitty Harris had a very different end. She had spent the rest of the war continuing her career as a successful intelligence agent in Mexico, and in 1946 was brought to the Soviet Union, where she stayed until her death in 1966. But once she reached Russia, she found that the society for which she had worked so tirelessly and at such risk to her own safety fell far short of her dreams. 'The only thing I know is that I am terribly lonely,' she wrote in her diary during her last years. 'My life is in pieces.'[9]

Those details were intended to tell us that Kitty Harris could not possibly be the same woman as Kitty Oppenheimer. The two parallel and contradictory biographies were 'the result of purges in the 1930s and late 1940s under Stalin, and again in Khrushchev's ascent to power in 1953'.[10]

The Russian mind works like a maze designed to ensure that opponents lose their way, or turn their back on the inextricable confusion confronting them. It was all part of their mastery in concealing all evidence of their criminal footprints.

Sudoplatov, the former KGB spymaster, now retired, claimed in his revealing memoirs to have 'worked with Oppenheimer, Fermi, Szilard, Bohr, and many others – and [admitted] how the Soviets stole the secrets of the atom bomb'. He also 'named Oppenheimer, Szilard, Fermi, Bohr, Pontecorvo, and Gamow as scientists who knowingly cooperated with Soviet intelligence'.[11]

He was only partly right, because the most crucial evidence about Kitty Harris had been withheld from him by concealing it in the false narrative about the fictional Kitty. He was close to the truth, but not near enough to see the trickery that concealed it. In the course of his and his agents' work, which was to befriend the scientists at Berkeley, Los Alamos, and elsewhere, Moscow Centre had decided it would suit their purpose best to muddy the records retrospectively by introducing a fake Kitty Harris into the mystery in which Mrs Katherine Oppenheimer might still be trapped in Lansdale's and Groves's security web. Evidently, the Kremlin had not informed Sudoplatov that they were the same individual.

Sudoplatov wanted to correct his official biography and exonerate himself from the trumped up charges of treason that had been made against him after Soviet secret police Chief Lavrentiy Beria was arrested and executed – this time by Nikita Khrushchev in December 1953 – in yet another effort to remove another chief of secret police who knew too much.

All of that had been concealed by distracting Sudoplatov, as well as the public, with false news about what was going on. He was targeted because he 'had been head of the Poison Laboratory whose products were used to kill Stalin's enemies'. So he too knew too much and had to go. But he, at least, had managed to escape execution.

He admitted in his memoir to 'being in charge of four assassinations under orders. One of them was the assassination of Leon Trotsky in Mexico.'[12]

He was unlucky to be on the wrong side in the power struggle when Khrushchev was in the ascendancy after Stalin's death.[13]

Problem Number One

G. Ovakimian was in charge of the American and British desk in Moscow for the NKVD when they prepared a summary of the atomic energy situation in April 1943. His name appeared at the foot of the report. It contained a footnote stating that the names of British, American and German scientists who provided the research information had been deleted. The report was obtained by the FBI, who had arrested and deported him from New York for spying.[14]

Its contents included a complete description of Enrico Fermi's first reactor and emphasised that the scale of research in America was 'considerably larger than in other countries. Hundreds of highly qualified scientific workers were engaged in the project and their work produced substantial results. Due to this, the results of British research work summarized here do not merit great attention.'[15]

Beria removed the report when he left the NKVD, since Stalin gave him the leadership of all atomic intelligence work for Russia to develop an atom bomb. Beria's mission at that point was 'to undertake measures for the organisation of foreign intelligence work on obtaining more full technical and economic information on the uranium industry and the atomic bomb'. It was described as Soviet Russia's 'Problem Number One'.

22

The Race for the Atom Bomb

The new President of the United States after Roosevelt died on 12 April 1945 was former vice-president, Harry S. Truman. He would be briefed very quickly on the war situation and on the present status of the Manhattan Project in the secret city of Los Alamos, where snow lay on the ground and the Stars and Stripes stood at half-mast out of respect for FDR. Oppenheimer's tribute to the extraordinary man who was perhaps the greatest American president of all time, was: 'In the Hindu scripture, in the Bhagavad-Gita, it says, Man is the creature whose substance is faith. What his faith is, he is.'

Brigadier General Groves and Secretary of War Henry Stimson met at the White House to brief the new president on the Manhattan Project in the Oval Office a few weeks later. Groves brought with him a document he had prepared for Henry L. Stimson, which they now wished to share with President Truman. Its twenty-four pages were entitled 'Atomic Fission Bombs'. It described in clear and unambiguous words the weapons under development at Los Alamos, and their scientific and military implication. By now, a huge network of manufacturing plants had been built to produce nuclear materials.[1]

'The successful development of the Atomic Fission Bomb will provide the United States with a weapon of tremendous power which should be a decisive factor in winning the present war more quickly with a saving in American lives and treasure. If the United States continues to lead in the development of atomic energy weapons, its future will be much safer and the chances of preserving world peace greatly increased.'[2]

To make sure that Truman understood the implications, Stimson told him that 'the future may see a time when such a weapon may be constructed in secret and used suddenly and effectively with devastating power by a willful nation or group against an unsuspecting nation or group of much greater size and material power ... although probably the only nation which could enter into production within the next few years is Russia.'[3]

None of the men in the Oval Office knew that the Soviet Union had been working on an atom bomb since 1943 as their 'priority number one'.

Oppenheimer's Progress

Progress in the laboratory at Los Alamos had been slow since 1943, but now they were relieved to feel they were finally close to achieving the first critical assembly of U235 at the Omega site, which had been located for safety in an isolated canyon. They would know the exact weight of the critical mass as soon as they did so. Other scientists were just as close to learning the optimal division of uranium in the gun between the target and the projectile. They expected the uranium gun to be ready by 1 August.

The code name for the uranium bomb was 'Little Boy'. The plutonium bomb would be named 'Fat Man'. Its progress was less forthcoming. The objective of the Trinity test was to discover if 'Fat Man' would work, otherwise no one would know for sure until the first weaponised atomic bomb was dropped on a target. The 'Gadget' was planned to be detonated at the top of the Trinity tower for the first test. It would become 'Fat Man' only when weaponised to be dropped on Japan. At the end of June, Oppenheimer advised Groves that the U235 in 'Little Boy' would be coated in cadmium to increase safety.[4]

'Fat Man's' problem was its complex design, which presented huge challenges for scientists trying to assemble the implosion bomb. A high percentage of each batch of new explosive lenses had to be abandoned every time because of defects like cracks, bubbles, and chips. None of them were perfect enough for what was required. Groves was alarmed at the passing of time without results. The news on 28 April was not good, with the 'Fat Man' bomb holding back their anticipated schedules. Groves arranged to meet with the suppliers.

Nearly a week passed before Groves informed Oppenheimer that his meeting with a manufacturer in Detroit had gone well and that the lab should place a new order with them immediately.

Then the tests with the detonation system were unable to proceed because the contractor for the firing circuits failed to meet the agreed deadlines. Milestones for events were long since passed, due to the failures of one essential activity after another.

> Waiting anxiously at S Site for new molds, men found themselves with tons of raw explosives in brand new buildings erected to handle the increased demands, but without production equipment. With the July and August deadlines closing in with alarming speed, the hopeful spring turned into a problematic summer.[5]

With so many separate workshops, labs and factories to juggle with by now, like Hanford and Oak Ridge in Tennessee, Argonne National Laboratory, and Chalk River Laboratories, Oppenheimer needed more machinists and other workers, and Groves recruited two hundred and fifty or three hundred men at a time. They employed 120,000 American men and women in the end. But there was plenty of lost time that could never be recovered, even though Groves speeded up his own travel times visiting sites and plants all over the country, while attempting to keep the pressure on every supplier of every component to be used in the entire Manhattan Project.

His discussions with Oppenheimer in the spring of 1945 always seemed to centre on progress. Every one of their conversations resulted in some action or other from Groves to accelerate supplies and workers. He met Tolman in his office for fifteen minutes on 30 May, then Oppenheimer for forty-five minutes. Parsons, Szilard, Fermi, and Ernest Lawrence came soon after, in between numerous phone calls and being summoned to meetings. June and July were just as hectic, since they were aimed at a critical milestone named 'Trinity'.

The secret camp known as 'Project Trinity' was both a location and a proposed event to test the first bomb at the desert site, where 'Fat Man' was to be tried out to see if it worked. When it was finally ready to test, Cyril Smith's division reported on 26 June that they were only a week away from delivering the finished plutonium core for Trinity. It was delivered to Bacher on 2 July. Hanford shipped the next lot of Pu239 according to schedule. The Trinity core was taken to the Omega site and put in a mock-up of 'Fat Man' for examination on the Fourth of July.

Journey of Death

Oppenheimer looked strained the next day. It was only six days after enough plutonium had been released. He had sent a coded telegram to the head consultants, Compton in Chicago and Lawrence at Berkeley: ANY TIME AFTER THE 15th WOULD BE A GOOD TIME FOR OUR FISHING TRIP, BECAUSE WE ARE NOT CERTAIN OF THE WEATHER WE MAY BE DELAYED SEVERAL DAYS.[6]

Success or defeat for the enterprise would mean the difference between shortening the war, or spending $2 billion on a failed attempt to end it. The tension and strain was shown in the faces and postures of Groves as well as Oppenheimer, and on all the physicists who had contributed their theories and skills for years. All felt anxious that their contributions might end in failure.

The first atomic test had been thought through, planned, and prepared for by a special group, led by a Harvard physics professor, Dr Kenneth Bainbridge. Frank Oppenheimer was transferred from the Oak Ridge plant to help him. The Trinity explosion would be a rehearsal for dropping an atom bomb on the enemy from the air. Oppenheimer and Bainbridge had chosen a site in the desert called Jornada del Muerto (Journey of Death). It was 300 miles south of Los Alamos. The nearest towns were over 20 miles away.[7]

Implosion had never been tried before, and not enough plutonium had ever been assembled to achieve a chain reaction, so no one could be sure it would actually work. 'Fat Man's' heavy shape matched its name. It was 5ft in diameter and difficult to hold together. The shell had to be improved in a simpler form code-named Y-1561.

Despite the unprecedented situation, Groves's reports to the War Department became more and more optimistic 'about the probability that two types of fission weapon would be ready for use against Japan in midsummer'.[8]

With that thought in mind, Oppenheimer now strongly urged that, 'He thought it might be wise for the United States to offer to the world free interchange of information with particular emphasis on the development of peacetime uses … If we were to offer to exchange information before the bomb was actually used, our moral position would be greatly strengthened.'[9]

Oppenheimer had never stopped considering the moral aspects of using the bomb, ever since Niels Bohr had arrived at Los Alamos in the evening of 30 December 1943. Bohr's first question to Robert had been, 'Is it really big enough?'

What Bohr had meant was, would it be powerful enough to deter any nation from making further wars in future?

Leo Szilard showed more emotion than the other two scientists. He was acutely aware that time was running out, and that atom bombs were close to being ready for use. If so, they would almost certainly be used on the Japanese in an attempt to halt the war. He had been the first scientist to urge Roosevelt to initiate this programme to build atomic weapons; now he made continual attempts to stop them being used. He wrote to caution Oppenheimer.

Robert did not reply. He had already told him this weapon would be no use in war. 'The atomic bomb is shit,' was what he had said. But he thought the Russians should be informed in advance.[10]

'Is it really big enough?'

Oppenheimer reported a last-minute problem that Groves found difficult to understand. It required a critical decision about a complex mixing of layers of materials that might prevent the assembly of a critical mass of plutonium.[11]

Oppenheimer had been glad to have had Niel's Bohr's advice. The older Danish physicist had been fifty-seven in September 1943 when he had been rescued from the Germans in Copenhagen and smuggled out of Denmark in a motor launch. When taken to Stockholm in Sweden, he had been the victim of an assassination attempt by the Nazis, who recognised his value. British airmen had rescued him again by concealing him in the bomb bay of a Mosquito bomber. They had landed him in Scotland, where his colleague and friend, Chadwick, took him to London and told him about the Anglo-American atom bomb project. Bohr had been amazed.

Groves had not been too happy about allowing the physicist to visit Los Alamos that first time, but the Dane's prestige was so huge that he could not refuse, although he knew he was a loose cannon. Bohr had already spoken to the British press about the possibility of an atomic bomb, and feared that its development would lead to a nuclear arms race.

To prevent an arms race, 'he insisted it was imperative that the Russians be told about the existence of the bomb project, and be assured that it was no threat to them'.[12]

Groves was horrified to hear such dangerous opinions from scientists. He intended to isolate the Dane at Los Alamos to prevent outsiders from hearing his views. To make sure that Bohr did not cut loose and breach protocol, as he had done several times before – like barging in on the King at his palace in Denmark, and visiting Britain's ambassador Lord Halifax in Washington, and Roosevelt's friend Felix Frankfurter – Groves personally accompanied Bohr and his son on the train from Chicago, to keep a watchful eye on him until he could be confined in Los Alamos.

Groves and his scientific adviser were obliged to listen for hours on end to Bohr's characteristic whispering mumble that seldom ceased as he rambled on and on, barely listening to anyone else in his typical absentminded way. The general was relieved to deliver Bohr to Los Alamos, but was disconcerted to hear that the mumbling Dane was already disclosing all sorts of things he had promised not to divulge.

The German Physicists

Bohr had told Oppenheimer that Heisenberg was working intently on a uranium reactor for the Nazis that could produce a runaway chain reaction, 'and thereby create an immense explosion'. Oppenheimer had instantly called a meeting next day to discuss the serious possibility of a German bomb.

The scientists who attended the meeting possessed some of the best brains at Los Alamos. They had included Bohr, Aage, Edward Teller, Richard Tolman, Robert Serber, Robert Bacher, Victor Weiskopf, and Hans Bethe. Bohr did his best to inform them of his surprise encounter with Heisenberg in September 1941.[13]

He described how his brilliant German protégé had obtained special permission from the Nazis to attend a conference in German-occupied Copenhagen. Although Heisenberg was not a Nazi, he was a patriotic German who had decided to remain in Germany during the war, where he was the most outstanding physicist. So, naturally enough, all the scientists on the Manhattan project had been curious to know what Heisenberg knew, and what he was doing, since he was the obvious choice to head a nuclear project for Nazi Germany. It appeared that Werner had sought out his old teacher to ask or tell him something significant.

It would turn out that what the two old friends had talked about was a mystery, because Heisenberg was under surveillance by the Nazis and feared for his own life. Bohr was naturally apprehensive of the German officers who had accompanied Heisenberg. So apparently was Heisenberg. Heisenberg had been cautious in his approach, although it had clearly been deliberate. Evidently, he had had something important to tell the absentminded Bohr, who may have been too busy mumbling away to listen to him more intently.

By the time Bohr revealed what had happened at their brief moment of contact, he was unsure what exactly Heisenberg had intended to tell him. The gist of what he had managed to take away with him from his conversation with his former student was that apparently a German fission weapon was possible, and that, if developed, it could be decisive in the war. But Heisenberg and other German physicists 'wanted to persuade the Nazi regime that it would not be feasible to build such a weapon in time for use in this war'.[14]

Oppenheimer chose to view their surprise meeting in a somewhat different light. He believed that Heisenberg did not meet Bohr to tell him what the German scientists were up to, but rather to probe Bohr in order to discover if he or the Anglo-American scientists knew something that they did not. However each of them interpreted Bohr's encounter with Heisenberg, Bohr had come away haunted by a dreadful fear that the Nazis would end the war by using their own atom bomb on the Allies.

With the Manhattan Project apparently so close to testing the new American nuclear bombs, Oppenheimer, Groves, and the other scientists, worried anxiously, once again, who would be first to end the war by using an atomic bomb? They had all imagined the monumental explosion of the first atom bomb and its devastating effects, with wonder and horror, many times before, and considered and reconsidered whether there was a future for the human race in a world of nuclear weapons.

23

The Future of the Human Race

While Oppenheimer had been glad of Niels Bohr's advice and help at Los Alamos, he had been uneasily aware that the Dane's mind had been distracted from the technicalities while he envisioned launching a political campaign against the nuclear bomb. Robert was more guarded in his attitude, whereas Bohr rambled on as if thinking out his political tactics aloud. Bohr appeared to have become more concerned about the openness of science and international relations. Having heard his ramblings during their train journey, the security-minded Groves viewed him as a very dangerous man.

Now that Oppenheimer had been given time to think while confined to his administrative duties, Bohr's persuasive influence had stirred up his moral outrage at the bomb. But to calm Groves's apprehension about the Dane, Robert hurriedly assured him that the highly esteemed Bohr's presence had lifted the morale of all the scientists.

Groves saw the bomb as an essential military weapon to end the war quickly and save Allied lives, while Oppenheimer had already begun to view the bomb more as a political tool than a useful military weapon. Even before it was tested, he had dismissed it as a tactical weapon. But Bohr called it 'The Great Hope', since its possession might prevent all future wars. On the other hand, the military looked upon it eagerly as a major weapon with far greater destructive power than all the others put together.[1]

Bohr's view was far more grandiose than Oppenheimer's, because it was not confined to a single purpose. He believed in 'complementarity'; that the contradictions in life were all of a piece. 'They were building a weapon of mass destruction that would defeat fascism and end all wars – but also make it possible to end all civilization.'[2]

Bohr had even begun to write drafts of a memorandum that would convey his philosophy. He showed it eagerly to Oppenheimer. The Dane evidently imagined he had finally put together a persuasive report by 2 April 1944. His argument was that, regardless of how things might turn out, 'it is already evident that we are presented with one of the greatest triumphs of science and technique, destined deeply to influence the future of mankind'.

The philosophical Dane was openly contemptuous of Hitler and felt optimistic that the combined brain power and skills of the scientists at Los Alamos would surely defeat the Nazis' ambitions for total military power over the world. The good news was that the bomb would completely change the conditions of warfare. The bad news was that unless some agreement could be obtained about control of its use in time, any temporary advantage may be outweighed by *a perpetual menace to human security.*

According to Bohr, it required a new approach to international relationship. Secrecy must now be banished. The open world he imagined already existed in the internationalism of scientists everywhere. What was required now was international control of atomic energy. He wrote in his memorandum that, 'Knowledge is itself the basis of civilization'. Any enlargement of that knowledge imposed increased responsibility on individuals and nations to shape the conditions of human life. Each nation in the post-war world must feel confident that no potential enemy was stockpiling atomic weapons. It required international inspectors with full access to all military and industrial complexes and complete information about any new scientific discoveries.[3]

In spite of the nuclear bomb not having yet been tested to discover if it worked, Bohr's mind assumed it was a fact requiring the Soviet Union to be invited to participate in post-war atomic energy planning before the bomb was used and the war was over. He insisted that Moscow would have to be informed of all work on the Manhattan Project, and be assured that it posed no threat to the Soviet Union.

Oppenheimer agreed in principle with Bohr's attitude. But what the Dane's rambling philosophical monologue assumed was that Soviet Russia possessed a high-minded morality like his, when in fact most people in the real world did not. The world was riddled with subversive elements and criminal gangsters who might be little different from Hitler and the Nazis.

Bohr and Oppenheimer were either extraordinarily naïve or remarkably ignorant of the real tawdry world outside of their own lives and careers dedicated to science. Their naïve trust in human nature and public ethics and in the dubious honesty of Soviet politicians was shown by what Bohr thought of a letter he received from one of his former students in Moscow in the spring of 1944.

The Kapitza-Bohr Correspondence

Peter Kapitza was a leading Soviet Russian physicist who had been well regarded in the West. He had won the Nobel Prize, and been elected as a Fellow of Britain's Royal Society in 1929.

After the Nazis occupied Denmark, Bohr's former student invited him to settle in Moscow, where he claimed 'everything will be done to give you and your family a shelter and where we now have all the necessary conditions for carrying on scientific work'.

However warm Kapitza's greeting and his generous offer were, it should have been obvious that Soviet Russia wished either to pick Bohr's brains, or prevent him from continuing to work for the Anglo-Americans on the atomic bomb. Kapitza conveyed greetings from several other Russian physicists whom Bohr knew. The lure of his letter was intended to show what a happy team they would all be, working together with a single purpose under the direction of their former mentor.

Having Bohr's help might well solve the Soviet's Problem Number One. And Bohr thought it was a magnificent opportunity to solve his own problem, which was how to arrange public disclosure of the making of an atom bomb. He even imagined that Churchill and America's president 'would authorize him to accept Kapitza's invitation'.

Oppenheimer explained Bohr's delighted reaction to the invitation to his colleagues as an opportunity to 'propose to the rulers of Russia, who were then our Allies, via these [Russian] scientists, that the United States and the United Kingdom were willing to trade their atomic secrets for an open world ... that we propose to the Russians that atomic knowledge would be shared with them if they would agree to open Russia and make it an open country and part of an open world.'[4]

Oppenheimer was more cautious and circumspect while the war continued. He knew he was under constant surveillance from several security forces, and was careful not to be drawn into such a political quagmire.

On the other hand, neither Churchill nor General Groves shared Bohr's delusions of trust in the Soviet Union. General Groves never considered the Russians to be true allies: they were the enemy as surely as the Nazis were. Prime Minister Winston Churchill took the same view of the Kapitza-Bohr correspondence as Groves did. Churchill had been through that type of deceptive seduction by the Soviet Union before. He had watched the Soviet secret police when he had been Chancellor of the Exchequer, and they had offered the same type of invitations to an anti-Soviet leader he had admired, named Boris Savinkov. Savinkov was persuaded to return to Russia back in 1924, and been slapped into a cell in the Kremlin, from which it was claimed he had committed suicide by throwing himself out of the window onto a concrete yard.

Soviet Spies

The Russians had done an extraordinarily efficient job in solving their Problem Number One by using several of their own dedicated agents to befriend the most valuable British and American nuclear scientists and encourage them to talk freely about their work. They had also been assisted bravely and effectively by a number of voluntary agents in the West, like Donald Maclean and the Cambridge Five so-called spy ring, who were just as dedicated in choosing to fight against the Nazis by providing nuclear information for Soviet Russia from British and American top secret files. Those agents were as idealistic as Niels Bohr, but more realistic, untrusting and practical, because they knew the enemy and Bohr did not.

An example of different thinking came from a Polish physicist named Joseph Rotblat. He admired the stand that Soviet Russia had taken against the Nazi invasion of their country by never giving in. However cruel and brutal the fighting was against such immense German forces, the Red Army fought back just as violently to the last moment, the last bullet, and the last man. He had found himself left in England when the war began. Now he worked for James Chadwick on the bomb project at Los Alamos, where he heard cynical remarks from Groves and others about the need to curb Russia's post-war military ambitions by concealing as much as possible from them.

As a lifelong military man, General Groves regarded the Russians as a threat, whereas Rotblat admired the Russian soldier for his aggressive tenacity in putting up with every hardship they all had to suffer to drive the Germans off their land or destroy them. He was shocked by any mention of subduing those brave men in the Red Army who were dying by the thousand every day in unimaginably horrible circumstances.

Until then he had thought the Manhattan Project was working for a victory against the Nazis. Now it was nearly the end of 1944 and, sometime soon, the Allies would be ready for their cross-Channel assault on France. Rotblat was convinced the war against Germany would be over very shortly, so he resigned from his job on the Manhattan Project in December.

Only a few months earlier, Moscow Centre had received the first direct intelligence report from a scientist named Klaus Fuchs who also worked at Los Alamos.

Klaus Fuchs

Klaus Fuchs had been born in Germany before the First World War. His father was a pastor in the Lutheran church, and well respected for his high moral principles. He had joined the Quakers later in life and become professor of theology at Leipzig University. There appeared, however, to be a hereditary flaw on the maternal side that drove Fuchs's grandmother, mother, and a sister, to commit suicide. The answer as to why seemed to be solved by the medical diagnosis of his other sister who suffered from schizophrenia, which is often hereditary.[5]

Klaus studied physics and mathematics at the University of Leipzig. He joined the German Communist Party in 1931, but was obliged to flee from Germany when Hitler took power only two years later. He taught for a while in Paris before moving to England and becoming a theoretical physics student at the University of Bristol, where he obtained his PhD. He took a Doctorate in Science at Edinburgh University under the guidance of Max Born. It was his first link to Robert Oppenheimer, who had also been mentored by Born.

Fuchs was interned in a high-security camp on the Isle of Man with about 80,000 other men and women under Defence Regulation 18B when the war erupted. They were viewed as possible spies or potential traitors who might assist enemy invaders. His loyalty to secret communism hardened as a faith to hold on to in a fluid situation. He sympathised with Soviet Russia when it was invaded by massive German forces. He was given some addresses by someone who had fought in the International Brigade in Spain.[6]

Klaus Fuchs was released after intervention by several distinguished scientists who claimed his skills were being wasted, and recruited as a research assistant on atomic weapons by Rudolf Peierls at Birmingham University, who was working on the top secret Tube Alloys project. Peierls would be Klaus's second link with the Manhattan Project. Peierls had him cleared by the security authorities, because work on the atom bomb had become a top priority.

But Fuchs believed that atomic secrets should be shared with communist countries and not confined solely to the United States and Britain.[7]

SOVIET SECRET AGENTS

24

Soviet Spies Saving the World

Klaus Fuchs began spying for the Soviet Union in August 1941, 'when he was recruited through the recommendation of Urgen Kuchinsky'. He was a German communist exile in Britain. Fuch's possible transfer to the American laboratory had been anticipated by Moscow Centre, and an NKVD liaison arranged with him. He passed on his first intelligence information to his controller, Ursula Beurton, in September 1941.[1]

He and Ursula spent more than a half hour together when they first met, as if they had arranged to take a little walk together. Both were encouraged and relieved to meet another dedicated German comrade.[2]

Fuchs joined Peierls in the Manhattan Project in 1943, and was based in a research unit in New York City, where he worked for Hans Bethe.[3] He met five times with his Soviet contact during the next two months. On 1 January 1944, the agent sent a report on Fuchs to the GRU (a so-called 'neighbour' of the NKVD and the KGB). The information that Fuchs passed on included 'a number of theoretical calculations on atomic fission and creation of the uranium bomb'. They were highly praised, and he was described as a devout communist. He received no financial rewards, only occasional friendly gifts. His courier now was Harry Gold, and Soviet intelligence officer Sam Semyonov was ultimately responsible for the GRU-Fuchs relationship. The NKVD chose Gold as his direct contact because Gold was an experienced group handler.[4]

It was Semyonov who had transmitted a report as early as late December 1942 on the world's first nuclear chain reaction, which was accomplished by Fermi in the Metallurgical Laboratory at the University of Chicago on 2 December, since Sam had received a call only a few hours after the pile of graphite went critical. The cryptic message said, 'The Italian sailor reached the New World.'

Surprisingly, the message came from Arthur Compton, who managed the Met Lab where the experiments were taking place.[5] According to Semyonov's son, his father had enjoyed an ongoing personal friendship with Compton since his days at MIT. But Compton had been entirely unaware that Sam Semyonov was a Soviet intelligence officer.

After Gold met Fuchs the first time in Santa Fe, he reported that, 'Fuchs obviously worked with our people before and he is fully aware of what he is doing ... He is a mathematical physicist ... most likely a very brilliant man to have such a position at his age (he looks about 30). We took a long walk after dinner ... He is a member of a British mission to the U.S. working under the direct control of the U.S. Army ... The work involves mainly separating the isotopes ... and is being done thusly:

The electronic method has been developed at Berkeley, California, and is being carried out at a place known only as Camp Y ... Simultaneously, the diffusion method is being tried here in the East ... Should the diffusion method prove successful, it will be used as a preliminary step in the separation, with the final work being done by the electronic method. They hope to have the electronic method ready early in 1945 and the diffusion method in July 1945, but (Fuchs) says the latter estimate is optimistic. (Fuchs) says there is much being withheld from the British. Even Niels Bohr, who is now in the country incognito as Nicholas Baker, has not been told everything.[6]

They met for a second time in Santa Fe on 25 February, 1944, where he turned in material with his personal work on 'Enormoz'. At a third meeting on 11 March, he delivered fifty additional pages.[7]

'He asked me how his first stuff had been received, and I said quite satisfactorily but with one drawback: references to the first material, bearing on a general description of the process, were missing, and we especially needed a detailed schema of the entire plant. Clearly, he did not like this much. His main objection, evidently, was that he had already carried out this job on the other side (in England), and those who receive these materials must know how to connect them to the scheme. Besides, he thinks it would be dangerous for him if such explanations were found, since his work here is not linked to this sort of material. Nevertheless, he agreed to give us what we need as soon as possible.'

On 28 March 1944, Fuchs complained to Gold that 'his work here is deliberately being curbed by the Americans who continue to neglect co-operation and do not provide information'. He even suggested that he might learn more by returning to England. If Fuchs went back, 'he would be able to give us more complete general information but without details'.

Saving the World

Major Pavel Fitin was the head of the NKVD's foreign intelligence unit. He described Fuchs as the most important figure in the project he had given the code name 'Enormoz'. In November 1944 he reported: 'Despite participation by a large number of scientific organisations and workers on the problem of Enormoz in the U.S., mainly known to us by agent data, their cultivation develops poorly. Therefore, the major part of data on the U.S. comes from the station in England. On the basis of information from London station, Moscow Centre more than once sent to the New York station a work orientation and sent a ready agent, too (Klaus Fuchs).'

Another memorandum from the NKVD stated that: 'Fuchs is an important figure with significant prospects and experience in agent's work acquired over two years spent working with the neighbors (GRU). After determining at early meetings his status in the country and possibilities, you may move immediately to the practical work of acquiring information and materials.'

American intercepts from Moscow Centre, and deciphering of thousands of coded messages sent out to their operatives over the years, would yield extraordinary information about the secret operations of the NKVD and the KGB. The Venona decrypts involved Alger Hiss by his code name ALES: 'Ales has been working continuously with the NEIGHBORS (code name for the GRU) since 1935.' (Hiss was an American government official accused in 1948 of spying for Soviet Russia in the 1930s.)

Venona was the tool by which the FBI identified Julius and Ethel Rosenberg as Soviet agents. Investigations by special FBI agents Robert Lamphere and Ernie van Loon traced the reports on the gaseous diffusion process, which also led them to Klaus Fuchs and David Greenglass. They discovered that Fuchs was a member of the British team of scientists at Los Alamos. Then he had left to work at Harwell Research facility, which was the British atomic laboratory.[8]

The British security officer at Harwell accused Fuchs of espionage, but he twice denied he had given away secrets from Los Alamos. William Skardon was the very experienced MI5 officer in charge of the investigation who questioned Fuchs, beginning in December 1944, by first making it clear to Fuchs that he had evidence against him, without mentioning the Venona decrypts, which were still top secret. Fuchs voluntarily sought out Skardon again, since he had been sympathetic, and confessed to his role in atomic espionage on 24 January 1945.

Fuchs's Lutheran conscience had evidently made him feel guilty that he had betrayed his fellow workers, whom he had evidently identified with after working with them for some time.

Six months before Fuchs was arrested, his Soviet case officer, Alexander Feklisov, had urged Fuchs to leave the West for his own safety. But Fuchs had refused, saying, 'No, there is still much work to be done. I know there is a dangerous minefield out there, but I will deal with it when the time comes.'

When Fuchs and Gold were arrested, the interrogation of Gold led the FBI to open up forty-nine new espionage cases.

Fuchs's former boss, Hans Bethe, was amazed when he heard of Fuchs's arrest.

'He worked days and nights. He was a bachelor and had nothing better to do, and he contributed very greatly to the success of the Los Alamos project.'[9]

Soviet spies who were overlooked at the time by American counter-intelligence also included Ted Hall, 'a precociously brilliant nineteen-year-old with a Harvard B.S. in physics'. Hall arrived in Los Alamos in late January 1944, while Fuchs came in August as part of the British team led by Rudolf Peierls. Hall worked on the calibration tests for the implosion-design bomb, and was one of the best young technicians there in creating a test implosion. He was socialist in his views, but not yet a communist.[10]

Hall took a train to New York City when on leave, and marched into a Soviet trade office to hand in a report on the Los Alamos project. He knew what they needed to know to make an atom bomb, and provided as much information as he could. His goal was to save the world from a nuclear war. In essence, every one of the Soviet spies from the West had the same motive, even if couched in different phraseology, like destroying the Nazis. Most, or all of them, believed that their fate might be nuclear extinction if the world ended because the United States had an atomic monopoly.

Bruno Pontecorvo

Italian physicist Bruno Pontecorvo managed to escape from Paris ahead of Nazi troops who were closing in on the capital city in June 1940, after defeating the French and British armies. He fled to the south of France on a bicycle after sending his wife and two-year-old son ahead of him by train. They crossed the border into Spain and Portugal, and then sailed to New York, where they arrived in August 1940. It was Bruno's twenty-seventh birthday.

Pontecorvo was a highly respected scientist. He worked with Klaus Fuchs in the nuclear physics division of the British atomic energy centre at Harwell, although they never became close friends.[11] When Fuchs was arrested, Pontecorvo was interviewed by the same security officer. KGB officers rated Pontecorvo's work as an atomic spy almost as high as Fuchs's.[12]

While on holiday in Italy, in September 1950, Pontecorvo would suddenly decide to defect by flying to Stockholm with his wife and three children, then entering the Soviet Union through Finland.

Ethical Qualms

Whether Oppenheimer knew any of that or not, he became aware that groups of scientists had begun meeting informally; many of them group leaders, about twenty at a time, to discuss the war and post-war politics, and their place in it. According to Rotblat, it was generally in someone's house in the evening. They would meet to discuss the future of Europe and of the world. As Rotblat remarked after Oppie turned up at one of their meetings, 'I always thought he was a soul mate in the sense that we had the same humanitarian approach to problems.'

By January 1944, Groves realised that the atom bomb would be unlikely to be ready to destroy Nazi Germany. He wrote to caution Sir John Dill of the Combined Chiefs of Staff that its use against Germany was now unlikely.[13]

In late 1944, with more satisfactory progress of the war against Nazi Germany, a number of the scientists who had been discussing post-war Europe began to express qualms at continuing to develop the bomb. Robert Wilson, chief of the lab's experimental physics division, took Oppie aside to discuss how it would be used. He came back to Robert sometime later, as if he had since talked to the others, and suggested that Oppenheimer should call a formal meeting to discuss the matter further. Oppie was reluctant to do so because he knew he'd be in trouble with the security people if he did. It was a military matter and he had to be seen to be philosophically detached from politics.

Wilson returned to the subject later on to suggest an open discussion on a matter of great importance. Oppie remained aloof. Then Wilson put up notices all around the premises advertising a public meeting to discuss 'The Impact of the Gadget on Civilization'. He was pleasantly surprised when Oppie turned up at the meeting and listened to the discussions that evening. Only about twenty other people turned up in the building that contained the cyclotron. It was an earnest discussion about why they should continue making the bomb since it was now clear that the Allies were about to win the war.

There was another occasion when the morality of continuing to make the bomb was discussed to a packed audience in the old theatre. Louis Rosen remembered that Robert was the speaker on that occasion, and that the subject was, 'whether the country is doing the right thing in using this weapon on real human beings'. He reminded the scientists that they had no right to a louder voice to decide on the Gadget's use than anyone else.[14]

Rosen thought he was persuasive. It did not seem to occur to anyone that they were merely suppliers of weapons to the military, or that the decision to use the weapons of mass destruction was a political matter that only the President could take. Evidently there were several other such meetings to discuss the morality of using a nuclear bomb on the enemy, who would most likely now be the Japanese, as discussions were beginning to take place as to whether the Red Army was the most suitable force to pin the Nazi leaders down in Berlin and encircle them. It was what Stalin wanted, since they had suffered more than any other nation from Nazi atrocities.

Memories vary on what exactly was decided, since no records were kept of the discussions. Weiskopf recalled a meeting in March 1945 where about forty scientists discussed the atomic bomb in post-war society. As to whether or not to use it, Oppenheimer insisted it was not their task to decide.

There was some doubt in both Wilson's and Weiskopf's memories as to whether anyone really thought of quitting. Oppenheimer favoured a similar 'openness' as Niels Bohr had argued for, so that the atom bomb would not remain a military secret: everyone should be told about it. He reminded them that the new United Nations organisation was due to meet in April 1945, and that the delegates should know about the existence of the atom bomb beforehand.

Any hope of that taking place was stalled by the military domination of the Poles by the Russians. U.S. military and political advisers warned against any more concessions to the Russians, and against disclosing any more information to them about the atom bomb. As Stimson remarked, 'We must find some way of persuading Russia to play ball.'[15]

But the Russians preferred to play their own hand, as the following Moscow Centre report would reveal.

> A description of the design of the first atomic bomb was reported to us in January 1945. In February, although there was still uncertainty in the report, our rezidentura in America stated that it would take a minimum of one year and a maximum of five years to make a sizeable bomb. The experimental test of one or two bombs would take only two or three months.[16]

25

The Experimental Atomic Test

Germany surrendered formally on 4 May. The end of the war in Europe did not prevent 'Project Trinity' from continuing. Bainbridge's High Explosives Group had been formed by Oppenheimer to direct and supervise the completion of a test weapon. The team initially consisted of only twenty-five men, and would rise to two hundred and fifty in twelve months. Bainbridge was an experimental physicist educated at Harvard. He had worked with Ernest Rutherford in Britain's Cavendish Laboratories. On returning to America he had brought with him the nuclear information in an official document code-named MAUD. He had designed and built a cyclotron at Harvard which had already been brought to Los Alamos in 1943.[1]

He had prepared a systematic plan for an experimental test based on using a bomb that would deliver an explosion that was the equivalent of 210,000 tons of TNT.

> Several imaginative methods of recovering the plutonium were proposed. One called for constructing a water baffle to contain the plutonium, another for exploding the device in the sand, and a third for detonating the bomb in a large solid container.[2]

Oppenheimer agreed with the third choice of using a huge metal container code-named 'Jumbo'. It was a 25ft-long steel cylinder, 12ft in diameter. Its shell was 6in thick and reinforced with steel bands that increased the thickness of the main part to 14in. It was completed and delivered to a railway siding in Pope, New Mexico, in May 1945. It weighed 215 tons and had to be sent to Ground Zero at Trinity. As it would cost more than $500,000 dollars to build a railway line to transport it, Groves refused to approve the cost. Instead, it would be conveyed across the desert in a trailer with sixty-four wheels at a cost of $150,000.

The next stage brought with it fear of a misfire, at which radioactive material would be scattered everywhere. Oppenheimer requested that the Chemistry and Metallurgy Division construct the most suitable facilities to handle contaminated material in Bayo Canyon, which was north-east of Los Alamos. By that time, their confidence in the effectiveness of 'Fat Man' had increased. So they abandoned 'Jumbo', which became nothing more than a $12 million insurance against the possible failure of 'Fat Man'.

Groves gave official approval for a full-scale experimental test of 'Fat Man', and reminded the scientists that the purpose of the Manhattan Project was to produce 'workable and deliverable' weapons. He officially approved the desert test site in the Jornada del Muerto in August 1944. Arrangements were made soon after, in September, with General Uzal Ent, who commanded the Second Air Force, to use the Alamogordo Bombing Range for the test. The site was approximately 18 miles by 24. The nearest town to it was 27 miles away.[3]

Groves gave Oppenheimer permission to proceed on 27 October, 'based on the assumption than a nuclear explosion will take place'.

A base camp was constructed about 10 miles away from the point chosen to detonate 'Fat Man'. It was completed in December, and Groves ordered a detachment of military police to guard the area and use a pass system for security. Bainbridge requested special radio frequencies for Trinity, so that two-way radios could be used and not monitored. More security regulations were enforced, and working days were increased from their normal ten hours to eighteen in order to have everything completed on time and ready to test 'Fat Man'.

Destroyer of Worlds

As a military man, General Groves was naturally sceptical of human beings and their claims, in particular their theories. He was a practical man. So he could only wait expectantly to see if 'Fat Man' could be detonated. And would the extent of its explosion turn out to be as huge as 10 kilotons of TNT? It was still problematic. There was an even more serious problem of any other unknown effects of a nuclear explosion. Bethe and Christy prepared a memorandum on the anticipated 'Immediate After-effects of The Gadget' – which was the original code name for the prototype.

> They predicted that within a radius of thirty feet of the explosion, the temperature would reach about one million degrees Fahrenheit. In less than a hundredth of a second, the central fireball would expand to eight hundred feet in diameter and cool to fifteen thousand degrees. Shortly thereafter, the fireball would rise into the stratosphere and in two or three minutes reach an altitude of over nine miles, with temperatures of about eight thousand degrees.[4]

They added that damage to a plane crew from neutrons would not be a danger since the altitude of the plane would be about four times the safe distance for neutron effects.

Groves checked uneasily with Oppenheimer on safety precautions. 'What about blast damage? And what if radioactive dust drifted over nearby towns?' There was a question of earth shocks, as typical of violent earthquakes. The possibility of radioactive fallout was uncertain. Oppenheimer had informed Groves in June that,

'The tests would be undertaken when the direction of the wind would not carry the cloud over any town for at least a hundred miles.'[5]

Accurate measurements would be taken by twenty men from Military Intelligence dressed as civilians and stationed in towns and cities up to 100 miles away. Plans were also made for Trinity staff to be evacuated if necessary. The lab's medical officer would be in charge of an evacuation. Each shelter would possess devices for detecting radiation. Bainbridge had already conducted rehearsals.

A 20ft Trinity tower was constructed of railroad ties and lumber on the chosen site. Another 18ft were added to reach a wooden platform. Jack Hubbard, the meteorologist for the Manhattan District, calculated that the weather would be ideal for undertaking the test at 4 a.m. on 7 May. Bainbridge agreed with the proposed date for the detonation and made the necessary plans.

As Russian tanks encircled Berlin in a broad search for Hitler, the aged, haggard, and defeated dictator, now with grey hair and a slight limp, committed suicide on 30 April in his underground shelter with trembling hands, before prowling Russian troops could find him.

Even though the atom bomb was no longer needed against the Nazis, the war was not over. But doubts about its use arose once again among the scientists at Los Alamos, who entered into further discussion on what they thought should be done. Leo Szilard was determined to talk with the President.

The Pacific War

Szilard was anxious at the prospect of the atom bomb being used on the Japanese. Japanese soldiers had been forced into war by a ruling hierarchy of militarists whom even Emperor Hirohito had been helpless to stop, since he was solely a spiritual leader. Their culture had taught them total obedience to authority. Most scientists thought the idea of using the bomb on them was unjust and barbarous, despite evidence of extensive Japanese atrocities. To militarists like General Groves, and America's political leaders, the mild Hirohito was viewed as 'a master war criminal that deserved to be hanged'.[6]

Szilard turned up at the White House by appointment, accompanied by Walter Bartky of the University of Chicago and Harold Urey from Columbia University. They were told they would be seeing the Secretary of State, not the President. They met with James Byrnes at his home in South Carolina, but their pleas not to use the atom bomb on Japan were unsuccessful. Byrnes even suggested that perhaps using the bomb on the Japanese would bring the Russians into line and persuade them to withdraw their troops from Eastern Europe.

Trinity

The same anxiety and worrying fear that had haunted all the participants in the Manhattan Project for years was intensified by their exhaustion and anticipation.

Would the Gadget work? It was considered essential to undertake a test to remove any doubts about its effectiveness. Every link in the chain intended to lead ultimately to a detonation and explosion were checked over and over again by the seven subgroups responsible for their own specialised category of planning and activities to bring Trinity to its intended conclusion. They were Services, Shocks and Blast, Measurements, Meteorology, Spectrographic & Photographic, Airborne Measurements, and Medical. Development, Engineering and Tests were added in a later reorganisation.[7]

Weather conditions were as had been predicted. The men needed for the experiment at Trinity began to assemble at the site after midnight. There was a thirty-eight-minute delay for the observation plane to arrive. Then, at 4.38 a.m. on 7 May, the Comp B was ignited from a number of positions within the tower. According to Tolman's official report on the First Trinity Test to General Groves, 'In an instant, an enormous, highly luminous orange sphere appeared. The light from it could be seen in Alamogordo, sixty miles away. It faded within seconds and passed through an oval configuration before assuming the shape of a mushroom and rising to fifteen thousand feet.'[8]

The tower on which the bomb had been positioned was completely destroyed, as expected. And the experimental pre-test was considered a great success. It was a useful rehearsal to make notes of numerous unforeseeable mishaps and other minor errors that occurred generally as a consequence of human errors or transport breakdowns. Cameramen forgot to start two cameras, for example. The stress of the occasion was clearly evident.

Robert Oppenheimer watched the pre-test with James Conant, Vannevar Bush, James Chadwick, Thomas Farrell, Enrico Fermi, Richard Feynman, Leslie Groves, Geoffrey Taylor, Richard Tolman and John von Neumann. The plutonium device implosion bomb was scheduled to be tested at Alamogordo on 16 July.[9]

The progress of Trinity had been observed from afar also by Moscow Centre, where Lavrentiy Beria was still in charge of solving the Soviet Union's Problem Number One.

Szilard would write later on that he was depressed and anxious at the possibility of a nuclear arms race between America and Russia that would end with them bombing each other.

Back in Washington on 30 May, he heard that Oppie was in town for a meeting with Secretary of War Stimson, and went to meet him. Oppenheimer thought that Szilard was interfering with a matter that was not his concern. They argued about the usual points. Oppie took the attitude that the bomb would make a big bang, but would be useless in war, although he agreed that the Russians should be informed in advance if the bomb were to be used on Japan.

Szilard argued that informing them would not prevent a nuclear arms race. He left feeling depressed because he had failed. All he could do now was keep a record to show that the scientists were against the use of the bomb on civilian targets.

THE EXPERIMENTAL ATOMIC TEST

Oppenheimer attended an important meeting the next day. It had been called by Secretary of War Stimson. Four scientists had been invited as consultants to advise the committee, which included Dr Vannevar Bush, James F. Byrnes, Stimson, Assistant Secretary of the Navy Ralph Bard, William Clayton, Dr Karl T. Compton, James Conant and George Harrison, who was Stimson's aide. The four scientists were Robert Oppenheimer, Enrico Fermi, Arthur Compton and Ernest Lawrence. General George C. Marshall was present with General Groves and two of Stimson's assistants.

Stimson's agenda did not include a decision on whether to use the bomb on the Japanese. He began by summarising his responsibilities to the President on military affairs. No one should be unclear that the military use of the bomb would be controlled entirely by the White House, with no input by those who had built it. But, Stimson assured the scientists, he had paid careful attention to all the implications. He told them that he and other members of the Interim Government did not regard the bomb as just another new weapon, but as 'a revolutionary change in the relations of man to the universe'. It could become a Frankenstein's monster or it could secure global peace. In either case, he emphasised, it 'went far beyond the needs of the present war'.

Both Oppenheimer and Lawrence provided information and advice to the committee. Stimson claimed that everyone agreed with Lawrence's proposal to make and stockpile weapons and industrial plants. Oppenheimer held a different point of view – he did not want the Manhattan Project to continue to dominate scientific thought after the war. Bush agreed: he wanted the scientists to return to their universities after the war and continue studying and providing new papers on new scientific theories.

The immediate concern had been to shorten the war. Now the Germans had been beaten, Oppenheimer thought it was time for a free exchange of information on developing peaceful uses of atomic energy. As for atomic weapons, he believed that a system of international inspection should be put in place by a central body.

While the scientists nodded in agreement, the military men present did not. General Marshall cautioned them about not placing their faith in an international body, when Russia was the main concern as the only country that could compete in an arms race. Oppenheimer expressed the opinion that Russia might be ready to co-operate. At least, Marshall remarked, we need have no fear that they will disclose such information to the Japanese.

Byrnes argued that once a limited amount of information was disclosed to the Russians, Stalin would not cease from demanding total involvement. Bush pointed out that even the British did not have blueprints of any of America's nuclear plants, and clearly any information provided to the Russians could be limited, without giving them the engineering designs of the bomb.

Byrnes was eager to stay ahead of the competition and use the bomb as a weapon of diplomacy. This was an arms race and America should exploit the opportunity of being ahead in research and development and productivity. Instead of sharing weapons technology they should improve their political relations with Russia.

Human Targets

When they resumed their meeting after lunch it seemed almost as if they had swept their previous attitudes and opinions aside to focus on the most important subject: it was how to put a stop to the Pacific War, which was costing a great many American lives, despite the extraordinary command of military strategy and tactics in the army with General MacArthur, and in the navy with Admirals King and Nimitz. It was also costing America a great deal in arms and armour, transport, landing craft, battleships and aircraft carriers. Those losses formed an ever-present background in their mind whenever they discussed the Japanese war.

They talked about 'the impending bombing' as if there was no other way to stop the Japanese before they took any more American lives.

Would the bomb be any more effective than all the previous bombing raids on Germany's industrial cities by the Allies? Oppenheimer claimed that the sight of one atom bomb exploding would be so dramatic it should stop everything. It would create a brilliant luminescence, and would endanger all life in a radius of at least two thirds of a mile.

After agreeing that the Japanese should not be given any warning beforehand, they discussed possible targets. They should attempt to make a profound psychological impression on as many people as possible. Conant suggested that 'the most desirable target would be a vital war plant employing a large number of workers and closely surrounded by workers' houses'.

General Groves complained that the atomic programme had been 'plagued since its inception by the presence of certain scientists of doubtful discretion and uncertain loyalty'. He was referring to Leo Szilard, who had wanted to persuade President Truman not to use the bomb.[10]

Since some of the scientists were evidently unreliable, it was recorded in the minutes that there was general agreement that the scientists should be severed from the bomb as soon as it was dropped.

What should they tell their colleagues, asked one of the scientists at the end of the meeting? The answer was that they had been given an opportunity to meet with a committee chaired by the secretary of war, and had been given 'complete freedom to present their views on any phase of the subject'.

26

A Japanese Target

What had not been revealed to the scientists at the meeting was that Japanese invaders had come closer to North America than the Pacific, and had even targeted the United States. The first news of a Japanese presence over America was transmitted to the Albuquerque Army Air Base when a fighter aircraft was flown on a search-and-destroy mission to see if missiles were being dropped by parachute or from balloons.[1]

A Japanese balloon bombing offensive against America's mainland had begun in autumn 1944. The first launch of Japanese balloons was reported on 3 November, after the navy found one floating in the sea off the coast of California. Another was discovered in the sky over Wyoming, and exploded. Soon afterwards, two men chopping wood in a Montana forest found the remains of a large balloon. Remains of other balloons were found in Arizona, Alaska, Iowa and Nebraska. U.S. fighter pilots were called out to intercept and shoot down balloons during the autumn. Only one balloon arrived in the area of the Manhattan Project's production site in Hanford, Washington. The remains of balloons were examined in military labs, while their existence was kept secret from the public.

The U.S. army organised a secret Firefly mission of up to three thousand soldiers to extinguish fires sparked by the balloons, while remains continued to be reported in Alaska and Washington, Colorado, Texas, Canada and Mexico. Government censorship organisations pressed secrecy on the news media in January 1945 to avoid civilian panic, and prevent the enemy from receiving news of the effectiveness of their launches from the east coast of Honshu. They had been planned to be picked up by high-speed winds to take them across the Pacific and over mainland America.

Nine thousand Japanese Fu-Go fire-bombs were sent off to North America, but due to malfunctions, only about a thousand actually landed. As far as was known, no deaths occurred. They were thought to be intended to cause panic, start forest fires, and demoralise Americans. It was a warning of what might come later if not prevented now.[2]

The Franck Report

A scientific panel met at Los Alamos on 21 June to report on the varying points of view. Szilard, who had originally persuaded Einstein to join him in warning Roosevelt of the danger of losing the war to a German atom bomb, had since become obsessive in his attempts to stop it being used. James Franck, who was the chairman, had been Oppenheimer's professor in Göttingen before the war. The aim of the Franck Report was to advise that, in the opinion of the scientists, 'a surprise atomic assault on Japan would destroy America's credibility and precipitate an arms race. It urged that a demonstration take place in the desert or on an uninhabited island, and thereby end the war without any further bloodshed.'[3]

It was felt that although the political bureaucrats had soothed the moral qualms of the nuclear scientists – with the exception of the stubborn Hungarian-American Szilard – James Franck's prestige could not be ignored by the White House, even though they had effectively blocked Szilard from protesting to President Truman. The report was signed by seven scientists and passed, with a covering letter by Karl Compton, on to Robert Oppenheimer.

Serber would recall later that, 'Given this background, we had no doubts about the necessity to use the bomb.' But they still imagined it was a psychological weapon to be used to end the Pacific War. On the other hand, Oppenheimer and Fermi believed that physicists were hardly competent to solve political, social or military problems: 'we see no acceptable alternatives to direct military use.'[4]

Oppenheimer had become convinced by then that 'the military use of the bomb in this war might eliminate *all* wars'.[5]

Nevertheless, many of them were troubled by their conscience; like Einstein, who now felt guilty at having produced the first significant atomic theory that had resulted in this quandary. He and Szilard, and the other scientists, felt helpless when faced with the ethics of whether it should be used on human beings. But was it really their responsibility, when they had merely been given orders by the military establishment and the White House to set up a project to produce a bomb? Robert Wilson had very strong moral objections to its use, but was it the wrong time to air them when the nation was still at war? They must leave the decision to the President, and to experienced leaders like Stimson and General Marshall, who were both capable individuals.

Oppenheimer stood quietly in the background to let them all have their say. He could not allow them to distract him from his work, which was to produce a number of bombs for the military. His persuasive summary of the meeting was aimed primarily at returning them back to work to fulfil their responsibilities to the armed forces and the White House.

Szilard made a final attempt at the beginning of July to persuade Edward Teller to support him by writing a petition to the President. But Teller's mind was taken up almost entirely with his plans to develop his Super Bomb. As far as he was concerned, the nuclear arms race was on, and nothing could stop it now.

The NKVD

Kheifetz and Liza Zarubin, and others, had been attempting to obtain Oppenheimer's co-operation since their first contact with him, for the same purpose; to defeat

Nazi Germany and end the war. Robert had distanced himself from their agents and the American Communist Party as soon as he realised they were seriously targeting him. That was before Stalin gave his secret police chief the responsibility of acquiring enough nuclear information to build a Russian bomb. Then somewhat ambiguous instructions were delivered to Beria by Vsevolod Merkulov, who had been Beria's deputy when he had headed the NKVD:

2 October 4 [1944] Top Secret
1107/M Urgent
Copy #2
People's Commissar for Internal Affairs of the USSR
General Commissar of State Security
Comrade Beria, L.P.

In accordance with your instructions of 29 September 1944, NKGB USSR continues measures for obtaining more detailed information on the state of work on the problem of uranium and its development abroad.

In the period 1942–1943, important data on the start of work in the USA on this problem was received from our foreign agent network using the contacts of Comrade Zarubin and Kheifetz in their execution of important tasks in line with the executive committee of the Comintern.

In 1942 one of the leaders of scientific work in uranium in the USA, Professor R. Oppenheimer while being an unlisted [*nglastny*] member of the apparatus of Comrade Browder informed us about the beginning of work.

On the request of Comrade Kheifetz, confirmed by Comrade Browder, he provided co-operation in access to research for several of our tested sources including a relative of Comrade Browder.

Due to complications of the operational situation in the USA, dissolution of the Comintern and explanations of Comrade Zarubin and Kheifetz on the [Vasili Dimitrovich] Mironov affair it is expedient to immediately sever contacts of leaders and activists of the American Communist Party with scientists and specialists engaged in work on uranium.

NKGB requests the consent of the leadership [*Instancia*]

People's Commissar of State Security USSR
Commissar of State Security First Rank
Signed/[Vsevolod] Merkulov

Handwritten note by Beria Inform about the approval, 2 X 44
[2 October 1944]
// signed Beria[6]

Those instructions would be used by the FBI as evidence that Oppenheimer was a member of the Communist Party, although that is not what it said. Whatever it might infer was only vague in translation. Although Stalin decided to disband the Comintern to replace his former hostile image with a more genial one for the Anglo-Americans, now that he was one of their Allies, an International Department continued to exist under Georgi Dimitrov.[7]

All that Merkulov's letter indicates is that information on atomic bomb research was received first from the American Communist Party network, which made approaches to nuclear scientists whom they imagined would be sympathetic. They were the scientists who feared that the Germans would develop an atomic bomb first, and felt that co-operating with the Soviet Union would ensure that Hitler would be beaten ahead of time. Others simply believed that it was not safe for any one country to possess nuclear bombs on their own.

The letter also confirms how effective the FBI was in its surveillance of America's Communist Party members. Merkulov asked Beria to have them vanish underground or become anonymous by severing contact with those who were working on the Manhattan Project. American communists would be replaced by trained professional intelligence officers from Soviet Russia. Zarubin suggested severing contact with Oppenheimer. But that did not necessarily imply he was a member of the Party. He had simply been a sympathetic contributor of funds, until he began to realise the danger of the Soviet regime to America's national security and to him.

'Moscow entrusted atomic espionage to only the most experienced and sophisticated intelligence officers, because they had to operate at the highest level of the world scientific community.' At the height of their activities they had twenty-nine agents in the Manhattan Project.[8] So, of course, they knew about the success of Trinity the moment it was achieved. Not unnaturally, their goal now was to persuade the Allies to share their nuclear secrets with them.

But the Allies were uneasy about what they saw as Russia's post-war aim to dominate Eastern Europe with the Red Army and their powerful force of tanks, which they had learned to use with menace against huge forces of German troops during Operation Barbarossa.

The Allies became even more anxious when mass graves were dug up in the Katyn Forest, to reveal thousands of bodies of senior Polish officers who had been executed. News leaked out about the finds in the *New York Times* and *The Times* of London. When the Polish Government-in-exile in London accused Stalin of the atrocities, he ignored them and set up a puppet Polish Government in Lublin who would do what he wanted.

27

Japan

Oppenheimer would claim later that, 'We didn't know about the military situation in Japan. We didn't know whether they could be caused to surrender by other means or whether the invasion was really inevitable.' They were also unaware that military intelligence in Washington had intercepted and decoded messages from Japan that suggested the Japanese Government knew they had lost the war and wanted to seek surrender terms.[1]

The Assistant Secretary of War, John McCloy, advised Stimson to recommend that the phrase 'unconditional surrender' be dropped from America's demands for capitulation. Roosevelt had stubbornly insisted on those terms of surrender for the Germans, against General Marshall's and Churchill's wishes, and may have prolonged the war as a consequence. OSS agent Allen Dulles informed McCloy that the Japanese Government insisted on one condition that they would not relinquish – that their Emperor and the constitution would continue as before; otherwise they feared a total collapse of all discipline and law and order.

On 28 May 1945, Acting Secretary of State Joseph C. Grew met with President Truman to advise that heads of the Tokyo Government were earnestly attempting to find compromise terms in accordance with Washington's demands. And on 18 June, Truman's chief of staff, Admiral Leahy – who had always been hotly antagonistic towards the Japanese – made a note in his diary: 'It is my opinion at the present time that a surrender of Japan can be arranged with terms that can be accepted by Japan ...'

On the same day, John McCloy advised President Truman that political steps should be taken for a full Japanese surrender before deciding whether to invade Japan's mainland islands. He added that 'the Japs should be told, furthermore, that we had another and terrifyingly destructive weapon which we would have to use if they did not surrender'.[2]

That political and military advice, and other persuasive arguments from elsewhere, persuaded Truman to note in his private diary on 18 July, 'Unconditional surrender is the only obstacle to peace ...' He referred to an intercepted cable quoting the emperor to the Japanese envoy in Moscow as a 'telegram from Jap Emperor asking for peace'.

Truman had persuaded Stalin that the Soviet Union could declare war on Japan by 15 August, the date that his military advisers had considered decisive. He had already diarised a terse reminder on the previous day: 'Fini Japs when that comes about.'[3]

He had also decided that the shock of a Soviet declaration of war on Japan should remove any necessity to use the atom bomb.

The Gadget

Robert Oppenheimer knew nothing about any decoded intercepts or the discussions taking place with President Truman in the White House, or any arguments between politicians and the military. He concentrated on his main objective, which was to organise and oversee the detonation of the Gadget in the official explosion on the steel Trinity tower at the Alamogordo bombing range in New Mexico on 16 July. He was wracked by excitement, anticipation, anxiety, and exhaustion; 'strained and emaciated', when the day arrived for the official detonation of the bomb.

Everyone at Los Alamos was restless and apprehensive while they wondered whether the official detonation of the plutonium bomb would replicate the same type of explosion and devastation as they had already observed at the experimental pre-test on the platform of the Trinity tower at Los Alamos.[4]

No test was planned for the uranium bomb. There had only been enough weapon-grade uranium available for one bomb. Only one uranium bomb, named 'Little Boy' was produced during the war.[5]

The transportation of the plutonium bomb had already been rehearsed using a dummy bomb with explosives on 3 July. A similar bomb, but with a dummy core, was tested, to find out how it would behave if it were hit by Japanese anti-aircraft fire at the plane before arriving at the target. They had decided it had a reasonable chance to survive unless a detonator was hit directly.

They spent nearly two days from 10 July continuously preparing the lenses for installation into the Trinity 'Fat Man' bomb. They checked for cracks and chips, or any other imperfections.[6]

The previous 100ton experimental shot explosion on 7 May had been 'extremely valuable, providing much necessary data for calibrating instruments and redesigning shelters for greater efficiency'. Lab scientists had now become accustomed to field work in correcting any mistakes and defects in Trinity's planning.[7]

'Fat Man's' components began to arrive in the desert, where two hundred and fifty scientists worked expectantly at the Trinity Camp in the intense heat of the sun. The plutonium core arrived in the rear of a sedan. They began to assemble the bomb next morning in a vacuum-clean room in a ranch house with its windows sealed with black tape. Men in white surgical coats assembled the plutonium globe on a table, while Oppenheimer wandered nervously in and out to check each stage of the operation. Every non-nuclear part of 'Fat Man' had been X-rayed beforehand for structural defects. On arrival at Trinity, explosive components had been taken to the base of the 100ft tower for final assembly in a canvas tent, supervised by Commander Bradbury.

'Holloway leaned over the bomb, his head inside it, directing the hoist by hand. Several scientists, including Oppenheimer, followed the operation in complete silence. They seemed outwardly calm, but everyone felt the tension in the air' as the core descended slowly into the hole ... [8]

The tent was removed next day at 8 a.m., and the 5ton bomb was hauled very slowly up by a hoist powered by a motor, to the top of the tower, into a specially designed house constructed out of sheets of steel. Once the entire device was safely in position, the fragile detonators were put in place, with the detonator crew climbing the tower for the final installation of the firing circuit. The assembly work was almost finished late at night on 14 July, when 'Fat Man' was left in the tower under armed guard.

Apprehension accompanied the initial success. Monday, 16 July, would be the official day for the Big Bang.

Anticlimax

There had been an anticlimax after tension had built up before the anticipated explosion, when a dummy 'Fat Man' had been detonated in a magnetic field in Pajarito Canyon in a test for symmetry. Edward C. Creutz headed the metallurgy group. He had been directed to find an effective way to make uranium slugs for the reactors. He had instantly sent a coded message to Oppenheimer to warn him that the *real* bomb waiting in the tower 'was not likely to work properly'.

Considerable pent-up anger had flared dangerously from several directions, particularly from General Groves. 'It would explode,' he was told, 'but not successfully, because the shock waves would not converge as required.' Most of his anger had been aimed at George Kistiakowsky, who had been responsible for the lens configuration, since two years of work appeared to have been wasted.

Kistiakowsky would write about the incident later on: 'Everybody ... became terribly upset and focused on my presumed guilt. Oppenheimer. General Groves, Vannevar Bush – all had much to say about that incompetent wretch who forever after would be known to the world as the cause of the tragic failure of the Manhattan Project.'[9]

The unfortunate incident had forced them to examine whether the analysis and calculations were wrong. Bethe had studied the results of Creutz's experiment very carefully, and finally concluded that the implosion *was* symmetrical, as intended. Now, all that Oppenheimer had to consider was the weather. The bomb was finally fired at 5.30 a.m. as originally planned.

Their reaction to the intense flash of light had been one of relief after the delay. Groves had been dazzled, and turned away silently to shake hands with Bush and Conant. The stunned silence at the vision of a typical mushroom shape appearing and instantly rising into the sky was broken by light applause.[10]

General Farrell said it was terrifying. Bainbridge was simply overwhelmed. Fermi watched the mushroom cloud rise speedily to over 30,000ft. Victor Weiskopf wondered how much radiation was being emitted – perhaps a thousand billion curies? William Laurence saw the explosion as full of great promise and considerable foreboding.

Oppenheimer and Farrell drove away afterwards, back to base camp in their jeep, and encountered General Groves. Farrell repeated his relief that the war was as good as over now.

'Yes,' General Groves said, 'after we drop two bombs on Japan.'[11]

28

Unconditional Surrender

President Truman's decision to bomb Japanese civilians was another anticlimax for the scientists. Some thought it appalling and unnecessary, while others, like Kistiakowsky, thought the bomb was no worse than the day and night bombing of German industrial sites had been, or the fire-bombing of cities like Dresden. After all, 'The Japanese had lost a hundred thousand civilians during the firebombing of Tokyo on March 9, 1945.'[1]

Dorothy McKibbin barely noticed the contentiousness of the issue. Life appeared to have returned to normal for her, with the usual mundane local suburban news in Santa Fe by the *Daily Bulletin* advertising supplies of Coca-Cola and what to do with empty bottles.

Robert and Kitty drove off to seek privacy on a holiday around the southern slopes of the Sangre de Cristos, and up the Pecos Valley to Perro Caliente. He looked forward to re-establishing contact with the outside world by correspondence, after having been confined for so long at Los Alamos, and took some letters with him that needed answering.[2]

Japanese Warlords

Another anticlimax had been Japan's negative response to President Truman. Truman was now feeling mighty pleased with himself at having taken a firm hand in standing up to Soviet Russia at a meeting, where he had warned Stalin that the United States now possessed 'a new weapon of unusual destructive force'.

Stalin had remained silent and inscrutable, in order to conceal the fact that he knew about it already. Truman had misconstrued his polite congratulations as submissiveness to a winner, whereas Churchill had noticed that Truman had suddenly become enormously self-confident, and wondered why.

According to Stimson's diary entry, 'He [Truman] told the Russians just where they got on and off and generally bossed the whole meeting.'[3]

Truman felt inflated by the successful result of the atom bomb test in New Mexico, and was in no mood to be dictated to by the Japanese. Moreover, the premier of Japan, Baron Kantaro Suzuki, had dismissed the Potsdam Declaration for unconditional surrender of all Japan's armed forces with contempt, by calling it 'Unworthy of public notice'.

Evidently, Japan was not prepared to submit to the Allies after all. Their military honour demanded that neither they nor the Emperor must lose face by agreeing to unconditional surrender. Truman, who had always been impatient with the posturing of European leaders, had no time for play-acting by Asian warlords either. How many more Allied lives would have to be lost in battle before Japan's military leaders were humbled? In his opinion, the Japanese needed encouragement. Churchill and Truman made plans to invade Japan, with assurances from Oppenheimer and Groves that two more plutonium bombs would be made ready.

They had even approved a deadline on 24 July to invade Kyushu on 1 November, when Truman decided to put a stop to any more loss of lives of American troops and wake up Japan's leaders to reality by dropping two nuclear bombs on Japan. And that was what happened.[4]

According to Henry L. Stimson, Japan's leaders had been warned, and Hiroshima was the headquarters of the Japanese Army defending southern Japan. President Truman spoke to the nation and the world by radio on 6 August, at 11 a.m. to announce that he had warned Japan's military leaders, who had chosen to continue the war. Consequently, American aircraft had bombed an important Japanese army base with an atomic bomb, named 'Little Boy'.[5]

Life at Los Alamos continued with its usual routines of looking after the children, visiting friends, and passing the time with card games. But, although the bomb was dropped on Hiroshima from a B-29 Superfortress aircraft named *Enola Gay*, and piloted by Colonel Paul Tibbets, on 6 August, it did not end the war. The fireball incinerated the city, but did not result in Japan's instant capitulation as had been expected.

Days later, the White House announced that a second bomb had been dropped on Japan, which had achieved its objective. 'Fat Man' was dropped from the air on Nagasaki on 9 August. But Nagasaki had not been the intended target: it had been the large weapons arsenal at Kokura.

The bomb was dropped from a B-29 named *Bockscar*, piloted by Major Charles Sweeney. A malfunctioning fuel pump had left him with limited fuel and time for his bombing mission, but he was prepared to take the risk. He took off in a storm that rocked the aircraft, and headed for Kokura with a live bomb. But when he arrived there, the city was hidden beneath a heavy screen of smoke and fog. It was impossible to locate his target.

After circling several times, he became conscious of his limited fuel, and was forced to fly further on to Nagasaki. His bombardier released 'Fat Man' over the city from 28,900ft. The bomb exploded at 1,650ft, causing an enormous flash of light, followed by shock waves that struck and buffeted the aircraft.

The ball of fire spread out beneath them and changed colours. Forty-four per cent of Nagasaki was destroyed by the explosion. The effect on Japan's military leaders was almost instantaneous: they were shocked into surrendering.

Apart from the lethal effects of the bombing on Japanese civilians – which would only later come to light after radiation spread across the cities and caused even more painful deaths – the reality struck the bomb makers forcibly. Kitty was in an unusual emotional state. She exclaimed to her friend Jean Bacher, 'Robert was just definitely beside himself.' The enormity of what had happened to Hiroshima and Nagasaki affected them both profoundly. Kitty, who generally managed to button up her emotions, shared her distress with everyone she encountered. Bacher went home after talking to an observer of the bombings and could not sleep. 'I just shook all night, it was such a shock.'[6]

But most mothers with young sons fighting in the appalling jungle conditions against fanatical Japanese troops, tropical diseases, and having to use their wits hourly against booby traps, were glad to have the massacres of their own children halted, so that they could return home and live a normal life again. They were the ones whom President Truman had in mind when he had made his decision.

The bombing was followed by a failed military coup in Japan, which had hoped to avoid the dishonour of the Emperor having to submit to defeat. A compromise was struck in the end, with General Douglas MacArthur ruling Japan with the authority of Emperor Hirohito. Fortunately, it worked.

Post-war America

Now that the excitement of the war had ended, America was left with the horror of the results, and the gruesome finds by the Allied armies as they swept up the remaining Axis forces in Europe and discovered one murder camp after another that the Nazis had concealed in the forests, where they had murdered their opponents by torturing them to death, and carefully removed any gold teeth they could find.

One of the letters that Robert Oppenheimer answered from his retreat at Perro Caliente was from his old student friend at Harvard, Frederick Bernheim.

> Cowles, N.M.
> August 27 [1945]
>
> Dear Fred,
> It was good to have your note, singularly and pleasantly unaltered by the two decades.
> It was in Muenchen I saw you last, I think, one hell of a long time ago for Muenchen, even if not for you or me.
> I'd like to come see you, & if I knew where to stay, would most warmly return the invitation. Kitty – who is the vague marriage – read your note & said as how you must be a lovely fella.
> We are at that ranch now, in an earnest but not too sanguine search for sanity. It ought to be, but it isn't, like the spring days when the paving would make a tentative show through the slush of Mt. Auburn St. There would seem to be some great headaches ahead.
>
> Yours
> Robert[7]

Oppie wrote to another of his close friends, Charles Lauritsen, to add to previous talks he had had with him and Richard Tolman about returning to Caltech. He was not so sure of its future direction when Robert Millikan retired after twenty-four years as president. Evidently what he was searching for now was permanence. It was an effect that the war had on most people of his age group, although not on younger students who wanted change.

It was one of his longer letters in which he probed with specific questions to find out who would be in charge and with whom he might be working if he chose to fill an opening there, since he'd had another offer from Columbia, who would pay him well and agree to whomever he chose as his research assistant.

He mentioned that he knew from Conant and von Neumann that the Princeton Institute and Harvard were both 'working up to offer me jobs'. John von Neumann, his old Los Alamos friend and colleague, was a professor at the Institute for Advanced Study. Then Millikan wrote that he wanted Robert at Caltech as 'part of the big job of the next three decades here'.

Tolman's view expressed the social and economic conditions of the times: that Caltech might not offer Oppie a job because he was not a good teacher, that his future contributions to theoretical physics were doubtful, and possibly Caltech 'already had enough Jews on its faculty'. Anti-Semitism still lingered in the post-war realms of the United States and the UK. Tolman added that 'two promising young men might be had for the same price'.[8]

Oppenheimer's search for permanence continued by visiting Washington on several occasions, where he emphasised that 'all of us would earnestly do whatever was really to the national interest, no matter how desperate and disagreeable ... All of us are willing to wait for a bit ...'

After only a couple of weeks away from the Manhattan Project, in the restorative atmosphere of New Mexico, Robert appeared to be recovering his sanity – or so he wrote to his old and loyal friend, Ernest Laurence. Whatever Laurence had said to him, Oppie could not resist writing that he was much more of an 'underdogger' than Ernest was. Ernest kept clear of politics and continually warned Robert to follow his example. But Robert wrote 'it is a part of me that is unlikely to change'. He appealed affectionately for 'a certain mutual respect for non-identical points of view'.[9]

His correspondence from Perro Caliente before returning to Los Alamos revealed that he was still acutely conscious of the need for the atomic bomb to serve as an instrument to establish and maintain peace. Scientists at all the Manhattan Project sites would soon begin to discuss the need to educate policymakers and the public on the implications of atomic energy, in order to establish a body to impose controls internationally to avoid a nuclear arms race.

Manhattan Project groups at the Met Lab, Clinton Labs at Oak Ridge, and Los Alamos 'produced almost identical statements of principles and purpose'.[10] Arriving at their sober conclusions was a thoughtful antidote to the heady mixture of euphoria and remorse that had descended on the Los Alamos laboratories, where the scientists now felt haunted by the Japanese victims of the atom bomb.

29

Back to Normal

Now that Hitler was dead, and Italian partisans had disposed of Mussolini with their machine guns, the defeat of the Japanese warlords returned the world to normalcy. And, as Churchill always asserted, history shows us that normalcy is war. Peace arose only intermittently and in short interludes, while the world always returned to war. This time it would be a Cold War with Soviet Russia that would place the world on the edge of extinction.

On his last day in office as secretary of war, Henry Stimson advised President Truman that 'we should approach Russia at once with an opportunity to share on a proper quid pro quo, the bomb'.[1]

Stimson left it in Robert's hands to do something about the bomb, since Oppenheimer had now become a global celebrity and a household name with extraordinary influence in high places. They were positions he found he enjoyed to be in. According to *Life* magazine, physicists were seen as supermen and Robert had become a national icon. He realised almost immediately that his celebrity status could influence people as assuredly as a well-established brand name that the mass market trusted. All he had to do was make his feelings and opinions known, and the news media would publish any or all of it. He warned that the bomb was a weapon for aggressors to use.

It was the same time when the highly esteemed professor of mathematics, Jacob Bronowski, was driven by accident through the ruins of Nagasaki to join a ship waiting in the harbour in November 1945. The sight and the atmosphere merged to become 'a universal moment'. His experience was 'the experience of mankind'. Bronowski wrote his book *Science and Human Values* as a consequence of his haunting experience. As he wrote, 'The practice of science compels the practitioner to form for himself a fundamental set of human values.'[2]

Both he and Oppenheimer were concerned about the responsibilities and obligations of scientists – as Einstein and Fermi and Bohr had been all along. 'The power for good and for evil has troubled other minds than ours. We are not here fumbling with a new dilemma ... Men have been killed with weapons before now ...'

They were haunted men who knew they must do something to prevent such crimes from being repeated. Oppenheimer visited Washington from Los Alamos that autumn to exploit his sudden media fame by influencing high-ranking government officials on behalf of all the scientists in the Manhattan Project. Soon after speaking to an audience of five hundred, Hans Bethe, Edward Teller, Frank Oppenheimer, Robert Christy and others drafted a powerful statement on the dangers of a nuclear arms race.

Oppenheimer sent the document to Stimson's former assistant, George Harrison, telling him that it had been circulated to more than three hundred scientists and only three had failed to sign it. He wanted the War Department to approve its publication. Robert asked for more copies, which he wanted to circulate, but cautioned that the War Department did not wish to have it released. All they could do was wait for it to be passed around and considered.

The Atomic Energy Commission

As time passed, the scientists became concerned that Oppie was being influenced into docility by the Government, instead of influencing its leaders. He replied that they were obliged to wait as a matter of courtesy to President Truman, since he still had to release his own communication on atomic energy to Congress in order to propose legislation. At the end of September, Robert informed Under Secretary of State, Dean Acheson that the scientists no longer wanted to work on the atom bomb, or any bomb. While doing so, he ignored Edward Teller, who was still eagerly proposing to build his Super Hydrogen Bomb.

Truman gave his message to Congress on 3 October. It urged them to create an atomic energy commission with the powers to regulate the nuclear industry, which he described as a revolutionary force. But Edwin Johnson of Colorado and Andrew May of Kentucky proposed a somewhat different and negative bill with 'harsh prison terms and hefty fines' for security violations by scientists. Oppenheimer supported the bill in order to settle the first stage as quickly as possible, although he sensed he was viewed by established politicians as an outsider. What he did not want was to be seen as 'a lefty and a troublemaker', like Szilard and Bohr.

The scientists were enraged by the small print in which the May-Johnson bill would place all control in the hands of nine members approved by the President. Military officers would be allowed to sit on the commission, whereas scientists were 'subject to prison terms of up to ten years for even minor security violations'.[3]

To Johnson and May, it was the scientists who were the problem, not the bomb. Those in the Manhattan Project had already experienced the possibility of being drafted into the army at the very beginning, when Oppenheimer had built up a personal relationship with Groves and gained his trust, so that being under strict military regulations had been postponed and then cancelled. Robert felt he could do it again with Groves and the War Department. But the other scientists were more distrustful, and suspected that Oppie had been duped by smooth-talking politicians.

Lawrence and Fermi refused to support the bill, since the devil was in the small print, which Oppie had not seen before he had eagerly co-operated with the establishment. He now realised too late that 'you could do almost anything under that bill'. The possibility triggered alarm.'[4]

Robert had been reassured by the involvement in the drafting of the bill by men of goodwill whom he trusted, like Henry Stimson, James Conant and Vannevar Bush. He was not accustomed to dealing with lawyers and bureaucrats who covered every possible eventuality in tiny print. Whereas he thought that 'nine good men' could be found to administer it – like General George C. Marshall, whom he respected – the other scientists were not so sure. Szilard and Robert's brother Frank were against the bill. Frank thought it was time to enter the public domain and educate citizens on the necessity for international controls.

On the other hand, Oppie now felt more comfortable with the scenario in Washington and, seeing that things were moving, he relied on the influence of his prestige to steer it in the right direction.

A Declaration of Independence

Robert Wilson was against the bill, and also thought it was time to go public. He was not afraid of being labelled as a troublemaker. He rewrote the original 'Document' that had been approved by most of the scientists and sent it to the *New York Times*. They splashed it across the front page. Wilson had learned – as he said later – that even the 'Best and Brightest' when placed in positions of power, could be overruled by other considerations and could not necessarily be depended on.[5]

Wilson's challenge in the *New York Times* was the beginning of a campaign against the bill by scientists who chose to bypass Oppenheimer. Their powerful lobbying was publicised by the news media and, remarkably, succeeded in defeating the May-Johnson bill. A new bill emerged by Brien McMahon from Connecticut, who proposed that control over nuclear energy should be given to a civilian Atomic Energy Commission (AEC). It was signed into law by President Truman on 1 August 1946. The bill had been so altered by then that the scientists began to wonder if Oppie had not been right after all with his ambivalent approach to the previous May-Johnson bill. He had at least understood the necessity for international controls over the manufacture of atomic bombs.

Oppenheimer had resigned from his position as director at Los Alamos almost a year earlier, in October 1945, when nearly a thousand people had turned up to wish their famously celebrated leader goodbye at an award ceremony marking his resignation. He was forty-one years old when he had received a scrolled Certificate of Appreciation for his work from General Groves.

Robert gave an acceptance speech, in which he emphasised the danger of a nuclear arms race. One of the eminent men present on the dais at the ceremony was Robert G. Sproud, the president of the University of California at Berkeley. He had been considering appointing Oppenheimer at Ernest Lawrence's recommendation to pay him double the salary, on the grounds that the Government would provide sizeable funding if Oppenheimer was there. But Stroud was a conservative man who had been annoyed at Oppie's support of the teachers' union in the past. Now he was undecided. So was Robert, who knew he had a record at Berkeley as a troublemaker, and did not wish to return there if Stroud viewed him negatively.

The problem in a nutshell was Robert's involvement in political activism – that obsession that Ernest Lawrence continually warned him against with no effect. It seemed that Oppie would always be a 'bleeding-heart' liberal.

True to form, he was back in Washington the very next day. Among the senators in his audience who listened to his warnings about the threats faced by the United States was Henry Wallace, who noted in his diary afterwards, 'I never saw a man in such an extremely nervous state as Oppenheimer. He seemed to feel that the destruction of the entire human race was imminent.'

The Russians are a proud people, said Oppenheimer; 'they will put everything they have into getting plenty of atomic bombs as soon as possible'.

Many of the scientists in the Manhattan Project were concerned about a possible war with Russia. As the notes made by Wallace in his diary continued, 'The guilt consciousness of the atomic bomb scientists is one of the most astounding things I have ever seen.'[6]

Crybaby Scientists

When Oppenheimer managed to meet with President Truman in the Oval Room of the White House on 15 October 1945, it was not a meeting of minds but emotions, in which one man sought compassion while the other was a more self-disciplined and restrained pragmatist. Both were charismatic individuals who felt they had to prove themselves worthy of public scrutiny.

Truman was naturally curious to meet this eloquent scientist whom the media never ceased to praise. He immediately insisted that, as opposed to Oppenheimer's plea for an international body to control the nuclear arms race, 'the first thing is to define the national problem'. But Robert was adamant that it was an international one.

The President asked him to guess when the Russians would produce their own atom bomb. Robert confessed he did not know.

'Never,' Truman snapped back triumphantly.

Oppenheimer was so amazed at Truman's lack of understanding of the situation that he found he was speechless. After a moment of thoughtful silence while each man weighed the other up speculatively, the prolonged adolescent in Oppenheimer piped up with one of his unfortunate phrases. 'Mr President,' he said in a hushed voice, 'I feel I have blood on my hands.'

Truman became angry as he considered his own formidable responsibility and was reminded of Japan. There are several different versions on record of his reply. According to what he told David Lilienthal afterwards (a lawyer who would later head the Atomic Energy Commission), 'I told him the blood was on *my* hands – to let *me* worry about that.'

'Blood on his hands!' the President was heard to repeat wryly afterwards, 'Dammit, he hasn't half as much blood on his hands as I have. You just don't go around bellyaching about it.'

Their meeting was still vivid in Truman's outraged mind a year later when he described Oppenheimer to Dean Acheson as a 'crybaby scientist'.

Despite all of Oppenheimer's intelligence, his erudition, and his otherwise calm and persuasive demeanour and loquaciousness, his liberal tenderness for the abstract and anonymous masses would continually rise up from his subconscious at important moments and act against his interests. One of his biographers described it as 'a form of intellectual arrogance that periodically led him to behave foolishly or badly, an Achilles' heel of sorts that would have devastating consequences. Indeed, it would eventually provide his political enemies with the opportunity to destroy him.'[7]

30

A World Transformed

In October 1945, Robert Oppenheimer was awarded the highest honour for an American civilian from President Truman. It was the Medal of Merit. He was considered to be a hero of the Second World War. But the dust from the havoc of a world war had still to settle. Britain was bankrupt from the role she had played in taking a sole stand against the Nazi forces for several years. The United States was now the wealthiest and most powerful nation in the world. And right-wing political leaders were doing their best to conserve the power and wealth that they and America had achieved.

Oppie was now mixing with influential and patriotic leaders of probity, like General George C. Marshall and Henry Stimson, and being applauded by them for his brilliance. This novel and apparently solid position in society gave Oppie a new perspective from which he could look upon the discontented and rebellious friends of his youth, who now seemed shallow and ignorant. Their discontent had arisen from the years of economic depression with millions unemployed, and a loss of faith in capitalism. But the rewards of supplying war material to its Allies had resulted in the highest standard of living for Americans, and the miseries of the past were swept away by an optimistic view of the future.

Robert regretted his previous left-wing political attitude and his funding of the American Communist Party, and did his best to edge cautiously away from his previous communist contacts. But he knew he had a left-wing and pro-trade union history with records that could be probed by the FBI.

Evidently, he felt that his prestige as a scientist and the continual publicity in the news media that gave him an aura of celebrity should be used to further the cause that was now dearest to his heart, which was international control of nuclear weapons. He hoped to prevent the type of arms race that had resulted in the First and Second World Wars. He proclaimed that physics and the teaching of physics, which had been his life, now seemed irrelevant with the constant threat of nuclear weaponry. Nevertheless, his visibility as a public intellectual continued to remind the FBI of his past associations with the Communist Party. It also made him an object of special interest to Soviet Russia.

In the years before McCarthyism became fashionable in the United States, Senator Joseph McCarthy was known to be friendly with the FBI's J. Edgar Hoover. They dined and wined together and had been recognised together at a race track. But the head of the FBI was frustrated because he had clear evidence of espionage by Judith Coplon. And yet, he could not have her sentenced because the proof had come through intercepting and decrypting secret messages from Moscow Centre that named her in code. As the 'Venona' ciphers were top secret, he could not divulge his evidence in court.[1]

Hoover took out his frustration on Senator McCarthy, as well as on his own staff.[2]

Judith Coplon had walked off free after being caught in the act of giving classified documents to her Soviet handler. She was the first Soviet undercover agent to be identified by 'Venona' decrypts. Hoover knew there must be other Soviet spies operating in the United States, but he was prevented from finding them.

On 15 November 1945, Hoover circulated a three-page summary of Oppenheimer's FBI file to the secretary of state and the White House. He reported that his agents had overheard Communist Party officials in San Francisco describing Oppenheimer as a 'regularly registered' member of the Party. And, since the explosions of the atom bomb, several of his old acquaintances from the Party had been interested in re-establishing their old relationship.

Hoover's agents most probably referred to Nelson, whom Oppenheimer had since carefully avoided, and never met again. The FBI information was vague and ambiguous, and likely to be inaccurate because several Party members had simply assumed that Oppenheimer was a member. Others thought it was time for him to come out of the closet and admit he was a member. Still, no one knew for sure.[3]

The White House and the State Department evidently saw the advantage of the FBI's illegal wiretaps, and made no move against them. Hoover instructed his agents to continue. He found the information his agents obtained was useful even if he couldn't use it in court. It often led to other links, and individuals who could be shadowed or bugged to discover even more communist members and their conversations. They bugged Frank Oppenheimer's home near Berkeley and heard Oppie talking to previous friends of his who still visited Frank.

Hoover continued with his illegal wiretaps, and documented about a thousand pages a year of reports, memos, and transcripts on Oppenheimer for eight years. The objective was to discredit outsiders and individualists and 'troublemakers' who would not toe the official line. On 8 May 1946, Hoover's agents set a wiretap on Oppenheimer's home phone at 1 Eagle Hill. They also attempted to turn Oppie's former secretary at Los Alamos, Anne Wilson, into an informer. Hoover even followed the activities of high-ranking members of Truman's administration. It was said that the more Hoover knew, the more secure he felt in his job.[4]

It was a time when the word communist began to be treated, not as a political alternative, but as a threat to democracy. Communist sympathisers and fellow travellers were automatically tainted as the enemy, and any previous trust in them was gone.

United Nations Atomic Energy Commission

It had occurred to Isidor Rabi that if the bomb was under national control, there would be international rivalries; so it must be under international control. He and

Oppenheimer also believed that the continuation of industrialisation depended on the peaceful use of nuclear energy. What was needed was an international atomic energy authority that would have the power to control nuclear weapons and the peaceful uses of atomic energy.[5]

United Nations representatives met in London, and Soviet Russia voted with the U.S. and other nations to exchange atomic information and establish an international body named the United Nations Atomic Energy Commission. Its aim was to control the manufacture, stockpiling, and use of atomic weapons. Negotiations finally resulted in agreement in January 1946. Oppie and Rabi were delighted, with Rabi claiming it had been his idea all along and Robert had been his salesman.[6]

At the end of January, Truman appointed a special committee to present a firm proposal for international control of nuclear weapons, with Dean Acheson as chairman. Other members were John McCloy, Vannevar Bush, James Conant and General Groves. Robert Oppenheimer was recommended as the most knowledgeable choice on atomic physics to advise the committee, with David Lilienthal to chair the advisory panel.

Early in 1946, the scientific project at Los Alamos was now solely under army management and on the verge of collapse. The infrastructure of the temporary artificial town was failing. 'The generators were on their last legs.' Power outages had become more frequent. Water was now in short supply as plastic pipelines from Guaje Canyon froze in the severe winter.[7]

By February 1946, Oppie was negotiating a return to Berkeley, where they showed their eagerness to have him back: 'Your old office is waiting, your old hat is on the rack, and your desk hasn't been cleaned out.'[8]

Lilienthal's first impression of Oppie, when he met him, was, 'I left liking him, greatly impressed with his flash of mind, but rather disturbed with the flow of words ... He is worth living a lifetime just to know mankind has been able to produce such a being. We may have to wait another hundred years for the second one to come off the line.'[9]

The Lilienthal group began work in earnest on 28 January 1947, while Oppenheimer tutored the advisory panel with an intensive course in nuclear physics. By 7 March they had compiled the Acheson-Lilienthal report, largely written by Oppenheimer. Significantly, he rejected earlier proposals made after Hiroshima to outlaw the bomb and create international inspectors to make sure that no nation was making them. He persuaded the committee to accept and advance his proposals, and Acheson endorsed the report. The plan became official United States policy.

General Groves, who had supported Oppie in the past, disagreed with him now. He thought the plan was unworkable. He complained that everyone bowed down to Oppie. 'Lilienthal got so bad he would consult Oppie on what tie to wear in the morning.'

The Washington Post announced that the report was statesmanlike and offered hope that the 'Great Fear' felt since Hiroshima had been lifted. But the Acheson-Lilienthal group was appalled when President Truman appointed Bernard Baruch to present the plan to the United Nations Atomic Energy Commission. They knew that the well-respected elderly statesman had little or no knowledge of the technical complexities of the subject. 'He immediately proceeded to introduce changes that distorted Oppenheimer's whole plan.' His emphasis was on punishing violators of the proposed treaty.[10]

Oppenheimer, who believed in a more co-operative, even conciliatory, approach to Russia, was repelled by Baruch's hard-line approach, and gave up hope of its effectiveness. He felt he had no other course but to resign, rather than stay to help to steer it in the right direction. He felt strongly that it was a backward approach rather than a progressive one.

In April 1947, Berkeley confirmed that Oppenheimer would not join them after all. Instead, he had accepted the directorship of the Institute for Advanced Study in Princeton. Professor Raymond Birge at Berkeley described the loss as 'the greatest blow ever suffered by the department'.[11]

Atomic Bomb Tests

The United States Government now began two atomic bomb tests, the first at Bikini Atoll in the Pacific, a coral reef in the Marshall Islands surrounding a 229.4-square-mile central lagoon.

Oppenheimer protested to Truman. He maintained that the tests were counterproductive and a waste of $100 million, when scientists could simulate the effects of the blasts on a warship. But the President had agreed to the request from the U.S. Navy who, after the shock of Hiroshima, wanted to be absolutely certain what damage nuclear weapons might unleash on the fleet.

The U.S. dropped an atom bomb over a group of battleships anchored in the lagoon. Observers were surprised at how little damage was caused – lending weight to Oppie's argument that the nuclear bomb was useless as a military weapon for waging war. The next one, exploded beneath the surface of the water on 25 July, produced an impressive water display, but little else.

One result of Baruch's changed or distorted report, and the atom bomb tests on Bikini Atoll, was that the Russians claimed the U.S. was negotiating in bad faith. It might have been a delaying tactic to allow them time to develop their own atom bomb. In any case they were encouraged by information from Klaus Fuchs that the sole possession of the secrets of the atom bomb by the United States was only a temporary event. So the Soviet Union abstained from voting for Baruch's plan.

Oppenheimer observed the first meeting of the UN Atomic Energy Commission as a member of the audience. He watched as all hope of preventing a nuclear arms race vanished. He had no doubt that America would continue producing more and more bombs, each more superior than the previous ones, while deluding itself that America's stockpiles were secret and no one else could ever catch up with them. When he heard Russia's assurance and defiance in its refusal to abide by the U.S. plan, he knew instinctively that it meant Russia had decided to conquer the world the moment it had developed its own atomic bomb.[12]

Hungarian-American physicist Leo Szilard conceived the nuclear chain reaction in 1933.

Italian-American physicist Enrico Fermi received the 1938 Nobel Prize in physics for identifying new elements and discovering nuclear reactions by his method of nuclear irradiation and bombardment..

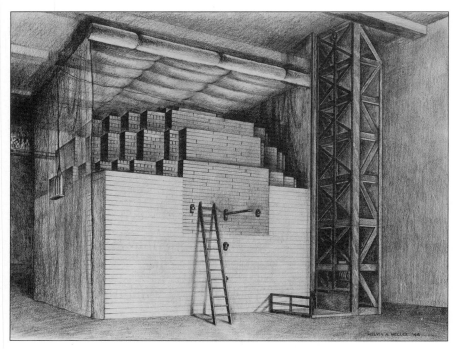

First nuclear reactor to achieve a self-sustaining chain reaction. Diagram of Chicago Pile-1, designed by Enrico Fermi.

Vannevar Bush headed the U.S. Office of Scientific Research and Development (OSRD), through which most wartime military Research and Development was undertaken. (1940-1944)

Award of honorary degrees at Harvard to Robert Oppenheimer (left), George C. Marshall (third from left) and Omar N. Bradley (fifth from left) in June 1947. Conant sits between Marshall and Bradley. Marshall announced the Marshall Plan to put postwar Europe back on its feet.

President Harry S. Truman presents James Conant with the civilian Medal for Merit award with bronze palm in 1948. Vannevar Bush on left.

Above: The 60-inch (1.52 m) cyclotron soon after completion in 1939. Standing, left to right: D. Cooksey, D. Corson, Ernest Lawrence, R. Thornton, J, Backus, W.S. Sainsbury. At back are Luis Walter Alvarez and Edwin McMillan.

Left: Robert Oppenheimer (Left) at the 184-inch cyclotron with Ernest Lawrence in 1946

1940 Police photo of nuclear physicist Klaus Fuchs who worked for the British and the Americans on the Manhattan Project. In 1950 he admitted to spying for the Russians since 1942.

Left: NKVD Spymaster Liz Zarubin (Elizaveta Yulyevna Zarubina) whom Kitty worked for. "One of the most successful operators in stealing atomic bomb secrets from the United States".

Right: British Diplomat Donald Maclean; Moscow Centre Spy and Kitty's former lover.

Left: Neils Bohr relaxing with Albert Einstein in December 1925.

Below: Oppenheimer with mathematician John von Neumann and his early computer.

English Physicist Paul
Dirac in 1933.

Werner Heisenberg when a student.

Above: Replica of the original Bomb code-named "Fat Man."

Left: General George C. Marshall in the 1940s.

Right: Katherine Oppenheimer Los Alamos ID at The Manhattan Project. Wartime staff security badge.

Below: Trinity atom bomb "Gadget" being readied for testing atop Los Alamos test tower, 15 July 1945. Norm Bradbury was group leader for bomb assembly. He would become the director of Los Alamos after Oppenheimer's departure.

J. Robert Oppenheimer Los Alamos ID in 1943.

Oppenheimer receiving the Army-Navy E Award on 16 October 1945 for the
Los Alamos Laboratory from Robert Sprout (left) with General Groves.

Mushroom cloud of 'Gadget' over Trinity, seconds after detonation. 16 July
1945. Copyright United States Department of Energy.

Official portrait of J. Robert Oppenheimer, first director of Los Alamos National Laboratory (1944). Copyright Department of Energy, Office of Public Affairs.

"Jumbo" was a massive steel bomb ordered by General Groves at a cost of $12 million, in case "Gadget" failed to explode in the first test. Copyright Atomic Heritage Foundation and National Museum of Nuclear Science & History.

Trinity test base camp, May 1945. Copyright Federal Government of the United States.

Left: The tower with "the gadget" used in the Trinity test. July 1945.

Below: J. Robert Oppenheimer and General Leslie Groves at the ground zero site of the Trinity test, 9 September 1945.

Isidor Rabi, Nobel Laureate in Physics in 1944.

Dr. Robert Oppenheimer received the Enrico Fermi Award from President Johnson. December 2, 1963. Photograph used with permission from Kitty Oppenheimer and the J. Robert Oppenheimer Memorial Committee.

Right: Colonel Paul Tibbets Jnr. waves photographers out of the way as he takes off for his mission to bomb Japan with a nuclear gadget in 1945.

Below: Robert Oppenheimer with wife Kitty and son Peter at the Fermi Award ceremony on December 2, 1963. Photograph used with permission from Kitty Oppenheimer and the J. Robert Oppenheimer Memorial Committee.

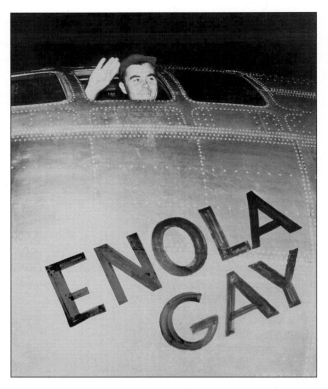

31

American Genius

British and American secret services like MI5 and the CIA continued to intercept coded messages emanating from Moscow Centre, but there were generally lengthy delays while some smart cryptanalyst worked daily to decipher the mysterious language to reveal its secrets in the Venona project. Real names of individuals were concealed by wrapping them in cover names. References to Churchill, for example, were transformed into the code name KABAN. Even those cover names were changed often to make decoding them harder. Klaus Fuchs was hidden beneath REST, and sometimes CHARLES. Alger Hiss was ALES. 'Other VENONA messages contained the code name HOMER for a British diplomat supplying high-level information to the Soviets. A message dated 28 June 1944 indicated that HOMER had gone to New York to be with his wife when she gave birth to their child.'[1]

In the case of Judith Coplon, who had so much annoyed Hoover, for example, FBI special agent Robert Lamphere had succeeded in tracking Soviet intelligence agents when stationed in the New York field office. He had now been transferred to Washington as a case supervisor. One of his colleagues introduced him to Meredith Gardner, who was a brilliant linguist and code-breaker with America's counter-intelligence. Meredith had made significant discoveries from secret Soviet traffic sources.

Both Lamphere and Meredith were cerebral men of great intellect, but very different from each other. Whereas the beefy Lamphere was a rough-and-ready individual who had worked his way through law school from the coal mines of Idaho, Meredith was a quiet and slender knowledge worker who was fluent in half a dozen languages, and a self-taught Russian speaker. Most importantly, they could communicate with each other at the same level and helped each other with clues and analytical speculations. One batch of messages they had studied together had referred to a woman code-named SIMA who worked in the Department of Justice. Those clues had led them to identify Judith Coplon in minutes, since she worked with secrets in the same building as the FBI.[2]

Thirty FBI agents had followed her through the New York subway system to arrest her as she was about to hand over classified documents to her Soviet controller.'[3]

Coplan would have been liable to up to ten years in prison, but appealed the conviction. Her appeal was upheld by the court since the reason for her surveillance and arrest lacked probable cause, as the FBI were prohibited from revealing the evidence of the top secret Venona decrypts that had led to her being shadowed and arrested. Venona was top secret.

Lamphere contacted Britain's MI6 in Washington to help with his search for HOMER. The British representative at the Washington embassy whom he met was Kim Philby – not yet unmasked as 'the spy of the century'. Philby listened mildly to Lamphere's description, whom he recognised as the first secretary at the British embassy, because he was Kim's fellow KGB spy in what would be called the 'Cambridge Five' spy ring. It was Donald Maclean. It was the first alarm signal received by Philby that he must persuade Maclean to defect to the Soviet Union before he was disclosed as a spy who had passed Britain's nuclear secrets to Moscow Centre. Maclean was back from his post in Cairo and working in London by 1948.

While in Washington, Philby passed on Britain's top nuclear secrets to his Soviet handler, Yuri Modin, in London. Cryptologist Meredith Gardner worked in an embassy office beside his, so that Philby had direct access to him. They soon became close friends, while Meredith studied the Venona code to search for HOMER, whom Kim knew was Maclean. Meredith's final discovery of Maclean would eventually lead him to the treachery of his newfound friend Philby.[4]

The Cambridge Five Spy Ring

All five of the Cambridge spies had been brilliant when young students at Trinity College in England. Each now worked in prominent positions in important government departments where they had access to secret files on such topics as relationships between the Allies, foreign affairs, and nuclear weapons, including the atom bomb. All possessed very high ethical principles. Several had either been brought up as strict Presbyterians or on moralistic Calvinist or Lutheran lines. They were shocked at the rise of Hitler and the Nazi threat to Europe and the rest of the world, and became passionately stirred to do something about it.

The reason they dedicated themselves to passing on valuable information about nuclear weapons to the Kremlin was to ensure that Nazi Germany would be defeated by sharing information to help the Soviet Union win the war. Each of the former graduates from Cambridge University was well placed in a particular government department to obtain most-secret files and have them photocopied and returned.

Kim Philby had been transferred to the British Embassy in Washington, where he lived two different lives simultaneously – as a senior civil servant and as one of Moscow's most valued KGB secret agents. Donald Maclean had worked in Britain's Foreign Office as head of the American Section, with access to Britain's Atomic Energy Commission. Guy Burgess joined Philby in the British Embassy in Washington, to work on Britain's policy towards China. James Cairncross also had access to secret information on nuclear weapons. So did Anthony Blunt. With those dedicated informants alone, Stalin knew more about how to make a Russian atom bomb than either the British or the American governments suspected. And there were others who were similarly dedicated to sharing secret information with the Soviet Union, like Klaus Fuchs. He was the son of a pastor with strict views on ethics.

'Maclean was the most important provider of political intelligence to Stalin.' He had been transferred back to London after embarrassing bouts of heavy drinking in Cairo and a nervous breakdown from the stress and anxiety of his double life at Britain's Foreign Office and as a KGB informer of Britain's nuclear secrets.[5]

Maclean had been responsible for nuclear matters at the Washington embassy, where he became suspicious of America's intentions. Since he had clearance to visit the Atomic Energy Commission's offices, he did so on about twenty occasions over several months, taking valuable information. It included records of the amount of uranium produced or planned for the manufacture of atomic bombs by the Americans.

Oppenheimer's Transformation

Robert Oppenheimer was not one of them. On the contrary, the speculation by the FBI as their agents continued to target him and pile up more and more information about him, was either false or out-of-date hearsay. His previous friends and communist acquaintances, and the scientists who had worked under him at Los Alamos, were all amazed at the transformation. It was as if the prolonged adolescent had finally come of age and taken on the responsibility for the terrifying problem of avoiding a nuclear war with Soviet Russia.

Oppenheimer was featured on the cover of *Time* magazine in November 1948 and treated as an 'American Genius'. He appeared again as 'No. 1 Thinker on Atomic Energy' on the cover of *Life* magazine in October 1949.

As for the others, they had committed themselves to continue to support the Soviet Union, even though the war against Nazi Germany was won by the Allies. Unlike Oppenheimer, they did not view Soviet Russia as a threat but as an opportunity to prevent the United States from being the sole owner of the secrets of nuclear power. They were convinced that those scientific discoveries belonged to the world and should be shared with the USSR.

Oppenheimer, on the other hand, appeared to be 'a member in good standing of the American Establishment'.[6] He was the 'Father of the Atom bomb'. He was Chairman of the Atomic Energy Commission's General Advisory Committee. He was president of the American Physicists Society. He was on the board of overseers of Harvard University. He rubbed shoulders with the great and the good of his time on a daily basis. When Harvard awarded him an honorary degree, he watched and listened to his much admired friend General George Marshall announce what would become known as 'the Marshall Plan'. It was a plan by Truman's administration to fund a programme to restore Europe's economy by supplying it with billions of dollars.

It was where the American intellectual and scientific genius belonged. He and the American poet Archibald MacLeish became close friends. They not only shared similar views about poetry and literature, but also liberal values that they both felt were threatened by the communists of the left and the radicals on the political right. McLeish furiously attacked the post-war utopia that had somehow become distorted into a dystopia. Although America was the most powerful nation in the world, many Americans had allowed themselves to be defined by Soviet Russia, which was dictating America's behaviour. They were 'willing to sacrifice their civil liberties in the name of anti-communism'.

A similar socio-political split had occurred in post-war Britain under a socialist Labour Government that created class hatred. The intolerance of others would gather momentum over the years to split other categories of people from the mainstream by degrading them or empowering them, not only by their different political views, but by their different class, gender, religion, or colour, as step by step, post-war society headed for the divisiveness of identity politics.

Oppenheimer's view of MacLeish's article in the *Atlantic Monthly* in August 1949 was that it was a masterful presentation of the current state of affairs in which the author had called for a restoration of the sovereignty of the individual, but he did not agree with it: he had become accustomed to the idea of a community in which each individual depended on his fellows. In responding to MacLeish's request to comment on his Libertarian article, Robert referred to a long discussion he had had with Bohr about the relations of the individual to society. MacLeish welcomed his contribution by saying, that 'is, of course, the central point of the whole business'.

The post-war search for an ideal society was, similarly, being discussed by intellectuals in the UK, at the beginning of the birth of the huge baby-boom generation who – when they became adolescents – would turn the West into an unrestricted permissive society, with a soaring crime rate that would vastly increase the level of peacetime violence.

In the meantime, Robert's old friends of the extreme Left were unsure what to make of his transformation. The old reasons for communism were irrelevant now the war against fascism was won. But to his other old friends who had refused to be politically indoctrinated, like Rabi, Hans Bethe, Robert Wilson and Ernest Lawrence, 'Oppie was the same man, with the same motivation.'[7]

Frank differed from his brother in believing that the Russians were not really a threat to America. But Robert was adamant in his belief that 'they were ready to march if they were given the opportunity'. He had changed his mind towards Truman and now supported his hard-line policy against the Soviet Union. He had been led to that conclusion by absorbing a great deal of information from a variety of different sources.

His old friend Chevalier had also remarked on the changes he had noted in Oppie when they had met again after the war in May 1946, and Robert had informed him openly of his different outlook. Chevalier thought it was to the political right, since Oppie had nothing good to say about communism or the Soviet Union. 'They are not what you believe them to be,' Oppie had warned Chevalier.

Meanwhile, Moscow Centre planted rumours through Klaus Fuchs that Fermi, Oppenheimer, and Szilard opposed the hydrogen bomb. The American physicists were unaware they were being used by Moscow. They had started as antifascists, and become political advocates of the Soviet Union.'[8]

FBI Interrogations

Chevalier had been upset when Berkeley had refused to give him tenure. He was puzzled as to why, and shattered at the blow to his academic career. He decided to work full-time on writing a novel that Knopf had agreed to publish. Then, some six weeks after he had met up again with Robert, two FBI agents appeared on his doorstep at home while he was working on 26 June 1946. They insisted he come with them to their downtown office in San Francisco. Other FBI agents called at George Eltenton's house and asked him to come with them to the FBI field office in Oakland. Each intensive interrogation lasted for about six hours. In both cases the FBI asked them about conversations they'd had in the early part of the winter of 1943 about Robert Oppenheimer.

Neither Chevalier nor Eltenton knew of the other's interrogation, but each gave the same replies to the questions that the FBI agents peppered them with. According to Eltenton, sometime in late 1942, when the Red Army was hard-pressed to resist the overwhelming German invasion of Russia, the Soviet consulate Peter Ivanov had inquired if he knew Professor Ernest Lawrence and Robert Oppenheimer. Eltenton had said he only knew Oppenheimer, but not well. The Russians needed help to withstand the German onslaught. As they were America's allies, they had wanted Robert to share information with Soviet scientists. Eltenton had replied that he had a friend who was close to Oppenheimer – meaning Chevalier. Eltenton asked Chevalier to approach Robert in confidence. After which Chevalier told him that Oppenheimer did not approve of the contact.

Chevalier replied much the same to the other FBI agent. They could not understand why the FBI kept pressing them about three other scientists. Who were they? They had no idea. Each was finally asked to sign an affidavit that he had approached no one but Oppenheimer. They did so reluctantly. The FBI agents left them wondering how they knew about the brief conversation with Robert in the kitchen of the Oppenheimers' home.

When, in July or August of 1946, Chevalier met Eltenton by chance at a luncheon of a mutual friend in Berkeley, it was the first time they had met in almost three years. Only then did each learn about the interrogation of the other by the FBI.

Robert invited Chevalier and his wife to a cocktail party at his home a few weeks later. They came early before the other guests arrived, which gave Chevalier an opportunity to confide in Robert about the FBI interrogations. Robert's face clouded over at once as he grew angry, and took his old friend outside – indicating that he knew his house was bugged. They walked into a wooded area in the back garden while Chevalier gave a more detailed account of his questioning by the FBI. He would write sometime later in 1965, 'Opje was obviously greatly upset … He asked me endless questions.' After which Robert reassured him and told him he had done the right thing.

'I had to report that conversation, you know,' Robert told his friend in the privacy of the garden, as he recalled the silly story he had told Boris Pash years ago on the spur of the moment, and became more and more annoyed with himself for his stupidity.

Kitty called out to warn them that their guests were arriving. And Oppie replied abruptly that he would be in momentarily. But his thoughts were on the past as he continued to pace the garden and ask Chevalier again what he had said to the FBI agents. Kitty came out a few moments later to remind him that he really should come in and greet his guests. Even when Oppie replied impatiently and spoke to her curtly again, she insisted. Then, to Chevalier's amazement, Oppie shouted angrily at Kitty in coarse language, calling her 'vile names and told her to mind her goddamn business and to get the ... hell out!'[9]

'Something was obviously bothering him,' wrote Chevalier, 'but he gave no hint as to what it was.'

Kitty's Mysterious Past

When Boris Pash had interrogated him all those years ago, Robert had said some idiotic things in order to shield Chevalier. He had told Pash he had been approached by three other scientists, so as to avoid Pash's counter-intelligence outfit from persecuting his old friend. By now he would have known that he had made a grave error with his misplaced schoolboy loyalty. It was the old dilemma of whether to be loyal to friends or country, and he had slipped up. He was angry at his stupidity, while his mind searched for some means of damage control.

As for his displaced anger at Kitty, nobody knew what went on between her and Robert after they were married, or what he knew of her complicated background. He was well aware by now that Soviet spymasters and spies were desperate to steal the plans to make their own atomic bomb at that critical time. He was also now convinced that Soviet Russia had no intention of co-operating with other nations to achieve peace, but was determined to dominate world affairs through the possession of nuclear weapons. Whether he knew that the artful Kitty's activities had involved her in global events once again was questionable. And yet, somehow she seemed to know what was going on.

> From [Maclean's] early days in the Foreign Office when he had Kitty Harris as his courier and lover, until his flight to the Soviet Union with Guy Burgess in 1951, Maclean was a valuable spy for Moscow Centre.[10]

Kitty had always been a go-between, carrying messages back and forth between the Kremlin and its secret agents. If Oppenheimer knew something significant, even critical, which had convinced him the Soviet Union was not what it showed itself to be to the outside world, and was a threat to world peace, whoever he tried to warn, like Chevalier or his brother Frank, he could not divulge the source of his information. That source had to be protected at all costs. Nevertheless, his conviction was so important that it had transformed his attitude towards Soviet Russia and allied him with President Truman's hard-line policy against the USSR, even changing his own personality in the process. Most probably, he could not disclose his source because the most likely information available to him about Soviet Russia came from his wife Kitty.

Kitty Harris had lived and worked with Earl Browder when he was head of America's Communist Party. She had revealed a gift for disinformation and obfuscation by lying at every opportunity, or reversing anything, however trivial, to prevent any possibility of being followed and identified. On her Moscow trip in October 1927 with Browder, for example, she had changed the name of the ship she was sailing on from the *Nordwyck* to the *Leviathan*. It had already become a habit to protect who she was and what she was doing from prying eyes.

WITCH-HUNT

32

Enemies in Waiting

The politics of the United States took an abrupt turn in 1950 into the fascism of McCarthyism, from which no one appeared to be safe, as Senator Joseph McCarthy interrogated one Hollywood celebrity after another as a potential communist to publicise himself as a powerful and influential politician. With all those star names his media coverage was vast. Apart from building himself up into a patriotic leader or a tyrant – depending on how the public viewed him – he managed to scare millions of Americans that there was 'a Red under every bed'. He made successful immigrants uneasy and insecure in his witch-hunt with its anti-Semitic atmosphere, by seeking to establish which one was really 'American', and who was 'Un-American', according to his own standards and those of the FBI. Once smeared as 'Un-American' by McCarthy's House Un-American Activities Committee, many talented people could no longer find work in Hollywood. His false or unfounded accusations of subversion and treason turned them into pariahs. Some left for work in Europe. A few committed suicide. His well-publicised witch-hunt made most film-makers insecure. Prominent producers, directors and screenwriters were caught off balance and on the defensive.

The hearings by McCarthy's committee had begun in 1947 as a reaction to the Cold War in Central and Eastern Europe, with the Soviet Union effectively stretching its elastic borders further and further out in an attempt to protect its own territory. It had spread alarm in Britain as well as the United States, and gave credence to Oppenheimer's constant fear of a Third World War, this time fought with nuclear weapons.

Washington was shocked in August when a senior State Department aide named Alger Hiss was accused of being a communist at a hearing. It was claimed that he was part of a Soviet cell planning to overthrow the United States Government. He would be found guilty on 21 January 1950.[1]

The revelation was quickly followed by another shock with news from London that Klaus Fuchs had confessed to being a Soviet spy who had passed nuclear secrets to Russia when working as a scientist on the Manhattan Project. A triumphant Senator McCarthy waved a piece of paper before a bunch of reporters, claiming that he had a list of 205 names of known communists who were 'working and shaping policy in the State Department'.[2]

Eager for more scandals, the news media encouraged the witch-hunt to probe further.

Oppenheimer, with his past history and questionable connections, had more reasons to fear McCarthy than any civil servant or Hollywood celebrity. And yet, he managed to carry on advising the State and Defense Departments on international control of atom bombs.

Wild and crazy rumours abounded with plenty of informers volunteering dubious information as evidence of a Soviet communist plot to influence the government. Who could be trusted? Apparently no one was safe from the Reds.

'Despite the fact that he knew he had many enemies, he made no attempt to temper his rhetoric.'[3] But, almost inevitably, as Oppenheimer followed Bohr's unpractical dream to halt the making of nuclear bombs for the sake of world peace and future generations, he invited attacks. His usual charm deserted him as he lashed back at those who criticised him. He made cutting remarks at people he considered ignorant. He humiliated people in public, in ways they could never forget, while admitting to friends in private that he was terrified of the Cold War, since he thought he knew how it would end. He was also afraid of McCarthy's Red Scare political tactics. But it seemed he could not abandon his and Bohr's ideal solution against using nuclear bombs that might spread radiation all over the world.

FBI director J. Edgar Hoover now had all the Manhattan Project security files in his possession, and sent a fat file of 'derogatory information' to David Lilienthal. The FBI claimed that the famous physicist Oppenheimer could be a dangerous security risk if he was a communist. Oppenheimer had 'already begun looking nervously over his shoulder to see if McCarthy's bloodhounds were on his trail'.

Although Lilienthal did not believe that Oppie was a security risk, he and his four AEC commissioners read the FBI dossier on Oppenheimer and realised they and the Truman Government could be involved in a political catastrophe if anyone leaked it to the news media.

He asked Conant and Vannevar Bush for character references for Oppenheimer. Both immediately stated there could be no doubt of his loyalty and patriotism. Conant wrote to Lilienthal accordingly: 'Any rumor that Dr Oppenheimer is a Communist or toward Russia is an absurdity.'[4]

They produced similar confirmation from General Groves and Secretary of War Robert Patterson: The FBI claims in their dossier on Oppenheimer were too vague and unsubstantiated to present an immediate hazard or require an official inquiry. Oppenheimer's security clearance continued.

Frank's turn to be exposed in the limelight of the news media came when the Washington *Times-Herald* told a story on its front page on 12 July headlined 'Atom Scientist's Brother Exposed as Communist Who Worked on A-Bomb'. Frank denied their claim, but was exposed to public scrutiny through McCarthy's Un-American Activities Committee. J. Thomas Parnell, the chairman of the so-called House Committee on Un-American Activities, thought differently than Lilienthal and the AEC about the Oppenheimer brothers. He too had his sights set on the 'Alger Hiss of science'.

There were plenty of victims and possible informants for McCarthy and the FBI's Hoover to vilify as they scrutinised old files from the Manhattan Project once again. There were masses of security memos too, which referred to leftist physicists on Berkeley's campus who had been possible security risks in the war and might have leaked atomic secrets, like Klaus Fuchs had done.

No one – not Oppenheimer or any of his friends – was safe from suspicion in the McCarthy and FBI witch-hunt. Robert Serber had been selected as another victim in 1948, and interrogated for his 'character, associations and loyalty', and his security clearance was questioned.[5]

Even brothers-in-law and fathers-in-law were suspected and smeared forever in the hunt for possible subversive elements, while the legitimacy of the HUAC committee was rarely, if ever, questioned. It had become so powerful that too many people were afraid of this revolutionary tribunal acting in the shadow of a guillotine and eager for their victims' exposure.

When Serber was cleared, Oppenheimer told him he had seen the final report on his loyalty and he had 'passed with glowing colours'.[6]

The Inquisition

McCarthy's Un-American Activities Committee continued to study all the old rehashed files for other names and other possibilities, like Joe Weinberg, David Bohm, Bernard Peters, Rossi Lomanitz – whom Robert had distanced himself from after Ernest Lawrence and Colonel John Lansdale had warned him about them.

Dorothy McKibbin and several of Robert's former colleagues from Los Alamos packed the HUAC hearing one spring morning on 7 June 1949, while Robert sat alone in a chair facing six inquisitors on their dais. He was isolated by strong lights deliberately focused on his eyes.

With so many people against him, and many out to destroy him, Oppenheimer had reached a uniquely elevated position of isolation, that might well have caused him to view himself as the one 'Just Man' in the Old Testament story whom God recognises can remove the sins of all living in those and other corrupt cities. But he was still so idolised by public acclaim that his interrogators were cautious while questioning him.

When Frank took his turn before the interrogating panel two days later, he was forced to admit publicly that he had lied about his membership of the Communist Party. Now he testified that his wife and he had joined the Party in 1937, hoping to find an answer to the large-scale economic and unemployment problems in America. He said that he had been disappointed and left the Party three and a half years later.[7]

As a consequence of his admission, the University of Minnesota stated they had accepted his resignation. Frank's career in research into cosmic rays was terminated, and he fled to his ranch in the countryside of Colorado.

Frank was now a threat to his brother as an example. Although Robert had not been proven disloyal or treasonous during his interrogation, he was brought back in front of another inquisition a week later, on 13 June. It was chaired by Senator Bourke Hickenlooper of the Joint Committee on Atomic Energy. He was encouraged by the public outcry for security to discredit the Atomic Energy Commission.

The silent force lurking in the background that had empowered Senator Bourke to discredit Robert Oppenheimer was Lewis Strauss. Strauss was a self-made financier and a self-righteous and conservative commissioner of the Atomic Energy Commission. He was also one of the enemies whom Robert had made by being too clever by half. For Strauss was a complex man, half filled with admiration for Oppie, and half filled with jealously at his brilliance and achievements. He had been deeply hurt by Oppenheimer's arrogant way of dismissing his wishes on the committee, as if he were irrelevant.[8]

Strauss had offered him the top job in the Atomic Energy Commission in 1947, despite knowing the contents of Robert's FBI file. Evidently Strauss had disregarded the accusations as vague or ambiguous and inaccurate at that time. Now he was determined to use the FBI file to destroy Robert.

Two years previously, he had been outvoted and his objections swept aside by the committee. Now he had decided to get his revenge by discrediting both Oppenheimer and the committee. His reason appeared to be that they had disagreed about research isotopes.

'The AEC had been steadily sending these overseas, filling more than two thousand requests in the spirit of Oppenheimer's international cooperation.' Most were small samples of non-secret radioisotopes for use solely in physics research. But Strauss strongly objected on the grounds that they could be used by foreign countries to apply to atomic energy for industry or radioactive warfare. He claimed they could even be used to build reactors for making atomic bombs.

Armed with so much complex nuclear information that he could not possibly understand, the senator had Oppenheimer on the stand to admit to the Joint Committee that the shipment was evidence of gross mismanagement and a violation of the Atomic Energy Act. Oppenheimer was scornful and scathing in his reply, saying you could use even a shovel for atomic energy, or even a bottle of beer. But, to put the matter in proper perspective, 'during the war and after the war these materials have played no significant part, and in my knowledge no part at all'.

Strauss, who had dropped in to watch Robert's humiliation at the hands of the senator, heard the laughter in the hearing room and was furious. Despite his business successes, he had not finished high school, and felt insecure at his lack of education and knowledge. Now Robert was humiliating him again, this time in public.

Robert had often made the mistake of being condescending towards Strauss, without realising that he was a vengeful man. Now he made the mistake of showing enjoyment at the laughter of his audience at the expense of the senator. One of the AEC commissioners, Gordon Dean, remembered the incident clearly, and 'the terrible look on Lewis's face'. David Lilienthal recalled it too: 'There was a look of hatred there that you don't see very often in a man's face.'[9]

'How did I do?' Oppie said triumphantly afterwards to his lawyer, Joe Volpe.

'Too well Robert, too well.'

33

Soviet Russia's Atom Bomb

Robert Oppenheimer's victory in the hearing against him had come at a price: his opponents had responded by ruining his brother Frank's career. Now they would stop at nothing to destroy Robert. His intellect, which had contributed to his extraordinary success in physics, now shielded him from reality by obscuring the typical behaviour of enemies who were desperate to prove their point at any cost. If he was vain enough to imagine he was above the petty emotions of the mob, he would now learn what it felt like to be overwhelmed by their huge numbers.

As he saw with Frank, who had been exposed as a 'closet communist', made men can be unmade. The committee leaked parts of Oppenheimer's secret testimony to the press over the next few weeks, revealing that he had acknowledged that a number of pre-war friends and associates were radicals or communists.

When the story was revealed in the *Times Union* newspaper that Robert had given evidence against his former student, Bernard Peters, in the hearing, 'it turned people's stomachs', because he appeared to have betrayed Peters to save his own skin.[1]

Caught in a web by his enemies, he made even more enemies by opposing the hydrogen bomb. He had always argued against the feasibility of a thermonuclear bomb, believing that both the costs and the technical challenges were too high for the questionable results. But his opposition suggested, by innuendo, that he was acting on behalf of the Soviet Union.

Then, on 29 August 1949, Soviet Russia exploded its first atomic bomb at the remote Semipalatinsk test site in today's Kazakhstan. It changed the entire global situation.

Oppenheimer saw the incident as typical of a nuclear arms race. And the U.S. Government was shocked into reacting by accepting Edward Teller and Ernest Lawrence's proposal to design and develop hydrogen bombs. Oppenheimer felt that it would end in total destruction in a Third World War. He led the General Advisory Committee in a powerful recommendation on 29 October to oppose Edward Teller, with Conant and all the other seven members supporting him.[2]

Teller had come to hate his old boss by now. And he accused Conant of having been 'unduly influenced' by Oppenheimer. At this time of a Cold War showdown, Teller was able to use the rising fear of a Third World War to gain support for his Super Hydrogen Bomb from Lewis Strauss and Senator McMahon, as well as the U.S. Army and Air Force, who could be powerful enemies.

President Truman was caught in a quandary – whether to launch a nuclear arms race or leave the United States vulnerable to a nuclear attack by Soviet Russia.

What swung the balance in favour of a super hydrogen bomb was the revelations that came out of the confession by Klaus Fuchs, 'his funneling of atomic secrets to the Russians while he was at Los Alamos, and his presence at high-level meetings in which the fusion weapon had been discussed'. It was now obvious that Soviet Russia had been in a race for nuclear superiority all along.

The Race for Nuclear Superiority

Truman felt he had no choice in the face of evidence of the Soviet threat to peace. On 31 January 1950 he ordered the Atomic Energy Commission to develop 'all forms of atomic weapons, including the so-called hydrogen or super-bomb'.[3]

As Oppenheimer described the situation, he visualised two Great Powers who would soon be in a position to destroy each other's life and civilisation, while risking their own lives at the same time. His opposition made him even more enemies, as it attacked the U.S. Air Force's goal of air superiority by using nuclear bombs for America's Strategic Air Command.[*]

Nor had Oppenheimer anticipated the media accusations against him of disloyalty in continually opposing U.S. military strategy. If the tortured Robert Oppenheimer had thought of himself as the One Just Man who could save the United States and the world, the news media did not. Instead, they blamed him for allowing the communists to get ahead of the United States.

After Truman decided to go ahead with the hydrogen bomb, the attitude towards Robert in Washington became poisonous. Now the Justice Department took its turn to destroy Oppenheimer once and for all.

In order to do so, they paid Sylvia and Paul Crouch to accuse Oppenheimer of being a member of the Communist Party. The two former communists duly testified that Oppenheimer 'had once hosted a Party meeting in his Berkeley home. Crouch alleged it had been in late July 1941.[4]

Oppenheimer made a written statement denying their allegation: 'I have never been a member of the Communist Party. I never assembled any such group of people for any such purpose in my home or anywhere else.' He did not recognise their names, but added that he had never made a secret of knowing plenty of people in left-wing circles. His denial was widely reported in the news media.

Paul Crouch was an odd but useful informant for the Justice Department to bribe, as he had been court-martialled when an enlisted man in the army and sentenced to forty years in prison for 'fomenting revolution'. He had been pardoned by President Calvin Coolidge after only three years in Alcatraz, and been turned into a double agent.

---

* Battleground activities in Russia's 2022 war against Ukraine would confirm Oppenheimer's insights that air superiority had been replaced by the superior effectiveness of ground-based rocket missiles fired by more accurate and less costly precision weapons of modern artillery.

Crouch's state of mind could be gleaned from his weird testament at his trial: 'I am in the habit of writing letters to my friends and imaginary persons, sometimes to kings and other foreign persons, in which I place myself in an imaginary position.'[5]

Evidently, his claim that Oppenheimer had held a Communist Party meeting in his home was also imaginary. But, by now, Crouch was 'the most highly paid "consultant" on the Justice Department's payroll.'[6]

When interviewed by FBI agents on 29 April and 2 May 1950, Oppenheimer pointed out that he could not possibly have held the alleged Party meeting at his home on the date alleged by Crouch, since he was not there – he was staying at that time at Perro Caliente, with his wife, in New Mexico. His alibi that he had been 1,187 miles away at that time was proof that Crouch had lied. Robert also provided evidence of being X-rayed at the hospital in Santa Fe. And Hans Bethe could confirm he had been a guest at the ranch and remembered when Robert had been kicked and injured by a horse on 24 July 1941. It was abundantly clear that the Oppenheimers had been in New Mexico continually from 12 July until 11 or 13 August. These facts were fundamental to the charges made by the Crouches being dismissed in court.

Darker Influences

The essence of Oppenheimer's arguments and protests against the nuclear arms race, which he was sure would result in an unwinnable war with Soviet Russia, was his old claim that the atom bomb was not an efficient military weapon. On the other hand, he was perfectly satisfied with the idea of using tactical nuclear warheads. After the Soviet Union had detonated its atom bomb in 1949, he had pressed the Truman Administration to build more such 'battlefield weapons' instead of the Super Bomb. He was entirely convinced that the number of atom bombs that America produced was irrelevant, since they were not needed for fighting a real war like they were presently doing on the Korean peninsula, where, once again, they were on the edge of an eruption of a Third World War because of China's involvement.

Although some of his friends might have imagined that Oppenheimer was guilty of poor judgment, as many other people did, there were two persistent individuals who had set their sights on him because they were convinced that Robert had darker motives for halting America's development of a super hydrogen bomb. One of them was William Liscum Borden, a young staff member of the Joint Committee, formerly educated at Yale Law School. He had previously been an admirer of Oppenheimer's intellect and leadership. But after the disclosures of the Soviet Spy Klaus Fuchs, he began to think differently about Oppenheimer and wondered if he might be more dangerous than a manipulator of other men's thoughts.

Borden's suspicions were encouraged by Lewis Strauss. The two men were quite close by 1949, and Strauss continued to be in touch with Borden after he himself was no longer involved in the Atomic Energy Commission and Borden had become the staff director of the Senate Committee now responsible for AEC activities. They soon recognised they shared similar suspicions about the motives behind Oppenheimer's views and actions.

Borden watched FBI director Edgar Hoover testify before the Joint Committee on 6 February 1950, when Hoover briefed them on Fuchs, but chose to speak at length about Oppenheimer. Senator McMahon and Congressman Henry Jackson sat on the committee. Jackson's district in Washington included the Hanford nuclear facilities. He was staunchly anti-communist and a strong supporter of nuclear weapons. He had met Oppenheimer and was amazed at his arguments that developing the H-bomb would not only fuel an arms race but also make America less secure.

Now they heard from Hoover about the Chevalier incident for the first time, when he had approached Oppenheimer in 1943 to suggest that Robert might have scientific information to disclose to their Soviet ally in wartime. Hoover rightly reported that Oppenheimer had rejected the overture, but Borden thought the incident seemed suspicious, even possibly incriminating.[7]

He wondered if Oppenheimer's opposition to the super bomb was motivated by loyalty to the Communist Party. Then, a month later, he met Edward Teller, who told him that Oppenheimer had wanted to close down the Manhattan Project after the war. Now Teller worked closely with Borden against Oppenheimer and fuelled his suspicions by telling him that the nuclear programme was behind because of Oppenheimer.

It was then that Borden heard for the first time that 'Kitty Oppenheimer had once been married to a communist who had fought and died in Spain'.

Borden still thought Paul Crouch believable, even though he had been discredited. It had become a case of believing what he wanted to believe. But to clarify the situation, Borden decided to send one of his staff aides, Kenneth Mansfield, to talk to Oppenheimer. Oppenheimer told him he believed that city-busters like nuclear bombs had only one purpose, to deter Soviet Russia from attacking the United States. Tactical nuclear weapons were a different matter altogether. He told Mansfield that the military usefulness of the nuclear arsenal depended far more on the wisdom of the war plan and the skill to deliver it, and not on making any number of atom bombs. His deep-seated view about nuclear bombs was best expressed when he claimed that, 'The United States and the Soviet Union are as two scorpions in a bottle, each capable of killing the other, but only at the risk of his own life.'[8]

Prejudiced doubters of his philosophy, who were antagonistic to him, like Lewis Strauss, were not trained scientists or even strategic military experts. Their biased personal opinions or politics prevented them from understanding the difference between the fantasies of a conspiracy theory, compared with what was actually happening in the real world around them. Oppenheimer understood the dangers of leaving super-important decisions in the hands of a small group of men who might decide to use a nuclear deterrent.[9] But he was far too impatient with lesser intellects to bother to explain the perils of being responsible for such vast destructive powers as the H-bomb was claimed to be.

Mansfield reported back to Borden in June 1951 that he thought Oppenheimer's 'fastidious mind finds the whole notion of strategic bombing essentially clumsy and heavy-handed. It is using the sledgehammer rather than the surgeon's scalpel ...'[10]

In the meantime, further complications were building up at the discovery, by the Americans and the British, of who the enigmatic HOMER was in the encryptions of the treasure trove of secret information being unwrapped by the clever American cryptanalyst Meredith Gardner. Gardner continued to work quietly and intently in the next office to Kim Philby, who was the top British KGB agent now working in Britain's embassy in Washington D.C.

34

Conspiracy Theories

Hardly a day would go by during the Cold War without another revelation in the news media of soviet espionage, either in Canada, Britain or the United States. Each time another KGB spy was uncovered, it raised yet another conspiracy in the minds of people and nations. It was very likely that the exposure of those Soviet moles that prevented Strauss and Borden from putting aside their suspicions about Oppenheimer, even though they had no evidence against him.

Neither Strauss not Borden was prepared to listen to reason where Oppenheimer was concerned. Both seemed more concerned to wreak revenge on him for some imagined slight. Their particular suspicion about him was that he had delayed the development and manufacture of the H-bomb, although he had stated his case against it on several occasions and thought it irrelevant how many atomic or hydrogen bombs a nation possessed, since they were not militarily strategic.

In fact, had they but known it, there was secret evidence to support their attitude. As Sudoplatov described it, 'Beria said we should think how to use Oppenheimer, Fermi, Szilard, and others around them in the peace campaign against nuclear armament.'

The delay would deprive the United States of the advantage of imposing nuclear blackmail on Russia. Russia kept up a peace campaign against American nuclear superiority with an H-bomb until they could explode their own nuclear bomb in 1949. 'Through Fuchs we planned the idea that Fermi, Oppenheimer, and Szilard opposed the hydrogen bomb.' They did not know they were being used.[1]

Moscow knew that Oppenheimer would remain influential in America after the war was over, and established a friendly and confidential relationship of sympathisers rather than attempt to run him as an agent. He and Fermi and Bohr opposed violence and would therefore do everything to prevent a nuclear war, 'creating a balance of power through sharing the secrets of atomic energy'.

In Strauss and Borden's conspiracy theory, Oppenheimer had used his influence to hinder the development of an H-bomb from 1950 until 1952, even though Edward Teller and Stanislaw Ulam had solved its design problem in June 1951, and Robert had proclaimed the design was 'technically sweet'.[2]

Evidently, Oppie had a change of mind between discouraging the super bomb and endorsing it. Something seemed to have happened to open his eyes to a realisation that his Soviet friends had been using him as propaganda against the H-bomb for their own purposes. Someone had assured him that the Russians had been pursuing a double agenda that was not favourable to his own views. 'Throughout the year following the war,' wrote Pavel Sudoplatov, 'atomic espionage was our primary preoccupation.'[3]

The most likely individual to open their eyes to the realisation that they had been duped was Kitty, who had apparently engaged in discussions – most probably with Elizabeth Zarubina in Santa Fe – and heard about the power struggles within the Kremlin after Stalin's death, that would result in the execution by poisoning of Beria, and other murders to conceal the plots of premier Malenkov, who had misjudged the situation, and the rising power of Khrushchev.

None of that interested Strauss or Borden, who were searching for clues to incriminate Oppenheimer, like the fact that he had rejected Teller's suggestion to build another weapons laboratory to produce Teller's super bomb. In fact, Oppie and his colleagues on the committee had felt that it would be counterproductive to develop two different bombs simultaneously in one weapons laboratory, since the division of ideas, scientists, and labour would be likely to hold back both type of bomb.

Nevertheless, Teller had gone straight to the FBI with a list of complaints against Oppenheimer. All contributed to his main theme that Robert had hindered the development of his H-bomb. Since Teller had no realistic evidence for his complaint, he used smear tactics. Having not proved that Oppie was a communist, he now attempted to destroy his credibility by claiming he had a personality disorder: 'In his youth he was troubled with some sort of physical or mental attacks which may have permanently affected him.' Teller said that he would do anything possible to ensure that Oppenheimer's services to the government were terminated.[4]

Project Vista

Others too disagreed with Oppenheimer and were dedicated to barring him from influencing the government. In September 1951, Air Force Secretary Thomas K. Finletter told a professor of geophysics at the University of California, David Tressel Griggs, that he seriously questioned Oppenheimer's loyalty. Griggs was chief scientist for the U.S. Air Force. Neither of them had any new evidence to support their suspicions. It was just another conspiracy theory, this time that they had seen a pattern of Oppenheimer's activities that hadn't seemed right to them.

Oppenheimer, on the other hand, questioned the sanity of the leadership of the Air Force. All he saw coming from them were murderous schemes. He had seen their strategic war plan, which demanded the obliteration of Soviet cities. He was shocked at their criminal readiness to commit genocide.

When Griggs led an Air Force delegation' to a conference in Pasadena with a group of Caltech scientists in 1951, the group was asked to write a confidential report on the role nuclear weapons might play in a Soviet invasion of Europe on the ground. The report was named Project Vista. Griggs and other Air Force officers were alarmed to hear that the report was against strategic bombing, and returned the army back to battlefields of small tactical nuclear warheads, instead of city-buster thermonuclear bombs.

The situation could simply have been the usual evolution of one technology being replaced by a more advanced and effective one. Each service guarded the empowerment of its own technology until it would be swept aside as obsolete. Economist Joseph Schumpeter had called it 'creative destruction'. But the users of technology that was due for replacement never saw it objectively and hung on to it for as long as they could, like cavalrymen with their horse in an age of tanks.

Oppenheimer had been asked to contribute to chapter five of the nuclear weapons report, which maintained that thermonuclear bombs could not be used for tactical purposes on a real battlefield. It suggested that Washington should publicly establish a policy of 'no first use' of nuclear weapons. The same chapter also recommended that Air Force Command should receive only a third of the nation's supply of fissionable material; the rest should go to the army for their tactical battlefield weapons.

Griggs was angry at the recommendations. Like many emotional men, he wanted to attack the author rather than know the reasons for the recommendations.

Oppenheimer was not a member of the panel, but he had been invited to contribute and clarify the conclusions by Caltech's President Lee DuBridge, who chaired the conference. In fact those general points had been discussed many times before the atomic bomb had even been thought of, soon after the First World War, by military philosophers, strategists and tacticians, like Captain Basil Liddell Hart and T. E. Lawrence.[5]

Griggs and Finletter failed in their attempts to suppress the report. Then, in December 1951, when Oppenheimer and DuBridge visited Paris to brief NATO, they persuaded General Eisenhower of the damage a few nuclear warheads could do against Red Army tank divisions.

The U.S. Air Force did not want Eisenhower to listen to Oppenheimer's military theories, particularly as the army would benefit with a greater share of the budget than the Air Force. In fact, it would turn out to be a useful lesson for Eisenhower the soldier, who had been more of an administrator in the past, and not a good strategist; as Britain's Field Marshal Alan Brooke had often complained during the Second World War.[6]

Lewis Strauss was angry too, and wrote later to Senator Bourke Hickenlooper that 'ever since Oppenheimer and DuBridge spent some time with Gen. Eisenhower in Paris last year I have been concerned over the probability that their visit was primarily for the purpose of indoctrinating him with their plausible but specious policy on the atomic energy situation'.[7*]

---

* When Eisenhower became President of the United States in 1953, his newfound strategic sense would help him to outfox Khrushchev by targeting Moscow with guided thermonuclear missiles, with nuclear warheads aimed from nuclear submarines concealed beneath the sea.

The Air Force Chief of Staff then removed Oppenheimer's name from the Air Force list of individuals cleared for access to top secret information.

Spymaster Pavel Sudoplatov was remarkably prescient in understanding how precarious and problematic Oppenheimer's position was, when he wrote in his 1994 memoir that, 'Oppenheimer reminded me very much of our classic scientists who tried to maintain their own identity, their own world, and their total internal independence. It was a peculiar independence and an illusion, because both Kurchatov [Soviet director of their atom bomb project] and Oppenheimer were destined to be not only scientists but also directors of huge government-sponsored projects. The conflict was inevitable; we cannot judge them, because the bomb marked the opening of a new era in science, when for the first time in history scientists were required to act as statesmen ... In the 1940s, neither government was in a position to control and influence scientific progress, because there was no way to progress except to rely on a group of geniuses and adjust to their needs, demands, and extravagant behaviour. Nowadays no new development in science can be compared to the breakthrough into atomic energy in the 1940s.'

Sudoplatov went on to inform readers of the Soviet choices: 'When the government wanted to speed up the test of our first atomic bomb in 1949, Kurchatov went along with copying the American design. However, parallel work continued on the Soviet designed bomb, which was exploded in 1951. In the United States, Edward Teller assumed a similar role later, when he was put in charge of the hydrogen bomb project.'[8]

A Bad-Luck Summer

Even though the charges against Oppenheimer made by Paul and Sylvia Crouch had been thrown out of court, Oppie was urged by his lawyer Joe Volpe to collect evidence in order to refute them, since the communist conspiracy theory was still believed about him and used by those who wished him harm. He wrote to Dorothy McKibbin to meet Volpe in spring 1952 and see if she could use diaries or other notes that would contradict their allegations. She was happy to help him.

Oppenheimer's problem was how to put the facts together after ten years had passed since then. And he had prudently decided to exclude the Serbers from his evidence because Bob Serber's wife, Charlotte, had communist ties, and so did her brother and father, who had been identified by the FBI as party members.[9]

Focusing his thoughts now on spring 1941, Robert recalled that he and Kitty had been overworked, tired and unwell. She had given birth to their son, Peter, on 12 May 1941, and had taken a long time recovering from post-natal depression, still feeling weak in July – so it was highly unlikely they would have thrown a large party in their home. They had gone to their ranch, Perro Caliente, in New Mexico, to recuperate. He gave Dorothy several names to contact as witnesses who could confirm their movements.

He recalled by then that Rose and Hans Bethe had visited them. And Robert and Kitty had dropped in at his old friend Katherine Page's guest ranch. It was at about the same time he had been kicked in the knee by one of their horses in the corral, seriously enough to seek a medical examination for possible fractured bones. Then Kitty had been involved in a car accident while driving the Cadillac to the ranch from Santa Fe. A truck had stopped unexpectedly in front of her, and she had jammed on her brakes to avoid striking it. Their car was badly damaged, and she had hurt her leg.

Priscilla Greene Duffield, who had been Oppie's assistant at Los Alamos, also attempted to recall where he had been from late July to early August. She remembered he had been involved in 'all the security stuff', because she had been so impressed by how close Kitty and Oppie were, and how much he depended on her. Kitty went all around Santa Fe asking questions and making notes of dates, even of prescriptions at the Capital Pharmacy, to prove that Robert had been in New Mexico at that time in 1941.

Dorothy's investigation began to produce results when she established that Robert and Kitty had been accompanied by Frank and Jackie when they turned up at Katherine Page's ranch on the evening of Friday, 11 July, and left the following Tuesday for *Perro Caliente*. The local grocery store was able to provide her with records that proved they had bought goods there on five different occasions between 12 and 29 July. As well as pharmacy receipts, she also found the receipt for the X-rays of Robert's bruised knee at St Vincent's Hospital on 25 July. Not only did both the Bethes remember the incident clearly, but Rose had taken a photo of the horse, which she had even dated.[10]

All were submitted in evidence, with another receipt from the garage in Pecos that had repaired the damaged Cadillac. The California committee had now put together an official dossier on Oppenheimer, but had taken no action against him so far. Nevertheless, the victimisation of Robert Oppenheimer was not over.

35

The Venona Revelations

America's counter-intelligence programme, known as 'the Venona Project', continued to be decoded by the American cipher expert Meredith Gardner in Washington D.C., as he eagerly shared extracts from a newly deciphered telegram with his newfound friend Kim Philby. The extracts came from several messages between Churchill and Truman, with comments by a KGB handling officer. The project had commenced on 1 February 1943, and cryptanalysts in Britain and the United States were still attempting to decode what they perceived as a gold mine of Soviet Russia's secrets, which had been transmitted, in turn, by the NKVD, the KGB, and the GRU.

The 3,000 or more Soviet messages would eventually take thirty-seven years to decipher in their entirety. But now, for the very first time, the name of the Soviet mole embedded at a top level in Britain's Secret Service was revealed as HOMER, a code name that Gardner had been trailing for some time, wondering who was concealed beneath that pseudonym.

Philby was unsure who HOMER was. But he assumed with some certainty that it was one of the Cambridge Five KGB spies. A few months later, Gardner told him they now knew for certain that the KGB mole responsible for the leak of nuclear secrets was employed somewhere in the Foreign Office in London. Philby hurriedly sent a message from Washington to the London resident KGB agent, saying; 'I think it's Maclean.'

Philby had not entirely overcome his engaging shy stammer, which he occasionally attempted to conceal by smoking a pipe. In spite of the tensions and anxieties of living a dangerous double life, he had maintained his outwardly friendly demeanour, which appealed to both genders in an affectionate spirit of loyal comradeship. He was 'one of us', and greatly admired by his American colleagues.

The Soviet secret agent whom Meredith was busy tracking so diligently on paper, without knowing who it could be, was Kitty Oppenheimer's former client and lover, Donald Maclean, whom she had been instructed by the NKVD to supervise and encourage as his courier. Moscow Centre knew HOMER was Maclean, but decided not to confirm Philby's suspicion.

In the meantime, Philby had reconsidered the situation and decided it was not as dire as he had first thought, because HOMER could be any one of hundreds of people who'd had access in London or Washington to the secret transatlantic messages from the Kremlin. MI5 was confronted with the appalling volume of work that would have to be done in the Foreign Office to settle on one individual to accuse for revealing top secret nuclear secrets. What guarantee was there that he or Maclean could be HOMER? HOMER could be in the Foreign Office in London or anywhere else.

J. Edgar Hoover's agents in the FBI focused their search instead on the domestic staff in the British Embassy in Washington.[1] It meant that Donald Maclean need not lose any sleep worrying about being a suspect – at least not yet; although he found his double life hard to handle without the comfort of alcohol.

His Soviet handler and controller, Yuri Modin, and his superior Korovin's, reports to Moscow Centre attempted to be detached in their evaluation of the possible damage to Maclean at the HOMER revelation. And Moscow replied briefly, 'Maclean must be kept in place for as long as possible.'[2]

The Cambridge Five Spy Ring

The main reason for getting Maclean out of the country was to avoid risking that he might give away secrets about Kim Philby and the other members of the so-called Cambridge Spy Ring, if interrogated by MI5. There were other important secrets that Maclean knew about the KGB spy who had been Kitty Harris and was now Katherine Oppenheimer. He might also conceivably incriminate Robert Oppenheimer, who was vitally important to Moscow; since – according to Soviet agent Pavel Sudoplatov – 'Katherine Oppenheimer was not mentioned by name in the reports, but we worked through a woman close to Oppenheimer, and it was my understanding then and is now that the woman was his wife.'[3]

During the final months of 1950, the number of suspects who might be code-named HOMER had been narrowed down to thirty-five. By January 1951 the investigators had reduced the names to four diplomats. It reminded MI5 of the Krivitsky affair in 1937, when that head of Soviet military intelligence had defected to the United States and written a book with a number of disclosures. When debriefed on arrival in the U.S., Walter Krivitsky had disclosed that a Soviet agent was working in Britain's Foreign Office; an Old Etonian who became an Oxford graduate.[4]

Krivitsky had not been wrong. He was found shot in the head in his Washington hotel room soon afterwards.

Philby continued to monitor Meredith Gardner's inquires until the shortlist for HOMER was reduced to only three names. Philby had discussed with Guy Burgess in Washington D.C. the possibility that Maclean could be accused at any moment. What they had decided was that Maclean and the KGB should be warned of the danger through the London resident agent, since there was none in Washington.

Burgess was now working at the British embassy in Washington and living temporarily in a basement apartment at Philby's family home. Although Moscow Centre disapproved of the security risk of two Soviet agents living under one roof, Philby had persuaded them that everyone knew that he and Guy were old friends from their time at Trinity College in Cambridge, so no one would question it.

Guy had put on weight, which appeared more prominent because of his below-average height. His features had become fleshy. But he still charmed admiring audiences with his witty erudition and superior knowledge of politics and history. And he had not lost his cheeky schoolboy sense of humour.

Deciding that a telegram would be too insecure, he planned to return to London to alert the Russian Embassy about Maclean's imminent danger. The question facing him and Philby was how he could leave his work in the Washington Embassy to go abroad without causing suspicion. Burgess's flights of fancy hit on the idea of misbehaving himself to get sent back home. It would be entirely in character with his reputation for being out of control. He loved fooling people and was tempted by this bizarre game of charades.

According to Modin, who was still their handler, 'Philby and Burgess concocted the whole simple stratagem to get Guy home to England.'[5]

Their carefully scheduled plan included Guy being deliberately rude to British colleagues and influential American friends, careless with confidential documents he left scattered around on his desk with his office door open, and misbehaving by speeding in his Lincoln. After deliberately behaving oddly for a diplomat – while secretly sniggering to Philby about the horrified reactions of his audience – the Americans were glad to get rid of Burgess. After which he pretended to throw a tantrum and stormed out of the British ambassador's room. The ambassador was pleased to let him go.[6]

HOMER Exposed

Philby and Burgess's plan was to warn Maclean in London that he was in imminent danger, and then organise his defection to Moscow. Neither knew how much time they had left. If they managed to get Maclean on to an aircraft to the Soviet Union, Burgess would remain in London and on no account lose his nerve and flee with him. If Burgess were to defect with Maclean, MI5 would not be slow to realise that his close friend Philby was implicated in the affair. Guy agreed that he would be loyal and remain in London.

Since it was a race against time, it was unclear why Burgess decided to travel to England on the *Queen Mary*, instead of by air, since it would take him at least five days by sea. It may have been a matter of more relaxed security.

Anthony Blunt was becoming agitated in London, even close to breaking point, according to Modin, because he had not heard from Maclean for some time. He feared that Maclean was a weak link with his occasional alcoholic slip-ups when he lost control.

Blunt was not a communist. He was three years older than Guy, who had once been his lover and was still his friend. He had decided with the other Cambridge undergraduates, at the age of twenty-two or twenty-three, that it was essential to use whatever help was necessary from the Soviet Union to defeat Hitler and Nazi Germany. He was austere and reserved in the English manner of the upper classes, and the son of highly educated parents. His father was a Church of England cleric. Blunt frequently played the role of courier between Guy and the KGB. Behind Blunt's sangfroid was his disdainful view of the communist doctrine and the Soviet Union, which he found crass and hypocritical. He was a British patriot, and loyal to his friends.

Maclean had, meanwhile, become uneasy in the Foreign Office, on observing several signs that he might be under suspicion. His close colleagues had begun to avoid him, and confidential documents were no longer made available to him. An uncomfortable atmosphere had begun to surround him at work from day to day. He could sense that it was only a matter of time before something ugly was going to happen.

Burgess arrived in England and immediately contacted Blunt to describe the gravity of the situation. Both felt that exposure was imminent, and decided that Maclean should leave England for the Soviet Union as quickly as possible. Blunt agreed to warn Modin of the crisis right away.

Blunt appeared to be his usual calm self, although he was deeply anxious beneath his façade of inscrutability when he informed Modin that Burgess had returned to warn them that MI5's lead to HOMER now pointed directly at Maclean. He could be arrested at any moment. It was only a matter of days or hours before he would be exposed as a KGB mole and a British traitor. His interrogation could not only wipe out the entire Cambridge spy ring, but might also reveal several critical secrets about the Oppenheimers.

Modin listened silently to what he had been expecting for some time, as Blunt assured him that Donald was in such a state of nerves that he was ready to break down immediately MI5 questioned him. Even so, Modin felt he could not move without instructions from Moscow Centre. They agreed that Burgess should meet him in two days' time, and perhaps by then Guy might have come up with a novel way to ensure that everything required to be done could be carried out.

Modin signalled Korovin at the Soviet Embassy in London to contact Moscow for their orders and plans. The Centre moved fast to answer their questions, and replied; 'We agree to your organising Maclean's defection. We will receive him here and provide him with whatever he needs, if he wishes to go through with it.'[7]

Burgess was ordered to contact Maclean and convince him he had no alternative.

When Guy visited him at the Foreign Office, Donald was happy to see his old friend back in town. They chatted amiably while Burgess wrote out a message for him on a slip of paper to meet shortly at the Reform Club, as they were both sure that Donald was being heard and watched in his office.

Once at the club, Maclean told Burgess that he had been expecting a summons from the Foreign Office or MI5 any day: 'I'm being followed by the dicks.'[8]

But when Burgess told him the only course was to run for it, Maclean sagged visibly in his seat. After considering the situation wordlessly, he confessed he had no stamina for a confrontation with MI5 or the Foreign Office. He knew he was weak, but also knew he could not face months of denying everything whenever they chose to interrogate him. Melinda's new baby was due in three weeks' time – how could he possibly abandon her? He appeared to be completely helpless.

The Deciding Factor

In the meantime, Korovin and Modin took turns meeting with Blunt and Burgess. Burgess informed Korovin of his meeting with Maclean, and of Donald's confusion and hesitation. Moscow Centre's advice was: 'Homer *must* agree to defect.' Korovin told Burgess to insist.

Maclean became more agitated, confused and helpless, so that Burgess promised to find someone to go with him, since Donald evidently needed bolstering up to ensure he would see the defection through until he reached Moscow. He was simply not strong enough to face leaving home alone in his nervous state: he could no longer think clearly. And Melinda's fragile situation needed to be handled diplomatically. She was well aware of his KGB work because he had told her everything from the beginning. When Maclean explained the situation to her, she told him he must leave immediately.

But Maclean needed someone to organise and usher him through all the stages and formalities of defection, and keep him out of trouble so that he reached Moscow. Burgess was instructed to accompany him as a travelling companion, but was taken aback at the suggestion, feeling, uneasily, that he would never be able to return to England afterwards. He was anxious and insecure when he told them that they all knew he could only live in London. Korovin sought to reassure Burgess that all he had to do was accompany his friend, and then return to London afterwards to make it clear he'd had no intention of defecting. Why should anyone imagine his departure was anything more than a gesture to an old friend?

Modin was sceptical: he could not imagine that Burgess would swallow Korovin's glib story, and wondered if there was something more behind his boss's attitude. As he would discover, there was: Burgess was far too indiscreet to be left behind. Moscow Centre wanted him out, as well as Maclean. So Burgess finally, almost fatalistically, gave in to the idea that he was needed to bolster his friend's resolve by accompanying him on his flight, without considering where and when he and Maclean would part company.

Korovin knew that Burgess had lost most of his value to Moscow Centre by now, when their priority was to prevent Maclean from being interrogated by MI5. Philby had also added to the urgency by making contact with Burgess from Washington with a confusing message that ended in, 'It's getting very hot over here.'

Philby's warning seems to have been the deciding moment for Burgess, who was already overwrought. He and Modin considered alternative options while they strode through Regent's Park. Trains and planes had to be avoided because police would be watching out for Maclean at each border. Since he was already under investigation by MI5, the immigration services would have been informed. And it was impossible to forge false documents for him in England at such short notice. The idea of a rendezvous on the coast with a submarine was raised, and immediately rejected for the same reason.

It was the cool-headed Anthony Blunt who came up with the most practical solution. He recommended a cruise ship sailing from a southern port along the

French coast. One of the shipping lines left on Fridays and tied up at several Continental ports over the weekend. Blunt pointed out that immigration controls for those excursions hardly existed, as the weekend cruises had proved popular with senior civil servants and businessmen who brought along their secretary or mistress, whom they would take ashore for a night or a weekend.

Modin and Korovin studied travel and cruise brochures, and chose a suitable ship named the *Falaise*. It was scheduled to leave Southampton on Friday night and cruise along the French coast for forty-eight hours. One of its stopovers was Saint-Malo. There were two berths available on 25–27 May.

One problem that arose was that Maclean had noticed he was being tailed daily by someone, but only from the Foreign Office to his train station in the evenings, and then from the station to his office each morning. It meant his daily arrivals and departures were probably watched only in London. An immediate KGB counter-surveillance operation confirmed it was the case.[9]

Burgess's Charade

In the morning of 21 May, Burgess bought two tickets for a weekend cruise to Saint-Malo in his name and that of a new acquaintance, Bernard Miller, without Miller knowing. Miller had only just arrived in London and did not intend to go to France. But Burgess had been well primed by the KGB to organise several confusing distractions to misinform anyone who might follow his trail.

The imminent crisis sparked not only Burgess's loyalty, but a need for self-sacrifice. Those lifelong Peter Pans who had been emotionally damaged by the institutions of the establishment in their youth had nowhere else to turn to for kindness or help, except themselves. And Guy was determined not to let down his friends.

He bought a new suitcase at Gieves in Old Bond Street, accompanied by Miller, and also chose several other travelling items, while he chatted with the staff about his holiday plans. As well as creating a diversion, he took care to plant evidence of his innocence to be spotted by investigators when he returned, since that was what he intended to do.

That evening, he drove in the rental car to the Macleans' home in Tatsfield, Surrey, where Melinda was preparing a thirty-eighth birthday dinner for her husband. Burgess provided a cover story for her about his visit under an assumed name. Then Maclean went up to kiss his children goodnight at about 9 p.m., leaving Burgess waiting for him downstairs. When Maclean came down to bid Melinda good-bye, he told her he was going to end the evening in a pub with his friend as part of a cover story. Then the two men left in the rental car and disappeared into the darkness of the night.

Maclean's escape took place shortly after Foreign Secretary Herbert Morrison gave approval to interrogate him on Monday morning. Nothing could be done for the moment because they didn't have an arrest warrant.[10]

Alert warnings sent out about the missing diplomats went only to British intelligence. That was because Britain's Secret Service was determined never to disclose the results of Venona, as the decoding programme was top secret. And Venona was the sole evidence against code name HOMER.[11]

The news media were determined to create a conspiracy theory over the evidence that Maclean had fled on Friday evening and his interrogation was planned for Monday morning. They saw it as a suspicious indication that there must be a Soviet mole at the highest level of government or the intelligence services. But it was nothing more than a leap of the imagination.

As soon as the tabloids heard of the scandal of Burgess's and Maclean's defection to Soviet Russia, they picked on sex to sell more newspapers, and smeared and vilified them as drunkards and perverted homosexual traitors. It would be the image pasted on them by the tabloids for years to come, since homosexuality was still a criminal offence in Britain.

Heroes and Traitors

Older politicians like Harold Macmillan, Anthony Eden, and Stewart Menzies, the Chief of Britain's Secret Service and MI6, who had served as young officers on the Western Front in the First World War, viewed Burgess and Maclean differently from press reporters and their editors who were looking for scandals to increase their advertising revenues. Those old patriots evidently held them in silent esteem as among the first of the few who had dedicated themselves to standing up against Nazi Germany. As an American communist summarised the situation, 'We are working for universal truth and justice – so how could it be treason?'

The crux of the matter was that if Maclean had been left free to babble about his past experiences with Kitty, she might be seen as doing for Robert Oppenheimer what she had done for him – been his comforter and inspiration, and consoled him in the belief that he was being loyal to the ideals of the founding fathers of the United States and their constitution, which promised the pursuit of happiness and justice for all.

36

Witch-hunt

In the spring of 1950, J. Edgar Hoover had encouraged his agents to continue investigating Oppenheimer in every possible way, in the belief that he would be tried for perjury when more evidence could be shown to convict him. Hoover's old friend Senator McCarthy still led his House Un-American Activities Committee with political energy and a flair for publicity by confronting rich celebrities. Oppenheimer also had to contend with the Justice Department. All had their sights trained on him now.

FBI agents interviewed him on two occasions that spring in his Princeton office. According to Hoover's operatives, he co-operated with them politely and patiently. But Robert was openly worried that his name would be linked to the Communist Party and revealed at a public trial. He was particularly concerned about an alleged Soviet spy named Weinberg whom he had seen at a Physicist Society conference in 1949, soon after Weinberg was targeted by the Crouches and HUAC, who had identified Robert in a witch-hunt as 'Scientist X'.

The relationship between Oppenheimer as 'Scientist X' and the defendant had been ambiguous, and based largely on the HUAC suspicions hovering over Weinberg. Who knew what to believe? Was he another communist friend or a Communist Party enforcer? Oppenheimer edged away from any contact with Weinberg for fear of being tarnished by McCarthy's smear tactics. Weinberg seemed as stunned and confused as Robert was, but he knew he was being targeted for discussing the atom bomb project with Steve Nelson in 1943, and Nelson was a dedicated and zealous communist. Weinberg did not know that FBI agents had illegal wiretaps of their conversation.

What all of the victims who were smeared by McCarthy were afraid of was that the mix of innuendo, lies, and false accusations by others seeking to save their own skins from the Committee's and FBI probes could implicate them and destroy their reputations forever. They had family commitments to consider, and the real possibility of losing their careers: what then? Weinberg had been astonished at a false claim by the *Milwaukee Journal* that he had been a courier for the Soviet Union and had passed on a sample of uranium 235. It was a complete invention, but likely to stick. He felt trapped and helpless.[1]

Oppenheimer did, too. But the Justice Department had little real evidence they could use in court: it was all supposition. As the illegal wiretap was unacceptable as evidence in a court of law, the case against Weinberg collapsed. Despite that, they rounded up a second jury in the spring of 1952. But their only evidence was from Paul Crouch, who was now seen as unreliable. As for 'naming names', which was the seductive way for the inquisitors to trap the innocent, Weinberg refused to tell them anything that might convict anyone, including himself or Oppenheimer.

Robert was interviewed again about Crouch's false allegation. He denied knowing the Crouches, or Gregori Kheifetz (whom he had only known as Mr Brown). And he denied the claim that Steve Nelson had ever contacted him for information about the bomb. By now, there was no attempt at friendliness or courtesy, since his interrogators had become desperate for anything they might conceivably be able to use against him and obtain press publicity for themselves. When FBI staffers were rebuked by Robert's lawyer, they replied they thought they were being nice about it.

The lawyers prosecuting Weinberg recalled one of the 'dirty tricks' used several years earlier with success by future President Richard Nixon to trap Hiss when Nixon was a young California Congressman. It was to face Oppenheimer with his accuser so that he could be trapped in an indictment for perjury. It required the Justice Department's prosecutors to repeat their questions about Crouch all over again. Robert replied that he did not know Paul or Sylvia Crouch, who had claimed he had organised a Communist Party meeting in his Washington home, when in fact he had been in New Mexico at that time. The Justice Department lawyers then told Oppenheimer's lawyers that Paul Crouch was waiting in the next room to identify Oppenheimer. They requested the defendant's agreement to bring in Paul Crouch and see if either recognised the other. Robert and his lawyers agreed.

'The door then opened and Crouch walked up to Oppenheimer, shook his hand and said, 'How do you do, Dr Oppenheimer?' He then turned melodramatically to the lawyers and said that the man with whom he had just shaken hands was the same person who had been his host at a meeting in July 1941 at 10 Kenilworth Court. Crouch reiterated that Dr Oppenheimer had given a talk on the 'Communist Party propaganda line to be followed after the invasion of Russia by Hitler'.[2]

Oppenheimer and his lawyers, Volpe and Marks, were thrown off balance by the prosecuting counsel's trick and Crouch's allegations. Crouch went even further with his claims. He had evidently been well rehearsed beforehand, and described the inside of Oppenheimer's house. Crouch also claimed he had seen Oppenheimer at Ken May's housewarming party in the autumn of 1941, when Robert had danced with a Japanese girl. Oppenheimer admitted he had attended a party, which might have been at May's home. If he had thought his admission was innocent enough, he was wrong, since the incident linked him to Crouch's claim that he had seen Oppenheimer talking at that party with Joseph Weinberg, Steve Nelson and Clarence Hiskey, a physics student at Berkeley; all of whom were alleged communists.

When Crouch finally left the room, Oppenheimer repeated that he had never met the Crouches before. Then he departed with his lawyers to await the next move by the Justice Department.

One Person's Word

After another three days they learned that Weinberg had been indicted. But nothing was mentioned about Crouch's allegations or the alleged Communist Party meeting at Kenilworth. That was because Marks and Volpe had lobbied the Justice Department to drop the Kenilworth allegation from the indictment. But there was still Joe Weinberg's trial for perjury, and Oppenheimer was subpoenaed as a witness, so he had no choice but to be manipulated and victimised all over again.

The *San Francisco Chronicle* spread the story that government prosecutors said today 'that Dr Joseph Weinberg attended a Communist Party meeting in Berkeley, Calif. in a "residence believed to have been ... occupied by J. Robert Oppenheimer."'

Oppenheimer was called into the court next day as a defence witness. If Weinberg were convicted on a charge of perjury, it would open the way for Oppenheimer to be prosecuted on the same charge. But it was one person's word against another's. Marks and Volpe did their best to get their client untangled from the case, arguing that it was surely unnecessary to embarrass him and subject him to the grief. Why help the communists' game by smearing such an important scientist as Dr Oppenheimer? But, in the end, there was no choice.

Weinberg's defence counsel opened by stating that the case could be reduced to asking whether to believe a criminal like Crouch or the word of a distinguished scientist and outstanding American ...' In the end, the Justice Department suddenly realised it had no case against Oppenheimer and withdrew the subpoena. The case proceeded against Weinberg, his trial ended on 5 March 1953 with Weinberg being acquitted.

The case had cost Oppenheimer a great deal of anguish and stress, and $9,000 in legal fees. It was a lot of money in the 1950s. And the frantic jungle warfare was not over yet.

A Policy of Candour

Lewis Strauss had generously funded Eisenhower's presidential campaign and, in the usual way in American politics, had been duly rewarded for his support by being appointed as the President's adviser on atomic energy, and then further elevated to chairman of the Atomic Energy Commission. Now he took every possible opportunity to turn the President against Oppenheimer's recommendation for openness concerning the amount of atomic bombs that the United States was presently stockpiling. He managed to impress on the President his suspicion that 'Dr Oppenheimer was not to be trusted'.

Strauss also dropped in on FBI headquarters to warn one of Hoover's aides that Oppenheimer had an appointment to brief the President and the National Security Council, and Strauss was concerned at Oppenheimer's activities. 'He had just heard that Oppenheimer had hired a suspected communist named David Hawkins to work at Los Alamos in 1943.' Oppenheimer was also sponsoring a brilliant mathematician named Felix Browder who was the son of Earl Browder, who had been the leader of the Communist Party of America. Strauss also emphasised to the FBI how Oppenheimer had delayed work on the H-bomb against America's interests.[3]

Although the Board of Trustees voted against appointing Browder, Oppenheimer had already committed himself to hiring him. That type of dismissive high-handedness from Oppenheimer enraged Strauss.

> The initiation of Strauss's campaign to destroy Oppenheimer's reputation can thus be precisely dated: it began on the afternoon of May 25, 1953, with his appointment with the president. Ike would recall later that Strauss 'came back to him time and again about the Oppenheimer matter.' On this occasion, he told Eisenhower that 'he could not do the job at the AEC if Oppenheimer was connected in any way with the program.'[4]

Robert had already made his appointment with the new president, who watched with fascination and suspicion as Oppenheimer briefed the National Security Council on 27 May, having brought Lee DuBridge with him. He took five hours lecturing them and answering questions. The President watched how he held them all spellbound. Ike thanked Robert at the end, without mentioning Strauss's suspicions or his claim that he could not work with Oppenheimer. Strauss had sown the seeds of doubt in his mind as his first strike at Robert's integrity, and they had taken root. Ike was heard to remark sometime later that 'he did not completely trust' Oppenheimer.

37

The Problem of Survival

Robert Oppenheimer had served the United States Government for twelve years by now. He had reached a point of revulsion for the Air Force people who could think of nothing but planning to destroy masses of lives and cities with bigger and bigger bombs; so that – after all the attempts to discredit him – he found it difficult to treat them as intelligent, or even reasonable, adversaries. He would not step down to their level of self-deception, flights of fancy and false conclusions by joining in their delusions. He had become tired of arguing with them or justifying his conclusions. Nor was he prepared to play political or diplomatic games with them. It was a problem of his superior intellect and his high ideals that he simply wished to dismiss them from his mind and avoid wasting any more time with them. Even after the Red Scare tactics used by Senator Joseph McCarthy and the FBI to destroy the careers of any number of people, Robert still underestimated his enemies, because he viewed them as not worth his attention, rather than as dangerous antagonists.

Evidently, he still thought of himself as a lone frontiersman standing up for what he thought was right, or the 'One Just Man'. It was difficult to explore his complex mind to imagine exactly how he viewed his situation at a time when he was still admired by most people as an American genius and hero of nuclear science. Nor was it possible to penetrate Kitty's veneer, because of her complicated past and her mysterious connections with the American Communist Party and the Kremlin, about which little or nothing was so far known.

To judge from his self-confident writing in the Vista Report, in which he continued to pursue his military philosophy in 1951 that atomic and hydrogen bombs were not tactical weapons, and that launching guided missiles with nuclear warheads was more strategically effective, his visionary outlook had raised him well above the out-of-date arguments of his critics, which – through complacency and arrogance – he dismissed. As he had once said mistakenly of Strauss, 'He is not greatly cultivated but will not obstruct things.'[1]

Griggs and Finletter were also concerned at his influence over a classified MIT report by the 1952 Lincoln Summer Study Group that recommended 'long range interceptors, armed with relatively long-range guided missiles' as the best way to defend the country against nuclear attack. The U.S. Air Force, which was controlled by Strategic Air Command (SAC), was afraid that funding for air defence would reduce funding for its retaliatory force – which was what the Lincoln report recommended. Bomber pilots considered their planes were more important than artillery using nuclear projectiles, whereas Oppenheimer had apparently suggested that defending America with guided missiles was more efficient than bombing an enemy.

When Griggs complained to Rabi that Oppenheimer was impeding the development of the Super Bomb, Rabi defended Robert and told Griggs that if he read the minutes of the Atomic Energy Commission's thinking and discussions, he might understand how objective and fair Oppenheimer's influence was. Griggs agreed to Rabi setting up a meeting between him and Oppenheimer at Princeton on 23 May 1952.

Griggs met with Robert at 3.30 p.m. But it was not a meeting between equals. If Oppenheimer intended to get rid of Griggs and Finletter once and for all simply by producing a copy of the AEC General Advisory Committee's 1949 report, 'with its controversial recommendation against development of the H-bomb', he did not succeed in satisfying Griggs. On the contrary, Griggs became even angrier than before. Evidently he felt patronised, like Strauss did. Oppie would have done better to use his well-known charm. But he was impatient with mediocrity. 'He saw in Griggs just another idiotic pretender to power … He would not stoop to defend himself before such a man …'[2]

Griggs told Oppenheimer that he had heard his loyalty questioned and had discussed him as a security risk with Secretary Finletter and Air Force Chief of Staff Hoyt Vandenberg. At which Robert thought that Griggs must be paranoid. And Griggs left even more convinced that Oppenheimer was dangerous. When Finletter's aides finally thought it time for the two antagonists to meet again and iron out their differences informally, Robert and Finletter met for lunch. But neither gave an inch, and Finletter told the Joint Committee on Atomic Energy a few weeks later that it was an open question as to whether Oppenheimer was 'a subversive'.[3]

The Problem of Survival

The question of who was looking down on whom arose again when Joseph McCarthy attacked Adlai Stevenson, governor of Illinois, because he had been a character witness for Alger Hiss, who was alleged to have been a communist spy. Stevenson had been chosen as the Democratic Party candidate for the 1952 presidential election. It was a dirty campaign, with Stevenson defending himself from innuendo by maintaining that 'the whole notion of loyalty inquisitions is a national characteristic of the police state, not of democracy'.

Richard Nixon attempted to link Stevenson with the Soviet spy ring, and as good as succeeded. For whatever Stevenson said afterwards would have no value once he had been tarred with the same brush as Hiss. He called McCarthy 'a phony patriot', but it was feeble repartee in comparison with what they accused him of. The FBI continued to smear him by filing a nineteen-page memorandum listing material to damage his campaign, alleging he was a Marxist and homosexual.

In that climate of public opinion, Stevenson's defeat by the more popular Eisenhower was inevitable. Adlai Stevenson exemplified the power of lies to destroy an opponent's reputation and turn him into a two-time loser. The same fate hung over Robert Oppenheimer, who was surrounded by enemies using lies to tear him down from his pedestal.

Although Eisenhower was urged by his White House aides to expose McCarthy's reign of threats, blackmail, and character assassinations, the anti-communist hysteria McCarthy had whipped up was at its height, and Ike felt sick to his stomach to engage with the demagogue. Much like Oppenheimer faced with similar bigotry, Ike replied, 'I will not – *I refuse* – to get down in the gutter with that guy.'[4]

When Oppie met up with his old friends, Conant and DuBridge, for lunch as the Cosmos Club, early in May 1952, they had remarked on their poor reputation in Washington. Some of the boys, they noted, 'have their axe out' for all three of us on the GAC of the AEC. They 'claim we have dragged our heels on the H-bomb … Dark words about Oppie!'[5]

Conscious that there was a mood to remove them from the advisory committee of the Atomic Energy Commission, all three resigned. Oppenheimer decided to return to physics.

Despite his resignation, Oppenheimer was persuaded to take on a consultancy to the AEC, automatically extending his top secret clearance for a further year. Then, in April, he agreed to accept an invitation by Secretary of State Dean Acheson to join a special State Department Panel of Consultants on Disarmament. Sitting on the panel that had elected him Chairman were Vannevar Bush, Dartmouth College President John Sloan Dickey, CIA Deputy Director Allen Dulles, and Joseph Johnson, president of the Carnegie Endowment for International Peace.

Acheson also brought in McGeorge Bundy, who was a professor of government at Harvard. He and Oppie took an immediate liking to each other, and Bundy treated the great icon with reverence. He was a younger man at age thirty-three, and very articulate, witty and with broad and well-balanced views on the world and American politics, as he would have to be for each to enjoy the other's company so enthusiastically.

The Face-Off

Bundy already understood the fragile situation, and quickly learned that the face-off between the United States and Soviet Russia was one of two poised scorpions of a similar size and weight that presented a problem of survival – as Oppenheimer had described the circumstances. Oppie knew that Edward Teller and his team expected to test a preliminary design for his H-bomb later in the year; so he was interested when Vannevar Bush proposed that, before it was too late, Washington and Moscow should be encouraged to agree to a total ban on testing any thermonuclear devices. They discussed Bush's suggestion further with James Conant at Bundy's Cambridge home in June.

Conant was only an observer, but understood what it seemed no one outside of Oppie's circle could conceive; that although outsiders continually harped on about completing the development of an H-bomb, and using it, what was really at stake was the threat of destruction of every major city in the United States by the enemy. The problem was surviving. America and Soviet Russia were still poised, eye-to-eye, with stingers raised in warning and ready to strike. It might involve another war.

Nevertheless, Teller and his colleagues continued to prepare their H-bomb test, which was expected in the autumn. It was tempting fate. As Bush viewed the situation, 'A thermonuclear arms race could be stopped before it began'.[6]

Conant was appalled at the attitude of the American military establishment, who relied solely on using an H-bomb for victory in a total war. He proposed a 'no-first-use' policy. They advised Acheson accordingly: 'if the Russians learn that a thermonuclear device is in fact possible, and that we know how to make it, their work is likely to be considerably intensified.' The Russians would also be able to analyse the H-bomb test to determine the size and magnitude of the device, which was code-named 'Mike'.

They knew their attempt to stop the H-bomb test would be strongly opposed by the Air Force and on 9 October 1952, Truman's National Security Council rejected their proposal. Three weeks afterwards, the United States exploded a thermonuclear bomb in the Pacific that entirely erased the island of Elugelab in the Marshall Islands from the map.

Conant withdrew from the H-bomb scene in a state of despair, deciding that Washington had become a lunatic asylum, while the other members of the panel, including Oppenheimer, considered whether or not to resign in protest, since the government was disinterested in listening to the advice of experts. Oppenheimer and Bundy drafted a final report for Secretary of State Acheson's State Department's disarmament panel. But the secret report that warned the Government that nuclear weapons would threaten the United States was circulated among only a handful of the newly installed President Eisenhower's officials. Oppenheimer and Bundy did acknowledge that a nuclear stalemate might evolve into an uneasy stability in which both nations might decide that the price of suicide was too great.

What their report sought was total candour to inspire a spirit of trust, instead of continued secrecy and suspicion. Oppenheimer hoped the government would see the sense in what was Niels Bohr's policy of openness, rather than blindly attempt to keep ahead of the Russians in a nuclear arms race.

When Eisenhower invited Conant to become the U.S. High Commissioner to West Germany in 1953, he accepted the new position eagerly, to escape from the madhouse that was Washington. But Oppenheimer could not escape from his Washington enemies so easily.

From the Sublime to the Ridiculous

When Oppenheimer returned to Washington from giving the BBC's prestigious Reith Lectures in England in December 1953, he received a message from Lewis Strauss, who was now the chairman of the Atomic Energy Commission. Strauss requested a meeting in his office. Oppenheimer arrived on the afternoon of Monday, 21 December, most probably still elated by the adulation of his admirers in London, where he had spoken earnestly about the great minds of early scientific discoveries and the lack of boundaries to science.

Perhaps the closest he got in his lectures to the nuclear bomb predicament were his comments about innovation: 'The greatest of the changes that science has brought is the acuity of change; the greatest novelty the extent of novelty. Short of rare times of great disaster, civilisations have not known such rapid alteration in the conditions of their life, such rapid flowering of many varied sciences, such rapid changes in the ideas we have about the world and one another. What has been true in the days of a great disaster or great military defeat for one people at one time is true for all of us now, in the sense that our ends have little in common with our beginnings. Within a lifetime what we learned at school has been rendered inadequate by new discoveries and new inventions; the ways that we learned in childhood are only very meagrely adequate to the issues that we must meet in maturity.'[7]

He had not expected that Strauss would be accompanied by the AEC manager, Kenneth Nichols, and a general who had supervised the Trinity test with General Groves, who barely attempted to welcome him politely. Oppenheimer found himself back again in the mediocre world of self-important functionaries with small-minded ambitions who were jealous of superior intellects, abilities and skills. They informed him that the AEC had drafted a formal letter of charges against him to justify why he should be questioned by an AEC Committee. They informed him that his security clearance would be withdrawn in thirty days, unless he requested a hearing.[8]

Oppenheimer was stunned. He watched while Strauss and Nichols summarised some twenty-four formal charges made against him of 'derogatory information', which included a description of all his alleged left-wing activities in the 1930s; a list of undesirable associates, including his former girlfriend Jean Tatlock, his wife Kitty, his brother Frank, and his sister-in-law.

Also documented were suspicious, contradictory, and misleading statements allegedly made by Robert to security officials in August 1943 regarding Communist Party members, like Giovanni Rossi Lomanitz and Haakon Chevalier, as well as others. The final charge was that Oppenheimer had opposed the development of the H-bomb on moral grounds, and had done his best to impede its development.

Oppenheimer carefully reviewed all the charges in the AEC's letter of notification, while Strauss informed him of his rights under the Atomic Energy Commission's security procedures. Then they calmly discussed the relative merits of whether Oppenheimer should resign or face a legal hearing. After which Oppenheimer left the Commission's premises in a daze.

38

The Hidden Struggle for the H-bomb

Economist F. A. Hayek's definition of freedom begins with an analysis of a free society, while attempting to define personal freedom. He claimed that 'one is free when one is not coerced'. Coercion, Hayek maintained 'occurs when one man's actions are made to serve another man's will, not for his own but for the other's purpose'.[1]

Oppenheimer had so far preserved his freedom by refusing to be coerced, but he had done so at a heavy cost. Considering all of his huge number of reports and recommendations about the A-bomb and the super H-bomb, he appears, with hindsight, to have been totally and genuinely absorbed in their intellectual, strategic, tactical, and moral problems, and very much his own man in the Libertarian ethic. It had always been important to him to be independent. And it appears that as soon as he felt that any communists might be taking advantage of his reasonableness and leading him astray, he immediately detached himself from them to be sure of going his own way.

As a consequence of Robert's independent nature, he was genuinely unaware of Strauss's personal feelings towards him, and his single-minded determination to seek revenge for several real or imaginary offences against his self-importance.

Strauss now began to organise a press campaign against Oppenheimer. He used *Time* magazine, *Life* magazine, and *Fortune* to attack him. All three influential magazines were owned by Henry Luce. The articles also attacked the influence of scientists on the government's defence policy. One of them in *Fortune* magazine, in May 1953, described 'The Hidden Struggle for the H-Bomb'. It claimed to be 'The Story of Dr Oppenheimer's Persistent Campaign to reverse U.S. Military Strategy'.[2]

The article by an unnamed author claimed that Oppenheimer had influenced the Project Vista study by Caltech, to question the morality of a strategy of atomic retaliation. The anonymous author quoted Air Force Secretary Finletter in charging that 'there was a serious question of the propriety of scientists trying to settle such grave national issues alone, inasmuch as they bear no responsibility for the successful execution of war plans'.

The essence of the article sought to expose the parts played by Oppenheimer, David Lilienthal, and James Conant in trying to block the development of the H-bomb, and how Lewis Strauss had 'saved the day', etcetera. It accused Oppenheimer of a 'conspiracy to defeat the idea that the strategic bombing unit of the Air Force has the answer to our defense ...'

Lilienthal described it as 'another nasty and obviously inspired article attacking Robert Oppenheimer …' Oppenheimer, Rabi and DuBridge met with C.D. Jackson at the Cosmos Club about the unwarranted attack; after which Jackson – who was Henry Luce's right-hand man – told Luce he agreed with them that *Time* magazine's Washington bureau chief had engaged in 'an unwarranted anti-Oppenheimer crusade'.

Without Candour

That was by no means the end of Lewis Strauss's mean-spirited personal crusade against Robert Oppenheimer. He had now created a public platform from which he intended not only to destroy Oppie's reputation, but to go for the kill.

Oppenheimer's openness speech was published in *Foreign Affairs* on 19 June 1953, and given considerably more prominence by the *New York Times* and the *Washington Post*. He was quoted as having said that without candour, the American public would be 'talked out of reasonable defense measures'. He added that only the President was above the bickering, noise and lies about the strategic position of the atom bomb.

Strauss instantly went to the President to protest at the White House at Oppenheimer's 'dangerous' article. But he found that Eisenhower had cleared Oppie's article and was in general agreement with his argument. Ike added in a press conference on 8 July that he agreed with Oppenheimer's view that more candour was needed about nuclear weapons.

Oppenheimer had intended to open up the subject of nuclear weapons to public debate with his article, which was exactly what happened. 'Candour was necessary precisely because the public ought to be frightened at the prospect of an endless arms race.'

On one hand, Ike had to think like a soldier, but as President he did not want to scare the country to death. It was the old conflict between military necessity and political expediency, but in this case struggling in the conscience of one man.[3]

> Ike understood Oppenheimer's vivid rendering of the two major powers as 'two scorpions in a bottle.' Eisenhower had seen the Disarmament Panel report and he found it thoughtful and wise. Highly skeptical of nuclear weapons, he told one of his key White House aides, C.D. Jackson – who had been Henry Luce's right-hand man at Time-Life – that 'atomic weapons strongly favor the side that attacks aggressively and *by surprise*. This the United States will never do: and let me point out that we never had any of this hysterical fear of *any nation* until atomic weapons appeared on the scene.'[4]

The White House staffers were agonised with the problem of relying heavily on nuclear weapons and a policy of openness, and Ike agreed with some of Oppie's ideas, while Strauss continued stubbornly to disagree with the President. What Strauss wanted was to pursue his personal vendetta against Oppenheimer at all costs.

At the beginning of August 1953, Jackson and Strauss spoke over cocktails. After which Jackson made a note in his diary, 'Very relieved to get from Strauss his categorical denial any feuding between him and Oppenheimer and any reluctance pursue Candor, except for stockpile arithmetic.'

Despite Jackson's impression, newspaper headlines at the end of that month encouraged Strauss's appetite for revenge: 'Reds Test H-Bomb'. Only nine months after the American test, the American public was told that the Russians had been able to replicate their success,

In fact, Russia's bomb was not a true hydrogen bomb at all. Nor could it be dropped from an aircraft. But the impression created by the news media caused a new scare that the Soviet Union was about to overtake the United States with its nuclear weapons. It provided another opportunity for Strauss to prevent Oppenheimer's recommendation for openness from being implemented.

Eisenhower was obliged by events to modify his call for candour. In his speech to the United Nations on 8 December 1953, he proposed that the U.S. and the Soviet Union should 'contribute fissionable materials to an international effort to develop peaceful nuclear energy power plants'. The Administration planned to begin cutting defence spending on conventional weapons and increasing its nuclear arsenal.

It was a temporary public relations victory for the West, which retarded any idea of candour. The friction between the two nations was producing the type of nuclear arms race that Oppenheimer had wished to avoid all along, while Strauss eagerly encouraged it. Although the Russians had managed to steer the agenda again, Moscow made no response. Without the public knowing the inferiority of the bomb they had tested, their 'one-upmanship' gave an impression that they controlled world events. It strengthened Strauss's hand to maintain nuclear secrecy while the U.S. built H-bombs in increasing numbers.

Clearing His Name

Oppie had been considerably shaken by his personal clash with Strauss, which had prompted his decision whether to resign or be publicly vilified. Resignation would be interpreted by the media as an admission of guilt. Or he could fight Strauss in open court to retrieve his reputation.

As soon as he had left Strauss's office, after being offered the unattractive alternatives, he had phoned his lawyer's wife, Anne Wilson Marks, who had been his assistant. Hearing in his voice that he was evidently worried and unsettled, she drove to his home. Her husband, Herb Marks, soon followed. Then Joe Volpe, Herb's partner, joined them and Kitty. Oppie was evidently shattered, but his immediate reaction was to fight back at the insult to his pride. They pointed out that there were obvious disadvantages, and spent the next hours sitting in his study over drinks while arguing the odds.[5]

At ten o'clock, Oppie suddenly stood up, looking tired and overwrought, and said he was off to bed. A moment later, they heard a huge crash upstairs. When Kitty hurried up to see what had happened, she found her husband had passed out on the bathroom floor. She had given him something in his drink to calm him, and the side effect with alcohol had knocked him right out.

Newspaper reporters called first thing in the morning to interview him, while Anne stood out resolutely in the rain to tell them he was not at home.

Oppie spent the next day with Marks and Volpe, discussing whether it was worthwhile attempting to clear his reputation or leave quietly and lose his security clearance. Volpe advised him to resign and avoid public embarrassment. But Marks and Oppie felt it would leave him looking unworthy; in which case his government career would be over and no one would be likely to listen to his advice again.

And there was another significant part of the equation to consider. It was Senator McCarthy, who was now a major power on Capitol Hill. 'He and Roy Cohen were holding hearings on "Communist Influence" in the federal government, and had already targeted the Voice of America, the Government printing Office, and the Foreign Service. Because of the damage Fuchs's spying had done at Los Alamos, it would be easy for McCarthy to attack Oppenheimer and cast him in a sinister light.'[6]

They advised him that if he did not submit to Strauss's AEC hearings, McCarthy's inquisitors would have him. That, they had to admit, would be the worst case scenario.

At the last moment on 23 December, Oppenheimer informed Strauss by letter that he would not resign, and chose to appear instead before the tribunal of the Personnel Security Board of the Atomic Energy Commission. As he carefully explained for the records, the alternative course of action 'would mean that I accept and concur in the view that I am not fit to serve the government that I have now served for some 12 years. This I cannot do.'

Strauss now had Oppenheimer exactly where he wanted him, under the eyes and interrogation of a prosecutor of his own choosing, while Nichols, the Atomic Energy Commission's general manager, began the process of organising an American inquisition against him.

HUMILIATION

39

Trial by Hysteria

Rarely, if ever, had such a brilliant scientist of such great intellect been caught in such a web of deceit, lies and intrigue, as Robert Oppenheimer was between the machinations of Strauss and his AEC, McCarthy's HUAC, Hoover's FBI, and the U.S. Justice Department. It seemed impossible that he could hope to escape their grasp. America had set justice back by 300 years, to the inquisitions of Copernicus and Galileo by the Vatican in the seventeenth century. But, for Oppie, it was a matter of integrity. Otherwise, he could have simply resigned and walked away from them all, freeing himself of the burden and anguish that awaited him from this odd array of hysterical persecutors.

Kenneth Nichols, the general manager of the AEC, told staff lawyer Harold Green that Oppenheimer was a 'slippery sonuvabitch, but we're going to get him this time'.[1]

Two FBI agents visited Oppenheimer's home on Christmas Eve to recover any remaining confidential or secret documents he still possessed. The AEC informed him on the same day that they questioned whether his employment on any AEC work 'will endanger the common defense and security and whether such continued employment is clearly consistent with the interests of the national security'. In confirming the AEC's charges against him, FBI staff included all the old 'derogatory information', from their files, including Oppenheimer's known connections to the Communist Party of California, and his state of confusion over Haakon Chevalier, and his opposition to the development of the H-bomb.

Most of it had been brushed aside long ago as unimportant by General Groves, except for allegations about the super hydrogen bomb that came much later. The same applied to when the AEC had given him security clearance in 1947. It all boiled down to an autocratic philosophy of trashing anyone who disagreed with the establishment. The hysteria caused by the McCarthy inquisitions had made everyone suspicious of conspiracies, by equating dissension with disloyalty and even treason.[2]

Nevertheless, the political vendetta would be judged by an AEC security panel appointed by Lewis Strauss, who hoped it would be endorsed and taken up afterwards by the media and a court of law.

Oppenheimer had to work seriously and urgently to defend himself. Signs of his preparation were seen by his secretary Verna Hobson, when he and Kitty strode into his office for an earnest discussion, after which he confided his problem to his secretary, as if laying out his provisional defence before her. For an hour and a half he narrated a summary of his life, from childhood to his youth and the present, apparently as a panorama of events that had influenced his attitudes. It was the first time he had ever exposed his private life so thoroughly to anyone, in order to rehearse it before his trial.

He had thirty days to prepare his defence. Most importantly he had to establish a legal team. He approached his old friends Marks and Volpe, who advised him to obtain a skilled trial lawyer. They ended up by recommending William Lloyd Garrison, who agreed to defend him. Garrison possessed a prestigious reputation and was a member of the board of the Civil Liberties Union. The first thing he did was extend the date of the hearing.

Illegal Wiretaps

Strauss held several trump cards in his hand, the best of which was that the FBI kept him continually informed of Oppenheimer's defence plans through their illegal wiretaps, so that Strauss could constantly improve his own plans accordingly. FBI agents listened in to Kitty on her phone on 2 January 1954, and heard her try unsuccessfully to find out if Dean Acheson might know what was going on, while Strauss knew most, or all of it, as the glue at the centre of the web he had woven with care to catch Oppenheimer. As well as the daily summaries of their illegal wiretaps that he was being fed by the FBI, Strauss knew that Oppenheimer's lawyers would never know what was in the files on him, because they did not have security clearance.

Strauss would be the one who selected the members of the board at the hearings, and they spent a full week studying the contents of the full FBI files with all their innuendo, rumour and gossip, and derogatory information and misinformation. Everything was in Strauss's favour. And he made sure that Oppenheimer and his lawyers were not offered any of the normal rights given to defendants in the law courts.

Economist and political theorist F. A. Hayek was concerned 'with that condition of men in which coercion of some by others is reduced as much as is possible in society'. That was the way of the Founding Fathers of the United States who established its character. They knew full well that human beings are vulnerable to self-deception, flights of fancy, and jumping to conclusions. The corruption of America's institutions at that time would have come as a greater shock to Oppenheimer than to more cynical people. He had managed to shed any coercion by the Communist Party and the Kremlin, only to find he was drawing all the leading bigots and narrowly self-important rogues to focus their attentions on blackmailing him into submission. Strauss was well aware that the FBI wiretaps were illegal, and did not care.[3]

By that time, Robert had got into the habit of scrutinising every room of every home he entered to search for some kind of microphone concealed behind pictures hanging on the walls, because he finally knew he was being overheard. FBI agents also monitored the homes of others connected in some way to Robert or Kitty.

Strauss chose Roger Robb from Washington to lead the case against Oppenheimer. He was known as an aggressive trial lawyer who was successful at cross-examining defendants and witnesses. Strauss not only provided him with information about Oppenheimer, but sent him sporadic tips on how to question specific individuals from what he knew about them from the FBI files.

Robert studied all the AEC charges carefully in order to be able to answer them at the hearing, while Garrison listed possible witnesses and rejected those about whom he felt unsure, like Teller. Kitty, who had learned to be a street-fighter when she'd worked on menial jobs for the Communist Party, and Robert's secretary, Verna Hobson, thought that Garrison was far too gentlemanly, instead of planning to fight aggressively against the dirty tricks piling up against his client.

On the other hand, Einstein thought Robert ought to have simply resigned. His own experience of the Nazis in Austria, Germany and Hungary had made him wary of being caught in an enemy's gunsights. And he could see in McCarthyism the sinister shadow cast by the Nazi propaganda in Germany. But Oppenheimer loved America and did not wish to lose his place or influence by taking a half-hearted stand and being swept aside from major events. He felt certain that the United States needed his knowledge and influence.

On 2 March 1954, Garrison and Marks told Strauss that Oppie was beginning to think it might be wise to compromise, and they discussed a possible deal. But Strauss had no desire for a settlement, and requested Robert's resignation in writing as the only other option. At which Oppenheimer instantly reverted to his previous fighting position.

Meanwhile, rumours of the imminent hearing had spread, and friends dropped by in support. 'I think the whole thing is damn nonsense,' Oppie told them. But DuBridge replied that if it were just damn nonsense they could fight it – unfortunately, it went far deeper than that.

The time came when the Oppenheimers had to think of the safety of the children, and put them on the train to Rochester, New York, to stay with their old friends the Hempelmanns, while the hearings took place. Who knew what might happen to them otherwise, as a climate of treason was being brought to the boil by Strauss?

The AEC Hearings

Lewis Strauss was eager for the hearings to start, and feared that his quarry might escape from the United States in the meantime. He warned the Justice Department of the possibility. He was also anxious that the McCarthy hearings might take Oppenheimer's fate out of his hands and into HUAC's. When attacked by the esteemed CBS-TV commentator Edward Murrow, McCarthy claimed that the U.S. H-bomb project had been sabotaged. Strauss could see how his case against

Oppenheimer could easily be snatched from him by the Un-American Activities Committee.

Nevertheless, his dreams of revenge against Oppenheimer appeared to be in the course of realisation on 12 April 1954, when the Atomic Energy Committee's hearing board arrived at the old two-storey edifice known as Building T-3, on 16th Street and Constitution. It was situated on a Mall near the Washington Monument, where Room 2022 had been prepared as a temporary courtroom.[4]

The AEC tribunal sat behind a long table at one end of the long rectangular room, consisting of Gordon Gray the chairman, and Ward Evans and Thomas Morgan. Their importance was embellished by piles of black binders on the mahogany table, containing confidential and top-secret FBI files that Oppenheimer's lawyers had not been provided with. It was the first shock of the day for his defence counsellors. One of Oppenheimer's defence team, Allan Ecker recalled, 'they knew what was in there. We did not know what was in there … The proceeding was skewed at the outset.'

Another question in the minds of his defence team was what would Kitty say when she was called to the stand.

'Kitty had always been accident prone.' And she continued to drink a lot. There had been numerous episodes, and Robert knew her habits, although his brother Frank would recall that Robert was unwilling to admit to them, because he could not admit to failure. He accepted Kitty as she was, knowing she could never change. Nor did he want to force change on her, any more than she wanted to change him. As several acquaintances and friends said, 'She was his rock.' He was dependent on her. But she was full of surprises.[5]

The teams of lawyers sat facing each other across another table. Roger Robb and Carl Rolander Jr for the AEC were confronted by the defence team of Lloyd Garrison, Herbert Marks, Samuel Silverman and Allan B. Ecker. A separate wooden chair was positioned for the defendant and witnesses to face their prosecutors.

Kitty had suffered from one of her accidents that morning. She had fallen downstairs, and hobbled into the room on crutches. One of her legs was clad in a plaster cast. She limped slowly to a leather couch, where she sat next to Robert. By now he was only a few days away from his fiftieth birthday anniversary. Now all they could do was wait for the hearing to commence.

40

A Letter of Indictment

Chairman Gordon Gray opened the proceeding for the Personnel Security Board on the first day by reading the AEC letter of indictment against Robert Oppenheimer and his reply. He added that it was not a trial but an inquiry. Even so, over the following weeks no one could think otherwise than that Robert Oppenheimer was being tried for a number of crimes. They allegedly included joining several organisations that were fronts for the Communist Party, being 'intimately acquainted' with the late Dr Jean Tatlock, who was a known communist, associating with other 'known communists' like Dr Thomas Addis, Kenneth May, Steve Nelson, and Isaac Folkoff; employing such known communists as his former students Joseph W. Weinberg, David Bohm, Rossi Lomanitz, and David Hawkins, in the atom bomb project; contributing $150 per month to the Communist Party in San Francisco; and failing immediately to report his conversation with Haakon Chevalier in early 1943 about George Eltenton's proposal to funnel information about the Radiation Laboratory to the Soviet consulate in San Francisco.[1]

Journalist Diana Trilling described in the *Partisan Review* the passing show of colourful characters who wove their way in and out of the room during the following weeks. It was, she wrote, a conflict between the H-bomb proponents and the H-bomb opponents. She wrote of the multitude of alignments and groupings, commitments and cross-purposes ... the scientific 'in' versus the unscientific 'outs', the friends of Dr Oppenheimer versus the friends of Dr Teller. And the military versus the academics, the Air Force versus the Army versus the Navy, the Strategic Air Command versus the Air Defense Command, Los Alamos versus Livermore, MIT versus the University of Chicago, Dr Oppenheimer the individual versus individuals of a dramatically different disposition of mind ...[2]

Kitty Oppenheimer was asked to testify to her communist past, which she did, soberly and firmly claiming that she regretted nothing.

Yet another description of her past emerged under interrogation: Katherine 'Kitty' Vissering was born in Recklinghausen, Germany, on 8 August 1910. She was the only child of Franz Puening and his wife Käthe Vissering. 'Although she claimed that her father was a prince and that her mother was related to Queen Victoria, this was untrue.' Her mother was a cousin of Field Marshal Wilhelm Keitel. Keitel had been Chief of Staff in the German Army in the Second World War. He did what Hitler told him to do and was hanged as a war criminal in 1946 after being sentenced to death by the International Military Tribunal at Nuremberg when found guilty on four counts, without extenuating circumstances. It was not something that Kitty liked to remember, and was likely to have contributed to her troubled youth, her excessive drinking, and her possibly manic-depressive state, as she attempted to escape from any connection to her murderous relative who had been guilty of so many individual and mass murders.

She had arrived in the United States at the age of three on 14 May 1913 aboard the SS *Kaiser Wilhelm der Grosse*. Her father was a metallurgical engineer who had invented a new kind of blast furnace. It resulted in a position with a steel company in Pittsburgh. The family settled in the suburb of Aspinwall, Pennsylvania. Although her first language was German, she soon became fluent in English, speaking both languages without an accent. Her parents had regularly taken her with them on summer visits to Germany.[3]

Kitty would have been likely to have witnessed the rise of Hitler and the Nazis when living later on in Germany in the early 1930s. And, like many of her generation at that time who saw the global threat of Nazism to Europe and the United States, it could well have been her motivation for joining the Communist Party as the only choice to defeat Nazi Germany. The thought of her origins appeared to have haunted her life and affected her health and mental equilibrium. But, like the Cambridge Five and Klaus Fuchs, she had felt there was no other way to defeat Hitler and the Nazis.

However, it was Robert who was asked to testify first, and he made a complete mess of it – writhing with guilt and anguish as he had often done in inappropriate moments in the past. He uttered ambiguous or irrational statements about his own personality and experiences, and others that seemed to be condemnations of himself, like a penitent in the confessional. He seemed to miss the point entirely, which was whether he was a threat to the security of the United States or not. Instead, to those who knew him intimately, he appeared to be apologising obliquely to his parents, or the Ethical Culture Society, or Dostoevsky, or Tolstoy, for not having lived up to their high ideals.

Public Reaction

As far as the general public was concerned, when they read the newspapers the next day, 13 April, there was Robert Reston's exclusive on the front page of the *New York Times*. It stated, 'Dr Oppenheimer Suspended by AEC in Security Review. Scientist Defends Record. Hearing Started. Access To Secret Data Denied Nuclear Expert – Red Ties Alleged.' The full text of the proceedings was published with Oppenheimer's answers. Readers across the United States were confronted at last by Robert's public and private lives.

Opinions were instantly polarised between liberals who were shocked that such a prominent scientist who had been the hero of the Manhattan Project could now be attacked in such a ruthless and petty way, and more conservative critics like Walter

Winchell, who had previously announced that Senator McCarthy would soon reveal that a 'key atomic figure had urged that the H-bomb not be built at all'.

Winchell claimed that the famous atomic scientist had been an active Communist Party member and 'the leader of a Red Cell including other noted atomic scientists'.

'The trouble with Oppenheimer,' Einstein quipped, 'is that he loves a woman who doesn't love him – the United States government ...'

On day three of the hearing, Wednesday, 14 April, Oppenheimer was called to testify about his brother, Frank. It was described as the most humiliating day in Robert's life.

Perhaps the most important piece of evidence they chose to present against him was his error of judgment over the Haakon Chevalier affair. Roger Robb had already read several references in the FBI dossier beforehand about Oppenheimer's investigation by Lieutenant Colonel Boris Pash in 1943, which had been recorded. Robb had listened to Robert's first explanation of the incident, which differed from his later description to the FBI in 1945. Robb now asked him, 'Didn't you say that X had approached three people?'

'Probably.'

'Why did you do that, Doctor?'

'Because I was an idiot.'

Robert's public self-contempt was typical of his own private self-criticism for not living up to the high standards of his intellectual heroes that he had always set for himself. Now he had stepped into a trap set by a clever prosecutor who had put him in a state of anguish by his questions that had led Oppenheimer into admitting his foolish mistakes. His inquisitor, Robb, returned home jubilantly that night to tell his wife, 'I've just seen a man destroy himself.'

Robert knew that most people did not consider him to be an idiot, but he was not concerned about their standards, only his own perfect and unattainable ones. He had been misguided in fudging the truth to protect his old friend Chevalier, out of schoolboy loyalty, as General Groves had recognised.

What emerged, for those who were interested in the truth about the Oppenheimers' relationship with the American Communist Party and the Kremlin, was that, despite the past, when the Soviet Union and the Anglo-Americans were Allies, both Kitty and Robert hated Soviet Russia and were convinced that the Soviet Union was a danger to the world. As Einstein had remarked, they loved the United States and were loyal patriots.

What also became clearer was that Oppenheimer had instinctively mentioned three other suspects he could not identify by name because the official in the Russian consulate, Peter Ivanov, 'had initially suggested that he contact three scientists associated with the Berkeley Radiation Lab'. His memory had been at fault and led to the error.

Another intensely embarrassing interrogation by Robb was directed at Robert's intimate relationship with Jean Tatlock. It consumed some time, because the prosecuting counsel apparently decided that a sex scandal would tarnish Oppenheimer's reputation and invite publicity for the hearing. So that, for the public's benefit, the inquiry dealt with how many times he had had sex with Dr Jean Tatlock before he had married Kitty and afterwards. According to the prosecuting counsel, every sexual encounter had endangered security, because she was a member of the Communist Party.

Robb kept Oppenheimer on his toes all the time, so that he could think of nothing else except where the next punch might come from. His friend Herb Marks could only watch while Robb made a fool of Oppenheimer by using every court room trick he knew. Garrison had not expected foul play, and it was too late to change his tactics.

The reaction on Capitol Hill was cautious, as politicians and the media waited for the secrets in the FBI files to be revealed. The general public found it hard to believe that the man on trial was the same one who had been seen not many years previously as a knight in shining armour, a scientific genius who had done what no one else could have achieved in what the *New York Times* had described as 'the most awesome mission ever assigned to a private citizen – the mission to open the door to the atomic age'.

Destroying a Man's Life

Senator McCarthy's reaction to the hearings was that, 'It was long overdue … I think it took considerable courage to suspend the so-called untouchable scientist – Oppenheimer. I give Strauss credit for that.'[4]

Hans Bethe was the first scientist to be questioned. Not surprisingly, he spoke highly of Oppenheimer's achievements: 'nobody else could have done this than Dr Oppenheimer.'

But that was not why he was chosen for interrogation. It was, 'Which division was Klaus Fuchs in?'

'He was in my division which was the Theoretical Division.'

When James Conant was interrogated, he replied that he and Oppenheimer had worked together and generally agreed on policy, and he was puzzled as to why the AEC had chosen Oppenheimer to be pilloried. When Lloyd Garrison asked him what he thought of the AEC's letter of indictment, he said he thought it badly written if it intended to judge an important matter by accusing Oppenheimer of being a security risk on the basis of allegations about his previous work for the government, which had nothing to do with the charges.

Robb wrestled with him for a while before getting him to agree that he had not heard all of Oppenheimer's testimony, and that the AEC might be in a better position to judge from information in their possession. Conant grudgingly agreed that might be the case. So Robb got what he wanted from Conant, which was a general agreement.

Rabi was more astute and refused to be caught in the same trap as Conant. 'You have to take the whole story,' he said at the end. 'That is what novels are about.

There is a dramatic moment in the history of the man, what made him act, what he did, and what sort of person he was. That is what you are really doing here. You are writing a man's life.'

Led by Herb Marks, Rabi grew angry under further questioning, saying that Strauss's suspension of Oppenheimer was wrong and the hearing should never have occurred. 'He is a consultant, and if you don't want him to consult, you don't consult him, period.'

Robb recalled Oppenheimer to the stand and reviewed with him his 'tissue of lies'.

When Edward Teller was called to give evidence, he began by extolling Oppenheimer's virtues and confirming his loyalty, and then made a number of apparently carefully rehearsed remarks to denigrate him by innuendo, such as expressing 'a feeling that I would feel personally more secure if public matters would rest in other hands'.

Teller had always been more interested in developing the 'Super' hydrogen bomb, even when he was supposed to be working on the atomic bomb during the Manhattan Project. Now he had his own laboratory named the Lawrence Livermore National Laboratory. But it was not enough – he resented Oppenheimer's success, and could not forgive him for postponing the development of his own hydrogen bomb.

Very few people had thought Oppenheimer could win against Robb's antagonistic prosecuting style, and with FBI evidence withheld from him and his lawyers. Teller's betrayal was the last twist of the knife already thrust into his back by Strauss. And the inquisitorial atmosphere and character assassinations of McCarthy's witch-hunt prevailed everywhere at this time, in spite of the First Amendment that guaranteed the right of Americans to free expression and free association. Everyone was afraid of McCarthy. And Oppenheimer had been systematically cornered by Lewis Strauss, who was determined to destroy him.

When Lansdale was called to testify, he remarked, 'I think the hysteria of the times over communism is extremely dangerous.'

The final judgmental of the hearing took 25,000 words. Two out of the three judges voted not to renew Oppenheimer's security clearance. On 29 June, the AEC commissioners endorsed the majority opinion that Oppenheimer was a security risk and unfit to serve his country, as Strauss had claimed. Only the scientist on the AEC panel, Henry DeWolf Smyth, maintained that there was 'no indication in the entire record that Dr Oppenheimer has ever divulged any secret information'.[5]

Nevertheless, President Eisenhower revoked Oppenheimer's security clearance on 29 June 1954.

The scientists at Los Alamos felt it had been a dirty business. Rabi explained to Dorothy how Teller had given Strauss all he had wanted to hang Oppie. She would write afterwards, 'Has this nation no gratitude for the man who saved it?'

41

One Thing is Certain

Oppenheimer returned to his position as director of the Institute for Advanced Study at Princeton after the hearing. Those who knew him best could see that he was not the same man as he had been before his series of prosecutions. Many of the scientists who had worked with him would remark that he had been martyred or crucified at the hearing or in the press – to which he would reply wryly that he could still feel the blood from the nails. But the agony of the disclosures about his private life had been real, and he was humiliated by the knowledge that he was no longer trusted by the government. He was forced to recognise that his career as a consultant to the United States was now over.

Nevertheless, Oppie was indestructible. The scientific community still respected him. And he had his independent nature to maintain his compass bearings. He also had his friends. His relationship with Kitty was problematic, but it had always been ambiguous, and he seemed to expect it to be. Even so, his older and closest friends noticed a profound sadness had enveloped him and he seemed to have shrunk physically.

He was no longer viewed as the 'father of the atom bomb', but as a martyr of McCarthy's 'reign of terror'. Considerable news coverage had turned Robert into a popular celebrity, like the humiliated Captain Dreyfus who had been court-martialled and imprisoned at the end of the nineteenth century in France. Both he and Dreyfus had been innocent of the charges against them. They had come from wealthy Jewish families. And yet, both had been used as scapegoats by the establishment to distract attention from the real culprits.

Now the nuclear arms race continued without Robert interfering. The Soviet Union's successful test of the RDS-1 hydrogen bomb in August 1949 – which resembled the American 'Fat Man' bomb, even to its external shape – had encouraged Russia to develop their first megaton-range hydrogen bomb, the RDS-37, which they detonated successfully on 22 November 1955.

Moscow Centre had been warned by Klaus Fuchs's top secret information about the American hydrogen bomb programme in the late 1940s, which they had perceived as an American threat against them. Andrei S. Sakow would become known as the 'Father of the Soviet H-Bomb'. It enabled Malenkov gleefully to announce that the United States no longer possessed a monopoly on the hydrogen bomb.

Robert and Kitty appeared to be out of circulation for a time, while he took her for a holiday to the Virgin Islands. Strauss and the FBI thought they might defect, and had them anxiously watched, in case they managed to escape. Strauss envisioned a submarine emerging from beneath the sea to spirit them away to the Soviet Union, in a similar way to Pontecorvo's defection in 1950.

The FBI listened carefully to what their wiretaps told them was happening, and informed Strauss, while the Oppenheimers flew out to St Croix on 19 July 1954, and travelled on to the tiny island of St John, where they found a small and private hotel with no phones, no electricity, and only a few other guests. From then on they would spend several months there in isolation every year.

But old friends encouraged them soon to be seen circulating again at parties in Washington, looking relaxed and loving, while the FBI continued to keep them under close observation, and interviewed them from time to time, with Oppie as courteous and patient with them as he could be.

On 4 January 1955, Oppenheimer was interviewed on Edward R. Murrow's popular national television show called *See it Now.* Robert talked about secrecy in the twenty-five-minute segment. The trouble with secrecy, he told the public, is that it denies to the government the wisdom and resources of the whole community. Murrow asked him whether humanity now had the capability to destroy itself. Robert replied, 'Not quite. Not quite. You can certainly destroy enough of humanity so that only the greatest act of faith can persuade you that what's left will be human.'

His appearances brought Oppenheimer back to the notice of academia in late 1954, when the physics department of the University of Washington in the Pacific Northwest decided to renew an invitation of a short-term visiting professorship it had made to him a few years previously. It brought controversy in its wake and more press coverage. It changed his image from Washington insider to exiled public intellectual.[1]

When the crisis between China and Taiwan grew hot, questions arose as to whether the United States should destroy China with an atom bomb. Some generals believed they should do so before China became too strong. But Oppenheimer did not think so. Nor did he want to protest to the President over his Administration's drift towards war. His reasonable rhetoric convinced his Washington audience not to protest as they had intended. Nor was he interested in supporting 'Ban the bomb' protesters, like Bertrand Russell, Joseph Rotblat, Szilard, or Einstein, who often signed petitions against the arms race. Oppenheimer was troubled by their agenda. He had been close enough to organisations that fronted the Communist Party to be scorched. He would not fall into that trap again. He preferred to stand on his own feet.

In the spring of 1957, his old friend McGeorge Bundy, who was now the Dean of Harvard's philosophy and psychology department, invited Robert to give the prestigious William James Lectures. Some alumni threatened to withhold donations if he was allowed to speak. Bundy heard the protesters out, but had the strength of character not to give in to anarchy. He joined Oppenheimer's audience. The title for Oppie's six lectures was 'The Hope of Order'. An unusually large number of

1,200 people attended the first talk. Another 800 listened to it piped into a nearby hall. Armed police stood at the entrance to discourage mischief-makers.

The entire audience paid attention to what Oppie said from the moment he began to speak. He talked of the multi-talented psychologist William James in relation to his brother Henry, the unique American novelist and anglophile.

By 1958, Oppenheimer had visibly aged, and was stooped like an old man, although he was only fifty-four.

In 1959, Robert attended a conference in Rheinfelden in West Germany. It was sponsored by the Congress on Cultural Freedom. They discussed the fate of the industrialised western world. He spoke about nuclear weapons and how Americans viewed them. 'What are we to make of a civilization which has always regarded ethics as an essential part of human life,' but 'which has not been able to talk about the prospect of killing almost everybody except in prudential and game-theoretical terms?'[2]

An observer commented, 'He looked astoundingly like Pinocchio, and moved as jerkily as a marionette on strings.'[3]

Perhaps because there was now a Democrat in the White House in the early 1960s, Robert Oppenheimer was no longer viewed as a pariah.

Awards

In April 1962, the Kennedy Administration decided to remove the smear from Oppenheimer's name caused by the bigotry and ignorance, and misunderstandings during the McCarthy era. President Kennedy invited him to join a dinner at the White House for Nobel Prize winners.

In October that year, Soviet nuclear missiles were seen in Cuba and photographed from the air. Khrushchev's major threat to attack the United States mainland with nuclear warheads, and the battle of wits between him and President Kennedy, placed the world once again on the brink of a Third World War, until the Soviet Union was obliged to back down by the end of the month. It weakened Khrushchev in Russia's hierarchy as an adventurer who took unacceptable risks with nuclear weapons, and marked the beginning of his decline in power.

In May 1963, Oppenheimer gave a memorial speech for Niels Bohr at Los Alamos. He was frail, aged, and worn. His doctors cautioned him about making the trip to New Mexico with symptoms of a heavy cough, which had continued from his first attack of tuberculosis. But he felt he could not refuse the invitation to honour his old friend. Dorothy McKibbin drove him up the state highway, and they laughed at reminiscences of how the route had looked in the empty desert when he and General Groves had first considered it as a site for the Manhattan Project.

On 22 November, the media announced that President Kennedy wanted to present Oppenheimer with the Enrico Fermi Award personally. It was the highest honour given by the Atomic Energy Commission. But the U.S. President was assassinated on the same day in Dallas.

Then, when the Cold War hysteria had ebbed away on 2 December, President Johnson honoured Oppenheimer with the Fermi Award, saying: 'One of President Kennedy's most important acts was to sign the Enrico Fermi Award for Dr Oppenheimer for his contributions to theoretical physics and the advancement of science in the United States of America. It is important to our Nation that we have constantly before us the example of men who set high standards of achievement. This has been the role that you have played, Dr Oppenheimer.'

It was nearly two decades since the end of the Second World War. And, although the West had been brought to the brink of a Third World War on several occasions, the threat of what an uncontrollable nuclear bomb might do to the world had turned it into a deterrent – so far, at least.

That cautionary note always hovered over optimistic observations; because everyone knew what would happen if an antisocial psychopath possessed an atom bomb. The odds were that he would use it.

In 1983, President Ronald Reagan would award the National Medal of Science to Edward Teller for his work on the H-bomb.

A mystery still lingered about Kitty Harris. From all the information and disinformation available, it was still not entirely certain that the Kitty Harris allegedly born in London and the Kitty Harris said to be born in Germany were the same individual. But it would be an unlikely coincidence if two KGB agents of the same name should turn up simultaneously in Los Alamos, when and where the first atom bomb was built, and both Kitty Harrises were run by the same NKVD controllers, Elizabeth and Vassily Zarubin.

Kitty had worked under so many code names for the KGB and NKVD, like AIDA, ADA, GYPSY, NORMA, Eleanor Davies, and many others, that it had become impossible to separate and identify her multiple personalities.[4] According to one source, she had seventeen different cover names.[5]

Nevertheless, a remark on record states the following:

> One result of Kheifetz's sounding the alarm about an American superweapon was that he received assistance from Zarubin as soon as he arrived in San Francisco. Zarubin put his wife, Elizabeth, a captain in the NKVD, and her protégée, Kitty Harris, to work on the newly initiated operation. After they settled in Washington, Zarubin dispatched Elizabeth on frequent trips to California, where Kheifetz introduced her to the Oppenheimer family. Elizabeth became friends with Katherine Oppenheimer, with whom she could actively espouse her communist ideals and discuss the need for Soviet–American cooperation against Hitler. Through Katherine, Elizabeth Zarubin and Gregory Kheifetz convinced Oppenheimer to agree to hire 'anti-fascists of German origin,' a seemingly small success that paved the way for bringing the physicist Klaus Fuchs, a leading spy for the Soviet Union, from England to work at Los Alamos.[6]

That paragraph claimed there were two different Kitty Harrises. But was the intelligence that those authors acquired merely KGB disinformation to maintain Kitty Oppenheimer's reputation, or even Robert Oppenheimer's, while Soviet Russia imagined they could use him? The source for that claim is described simply as 'Russian Intelligence Archives'. No reference to a file number or a date was provided, which makes the authors' claim suspicious. And yet, for anyone who knows the circumstances, Kitty is hidden somewhere among that possible disinformation. If we compare it with another series of statements made in the memoirs of NKVD spymaster Pavel Sudoplatov, we find he claimed something similarly ambiguous:

> In 1941 Elizabeth Zarubina was a captain in the NKVD. After her husband's posting to Washington, she travelled to California frequently to cultivate the Oppenheimer family through contacts arranged by Kheifetz. Kheifetz provided Elizabeth Zarubina with a rundown on all the members of Robert Oppenheimer's family, known for its left-wing sympathies, to enable her to approach them. He then introduced Elizabeth to Oppenheimer's wife, Katherine, who was sympathetic to the Soviet Union and Communist ideals, and the two worked out a system for future meetings. Katherine Oppenheimer was not mentioned by name in the reports, but we worked through a woman close to Oppenheimer, and it was my understanding then, and is now that the woman was his wife.[7]

Evidently, the woman was Kitty Harris *and* Kitty Oppenheimer. With all we know now about Sudoplatov from his boastful memoir and his involvement with scientists at the Los Alamos Manhattan Project, it is almost inconceivable that he would not have known about her double exposure. And yet he never mentioned her in his confessions, because he was uncertain. Apparently her work on the U.S. atomic bomb project and her real identity were considered so important to Moscow Centre that they wove a tapestry of deceptions around her so tightly, that even Sudoplatov could not penetrate its secret.

It was 'the special circumstances in and around Los Alamos in 1942 that that had kept her [Kitty] in America for so long. In cabling permission to [Vassily] Zarubin, the Centre actually suggested advancing her departure date ... but he cautioned her that she should not be allowed to operate independently .... while Kitty was a quick-witted and conscientious courier and contact agent, with an outstanding memory, the ability to relay a complex report very accurately and a field operator who knew how to extricate herself from a difficult situation, she was unable to run agents who were her social and cultural superiors, especially those who required a great deal of thorough work and who looked to their handler as an authority. She simply did not have the tough, assertive personality to allow her to take control. Unfortunately, this comment was disregarded, as a result of which her assignment proved extremely difficult.'[8]

The profile of the London-born spy named Kitty certainly appears to match the description of the spy said to have been born in Germany: 'headstrong, naïve, undisciplined, moody, wore her heart on her sleeve and at times could be a little bit gullible'.[9] And yet, the former senior KGB officer Igor Damaskin, who authored a book about Kitty Harris, also seems to have been unaware that both Kitty Harris and Kitty Oppenheimer was the same woman.

I had meticulously followed the trails of 'both' KGB spies sometimes named Kitty Harris, before deciding they must be one and the same individual. I could find only two photographs of Katherine Oppenheimer, no doubt because her file is still classified Top Secret in the Kremlin. Both are reproduced here. Igor Damaskin's choice of photos of Kitty Harris was similarly limited to only two. One snapshot shows her leaning casually against a tree. He found another one deliberately disguised and distorted to avoid recognition. All the other photos feature the same KGB agent with the same mischievous eyes and happy-go-lucky grin. Regardless of whether they portray Kitty Harris or Katherine Oppenheimer, they are different photos of the same individual.

New facts emerged about Werner Heisenberg when General Groves's Alsos Mission captured him, Carl von Weizsäcker, and another eight German scientists in Nazi-occupied Europe in 1945. Two teams were working on the German uranium pile, one led by Heisenberg. Colonel Pash arrested him at Urfeld at the same time that Diebners's laboratory was seized on April 24. They were interrogated in Heidelburg and England. A case has been made that "the German atomic program to develop a bomb was farther along than most historians have believed and some have alleged that Diebner's team conducted the first successful nuclear weapon test of some type (employing hollow charges for ignition) of a nuclear-related device in Ohrdruf, Thuringia on 4 March 1945."[10]

Apparently, when Heisenberg had met Niels Bohr in Nazi-occupied Copenhagen in 1941, he had intended to betray Bohr to the Nazis and pick his brains because, contrary to assumptions, he did not know how to develop an A-bomb, and judged it would be better to use the funds on another so-called "secret weapon." He was highly emotional, ambitious, pro-Nazi, and anti-Semitic, although he and other scientists lied to pretend they had been against Hitler all along.[11]

Timeline

April 1939
Germany began a secret weapons programme named *Uranverein*; the 'Uranium Club', which alerted Stalin, the British Government and the United States to the nuclear threat of extinction if Nazi scientists were allowed to develop the first atom bomb.

August 1939
Physicist Robert Oppenheimer, who heads America's atomic bomb project, is introduced to Kitty Harris by a Soviet Russian spymaster at a party.

1 November 1940
Soviet spy Kitty Harris marries Robert Oppenheimer, the chief scientist for the Manhattan Project in Los Alamos.

1941–42
Soviet Intelligence (the NKVD) re-establish a safe house in Santa Fe they had used to assassinate Trotsky in 1940, now to engage with scientists in the Manhattan Project.

1943
Oppenheimer accidentally draws attention to himself by lying to U.S. Army Security and the FBI to shield a communist friend from exposure. Now he is suspected of being a Soviet Agent too, the FBI tap his phone.

1944
Moscow Centre receive details of each stage of planning, design and making of the first atom bomb at Los Alamos from a scientist in the Manhattan Project named Klaus Fuchs, who is a Soviet mole hired by Robert Oppenheimer.

1944
Kitty Oppenheimer is interrogated by the head of Manhattan Project Security, Colonel Lonsdale.

May 1945
Nazi Germany surrenders to the Allies after Hitler's suicide.

1945
Russia's Secret Police Chief Lavrentiy Beria receives a report from Klaus Fuchs that the first atomic test explosion was successful – also from British diplomat and Soviet spy Donald Maclean – so that Stalin knows as soon as President Truman does.

THE RACE FOR THE ATOM BOMB

6 & 9 August 1945   The U.S. drops an atom bomb on Hiroshima and Nagasaki after Japan's leaders refuse to stop the Pacific War despite a warning of a nuclear attack.

1946   Robert Oppenheimer is recognised post-war as a national hero, and becomes politically active.

May 1946   A 'Red Scare' in the United States with the Cold War against Soviet Russia.

1949   Russia completes its own atom bomb and threatens the West with nuclear war. (A nuclear arms race follows from 1950).

June 1949   The rise of Senator McCarthy's Un-American Activities Committee's 'reign of terror' against communists, who accuse Robert's brother Frank in court and ruin his career for lying about his communist membership.

25 May 1951   Two British diplomats named Guy Burgess and Donald Maclean disappear under suspicion of being KGB spies.

September 1951   Oppenheimer is victimised in a witch-hunt by America's Atomic Energy Commission and the U.S. Air Force, the FBI, Senator McCarthy, and the U.S. Justice Department.

May 1953   Chief of the Atomic Energy Commission, Strauss, strives to destroy Oppenheimer's reputation with President Eisenhower.

1954   Strauss charges Oppenheimer with being subversive for using his influence against making a super-hydrogen bomb and reversing U.S. military strategy.

12 April 12 1954   Robert Oppenheimer is prosecuted at a security hearing.

29 June 1954   President Eisenhower revokes Oppenheimer's security clearance. Robert becomes a martyr to injustice.

November 1962   President Kennedy decides to honour Oppenheimer with the prestigious Fermi Scientific Award, but is assassinated on the same day. President Johnson presents it to him personally.

About the Author

Author age 23 in 1948

John Harte's undercover work as an investigative journalist was focused, in particular, on the two extremist political regimes that caused the global crisis after the Russian Revolution in 1917 and the rise of the Nazis in Germany. In 1948, he discovered a plot by fascist organisations to take control of Britain. He spent a year travelling across the British Isles to compile a dossier of provincial fascist groups in several major cities, with photos and files on each leader who headed a splinter group under a different name, which Sir Oswald Mosley intended to merge when he was ready to make a political comeback. Mosley had been the leader of the British Union of Fascists in England before the war, and was a friend of Hitler, who had been the best man at his wedding.

Harte's dossier was presented in Parliament, while he simultaneously gave a scoop to the *Sunday Pictorial*, and *Picture Post,* by taking their photographers to a secret meeting where Mosley was briefing his regional *gauleiters*. The revelation of the scandal in the House of Commons and the news media resulted in protests by ex-servicemen and the end of Mosley's political career.

In 1961, the author drove through Tito's Yugoslavia to interview his youngest partisan and lived in his house to study the communist dictatorship. He revisited Zagreb years later during Croatia's war of independence from Yugoslavia. He lived in South Africa for twelve years from 1965 to study the apartheid regime, and drove north to Lourenço Marques (now Maputo) during the war for independence in Mozambique (formerly Portuguese East Africa), and through the Kingdom of Swaziland (now Eswatini).

John was educated at St Paul's School in London, and Carleton University in Ottawa where he studied Psychology. His home is now in Canada, where he writes non-fiction books about the shapers and heroes and heroines of modern history.

Author's website: www.johnhartebooks.com

Notes

Introduction

1. Kai Bird & Martin J. Sherwin. *American Prometheus: The Triumph and Tragedy of J. Robert Oppenheimer* (Knopf, NY, 2005), p.3.
2. Arthur Koestler. *Darkness at Noon.* (Macmillan, London, 1940).
3. Moshe Zimmerman. *Hans Mommsen (1936–2015): A History of Cumulative Radicalization* (The International Institute for Holocaust Research, 1997), p.150.
4. Igor Damaskin & Geoffrey Elliott. *Kitty Harris: The Spy with Seventeen Names* (Little Brown, Boston, 2004), p.203.
5. Pavel Sudoplatov. *Special Tasks: The Memoirs of an Unwanted Witness.* Appendix 2, Document 1 (Little Brown, Boston, 1994), p.174.
6. *Special Tasks:* Ibid., pp.177–8.
7. Anthony Cave Brown & Charles B. MacDonald. *The Secret History of the Atom Bomb* (Delta, NY, 1977), pp.xiii–xiv).
8. Ronald Hamowy. Ed. Introductory Essay to *The Constitution of Liberty* by F. A. Hayek (University of Chicago, 1960), p.1.
9. *The Labour Monthly*, August 1940, pp.445–6; Transcribed by Joaquin Arriola.

Chapter 1: Modern Times

1. E. Whittaker. 'Albert Einstein 1979–1955.'*Biographical Memoirs of Fellows of the Royal Society* (1 November, 1965), pp.32–67.
2. *American Prometheus*. Ibid., p.22.
3. *American Prometheus*. Ibid., p.10.
4. Ed. Alice Kimball Smith & Charles Weiner, *Letters & Recollections* (Harvard, Mass, 1980), p.2.
5. *American Prometheus*. Ibid., p.10.
6. Stephen Birmingham. *Our Crowd: The Great Jewish Families of New York* (Harper, NY, 1967), Preface.
7. Arthur Koestler. *Arrow in the Blue* (Collins, UK, 1952).
8. *American Prometheus*. Ibid., p.17.

Chapter 2: An Awkward Undergraduate

1. *Letters & Recollections.* Ibid., p.6.
2. *American Prometheus.* Ibid., pp.21–2.
3. *American Prometheus.* Ibid., p.23.
4. *Letters & Recollections.* Ibid., p.15.
5. *Letters & Recollections.* Ibid., p.11.
6. *American Prometheus.* Ibid., p.29.
7. *Letters & Recollections.* Ibid., p.28.
8. Santrock & Mitterer. *Psychology* (McGraw-Hill, Canada, 1997–2006), p.135.
9. *Psychology.* Ibid. (Killen & Smetana, 2005), p.143.
10. *Letters & Recollections.* Ibid., p.44.
11. *Letters & Recollections.* Ibid., pp.28–9.
12. *American Prometheus.* Ibid., pp.32–3.
13. *American Prometheus.* Ibid., p.34.

Chapter 3: A Tortured Adolescence

1. *Letters & Recollections.* Ibid., p.68.
2. *Letters & Recollections.* Ibid., p.70.
3. *Letters & Recollections.* Ibid., p.24.
4. *Letters & Recollections.* Ibid., p.54.
5. *Letters & Recollections.* Ibid., p.69.
6. *Letters & Recollections.* Ibid., pp.76–7.
7. *American Prometheus.* Ibid., pp.42–3.
8. *American Prometheus.* Ibid., pp.43–51.
9. *Letters & Recollections.* Ibid., pp.14–15.
10. *American Prometheus.* Ibid., p.44.
11. *American Prometheus.* Ibid., p.44.
12. *Letters & Recollections.* Ibid., pp.20–1.
13. *Letters & Recollections.* Ibid., pp.91–2.
14. *Letters & Recollections.* Ibid., p.94.
15. *Letters & Recollections.* Ibid., p.93.

Chapter 4: The Magical Spell of Physics

1. Phillip Knightley. *The Master Spy* (Knopf, NY, 1989), p.39.
2. *American Prometheus.* Ibid., p.52.
3. *American Prometheus.* Ibid., p.52.
4. *Encyclopaedia Britannica.* Uncertainty Principle.

5. *Letters & Recollections*. Ibid., p.96.
6. *Letters & Recollections*. Ibid., p.89.f.
7. *Letters & Recollections*. Ibid., pp.97–98.
8. *Letters & Recollections*. Ibid., p.127.
9. *American Prometheus*. Ibid., p.60.
10. *American Prometheus*. Ibid., p.61.

Chapter 5: Different Strokes for Different Folks

1. *New York Times*. 13 November 1988.
2. *Encyclopaedia Britannica*.
3. *American Prometheus*. Ibid., pp.64–5.
4. *Letters & Recollections*. Ibid., p.103.
5. *American Prometheus*. Ibid., p.65.
6. *Letters & Recollections*. Ibid., p.98.
7. *American Prometheus*. Ibid., p.66.
8. *Letters & Recollections*. Ibid., p.101.

Chapter 6: The World Beckons

1. *Letters & Recollections*. Ibid., p.113.
2. As described by Frank Oppenheimer in later years.
3. *Letters & Recollections*. Ibid., p.10.
4. *Letters & Recollections*. Ibid., p.197.
5. *American Prometheus*. Ibid., p.74.
6. *Letters & Recollections*. Ibid., p.125.
7. *American Prometheus*. Ibid., p.78.
8. *American Prometheus*. Ibid., p.82.
9. *American Prometheus*. Ibid., p.83.
10. *Letters & Recollections*. Ibid., p.149.

Chapter 7: Oppie

1. *American Prometheus*. Ibid., p.85.
2. *Letters & Recollections*. Ibid., p.130.
3. *Letters & Recollections*. Ibid., p.118.
4. *Letters & Recollections*. Ibid., pp.144–5.
5. The First Century CE Doctor of Jewish Law, Rabban Gamaliel. *New Testament*. Acts of the Apostles 5. Alleged teacher of the Apostle Paul. Acts. 22:3.

Chapter 8: The Red Scare

1. *American Prometheus*. Ibid., p.104.
2. *Letters & Recollections*. Ibid., p.195.
3. *American Prometheus*. Ibid., p.105.
4. *Holocaust Encyclopedia.* https://encyclopedia.ushmm.org/content/en/article/the-press-in-the-third-reich
5. A.L. Rowse. *The Poet Auden* (Methuen, London, 1987).
6. *American Prometheus*. Ibid., p.105.

Chapter 9: We The Living

1. *American Prometheus*. Ibid., pp.104 & 112.
2. Ayn Rand. *We the Living* (Macmillan, NY, 1936).
3. *American Prometheus*. Ibid., p.112.
4. *Letters & Recollections*. Ibid., p.196.
5. *American Prometheus*. Ibid., p.115.
6. *American Prometheus*. Ibid., p.115.

Chapter 10: Political Activists

1. *American Prometheus*. Ibid., p.118.
2. *American Prometheus*. Ibid., p.123.
3. *Letters & Recollections*. Ibid., p.205.
4. *Letters & Recollections*. Ibid., p.202.
5. *Letters & Recollections*. Ibid., pp.146–7.

Chapter 11: The Atomic Bomb Project

1. Jerrold & Leona Schechter. *Sacred Secrets: How Soviet Intelligence Operations Changed American History* (Brassey's, Washington, 2002), pp.46–50.
2. *Sacred Secrets*. Ibid., p.52.
3. Russian Intelligence Archives.
4. Pavel & Anatoli Sudoplatov. *Special Tasks*. Ibid., p.175.
5. *Sacred Secrets*. Ibid., p.48.
6. *American Prometheus*. Ibid., p.137.
7. *American Prometheus*. Ibid., pp.137–8.
8. As told verbally to the biographers of *American Prometheus* in 1982.
9. *American Prometheus*. Ibid., p.139.

10. *American Prometheus*. Ibid., p.147.
11. Physicist Victor Weiskopf, who had spent several months in the USSR.
12. *American Prometheus*. Ibid., p.140.
13. R. V. Jones. *Most Secret War* (Penguin, London, 2009), p.306.
14. Ibid.

Chapter 12: Who Was Kitty Harris?

1. *Special Tasks*. Ibid., p.190.
2. *Letters & Recollections*. Ibid., p.214.
3. *Sacred Secrets*. Ibid., p.51.
4. *Sacred Secrets*. Ibid., p.58.
5. *Sacred Secrets*. Ibid., p.59.
6. Spartacus Educational online. https://spartacus-educational.com/Litzi_Friedmann. htm
7. Spartacus Educational online. Ibid.
8. Spartacus Educational online. Ibid.
9. *American Prometheus*. Ibid., p.161.
10. United States Congress Senate Committee on the Judiciary. *Scope of Soviet Activity in the United States:* Hearing before the Subcommittee to investigate the Administration of the Internal Security Act and Other International Security Laws of the Committee of the Judiciary, United States Senate, Eighty-fourth Congress, Second Session [Eighty-fifth Congress. first Session]. Parts 12–24 (U.S. Government Printing Office, 1956), p.A86.
11. Igor Damaskin & Geoffrey Elliott. Ibid., p.47.
12. Igor Damaskin & Geoffrey Elliott. Ibid., pp.55–61.
13. Igor Damaskin & Geoffrey Elliott. Ibid., p.84.
14. Igor Damaskin & Geoffrey Elliott. Ibid., p.93.
15. Igor Damaskin & Geoffrey Elliott. Ibid., p.101.
16. Igor Damaskin & Geoffrey Elliott. Ibid., pp.146–150.
17. Igor Damaskin & Geoffrey Elliott. Ibid., pp.154–156.
18. Igor Damaskin & Geoffrey Elliott. Ibid., p.3.

Chapter 13: The Nuclear Programme

1. Robert E. Sherwood. *Roosevelt and Hopkins: An Intimate History* (Harper, NY, 1948), p.28.
2. Stephane Groueff. *Manhattan Project: The Untold Story of the Making of the Atomic Bomb* (Little Brown, Boston, 1967), p.43.
3. Stephane Groueff. Ibid., p.5.
4. Stephane Groueff. Ibid., p.26.
5. Stephane Groueff. Ibid., p.xi.

6. Stephane Groueff. Ibid., pp.27–28.
7. Stephane Groueff. Ibid., pp.29–31.

Chapter 14: Germany's Secret Weapons

1. R. V. Jones. Ibid., p.67.
2. R. V. Jones. Ibid.
3. Ibid., p.68.
4. Atomic Heritage Foundation. www.atomicheritage.org/history/german-atomic-bomb-project
5. Groves.
6. Atomic Heritage Foundation. Ibid. *Sacred Secrets*. Ibid., p.91.
7. *Letters & Recollections*. Ibid., p.173.
8. *Encyclopaedia Britannica* online. Ibid.

Chapter 15: The Intellectual and the Militarist

1. *A History of the United States Atomic Energy Commission*. Hewlett et al., pp.54–5.
2. James Kunetka. *The General and the Genius: Groves and Oppenheimer – The Unlikely Partnership that Built the Atom Bomb* (Regnery History, U.S., 2015), p.22.
3. James Kunetka. Ibid., p.26.
4. *Letters & Recollections*. Ibid., pp.221–3.
5. *Letters & Recollections*. Ibid., p.224.
6. *Letters & Recollections*. Ibid., p.229.
7. James Kunetka. Ibid., p.53.
8. James Kunetka. Ibid., p.56.
9. Jennet Conant. *109 East Palace: Robert Oppenheimer and the Secret City of Los Alamos* (Simon & Schuster, NY, 2006), p.39, 57.
10. Atomic Energy Commission. p.170.
11. *Sacred Secrets*. Ibid., pp.198–9.
12. *American Prometheus*. Ibid., p.250.
13. *American Prometheus*. Ibid., p.251.
14. *American Prometheus*. Ibid., p.187.
15. *American Prometheus*. Ibid., p.188.
16. *American Prometheus*. Ibid., p.189.
17. *American Prometheus*. Ibid., p.190. Footnote.

Chapter 16: Merchants of Death

1. Stephane Groueff. Ibid., p.75.
2. Stephane Groueff. Ibid., p.75.

3. Stephane Groueff. Ibid., p.76. Footnote.
4. Stephane Groueff. Ibid., p.82.
5. James Kunetka. Ibid., p.62.
6. Richard Hewlett & Oscar E. Anderson Jr., *A History of the United States Atomic Energy Commission,* vol. 1, *The New World, 1939–1946* (University Park, PA: Pennsylvania State University Press, 1962), p.115.
7. James Conant to Leslie Groves, 9 December 1942. MED.
8. Stephane Groueff. Ibid., p.39.
9. Stephane Groueff. Ibid., p.40.
10. Stephane Groueff. Ibid., p.63.
11. Stephane Groueff. Ibid., p.66.

Chapter 17: The Pied Piper of Los Alamos

1. Jennet Conant. Ibid., p.42.
2. *Letters & Recollections.* Ibid., p.238.
3. Jennet Conant. Ibid., pp.52–3.
4. *Letters & Recollections.* Ibid., p.273.
5. *American Prometheus.* Ibid., p.212.
6. *American Prometheus.* Ibid., p.209.
7. *Letters & Recollections.* Ibid., p.252.
8. Jennet Conant. Ibid., p.62.
9. Margaret Gowing. *Britain and Atomic Energy 1939–1945* (Macmillan, London, 1964), pp.248–250.
10. *Letters & Recollections.* Ibid., p.270.
11. Margaret Gowing. Ibid., p.261.
12. *Letters & Recollections.* Ibid., p.273.
13. *Letters & Recollections.* Ibid., p.257.

Chapter 18: Achieving Critical Mass

1. Steffane Grouffe. Ibid., p.43. Footnote.
2. James Kunetka. Ibid., p.95. Los Alamos Laboratory. 'Memorandum of the Los Alamos Project as of March 1943,' 14 March 1943, LANL.
3. *American Prometheus.* Ibid., p.230.
4. Steffane Grouffe. Ibid., p.232.
5. Steffane Grouffe. Ibid., p.234.
6. *Letters & Recollections.* Ibid., pp.276–7.
7. James Kunetka. Ibid., p.99.
8. James Kunetka. Ibid., pp.100–101.
9. Ibid.
10. James Kunetka. Ibid., p.101.
11. Steffane Grouffe. Ibid., p.237.

12. Steffane Grouffe. Ibid., p.238.
13. Steffane Grouffe. Ibid., pp.239–40.

Chapter 19: A Magical Place

1. Steffane Grouffe. Ibid., p.251.
2. Steffane Grouffe. Ibid., p.249.
3. 'K-25:' *Voices of the Manhattan Project*. The Atomic Heritage Foundation.
4. Steffane Grouffe. Ibid., p.253.
5. *Letters & Recollections*. Ibid., p.260.
6. Roosevelt to Oppenheimer, 29 June1943, F.D. Roosevelt File, Box 62, Oppenheimer Papers.
7. Jennet Conant. Ibid., p.167.
8. *Special Tasks*. Ibid., p.190.
9. *Sacred Secrets*. Ibid., p.63.
10. *History of the Soviet Atom Bomb Project, 1938–1949,* vol. 1 (Moscow: Ministry of Atomic Energy, 1999), p.223.
11. Jennet Conant. Ibid., p.168.
12. *Letters & Recollections*. Ibid., pp.262–3.
13. Hans A. Bethe. 'Oppenheimer: "Where He Was There Was Always Life and Excitement."' *Science*, p.155. (3 March 1967) 1082.
14. Charles L. Critchfield, 'The First Implosion at Los Alamos', *Behind Tall Fences* (Los Alamos: Los Alamos Historical Society, 1996), p.171.
15. Jennet Conant. Ibid., p.147.
16. Jennet Conant. Ibid., p.150.

Chapter 20: Dangerous Associations

1. *American Prometheus*. Ibid., pp.256–7.
2. Steffane Grouffe. Ibid., p.291.
3. James Kunetka. Ibid., p.130.
4. Jennet Conant. Ibid., pp.180–1.
5. *American Prometheus*. Ibid., p.182.
6. Jacob Bronowski. *Science and Human Values* (Harper, London, 1956).
7. *American Prometheus*. Ibid., p.182.
8. Jennet Conant. Ibid., p.183.
9. Jennet Conant. Ibid., pp.183–4.
10. Jennet Conant. Ibid., p.184.

Chapter 21: Problem Number One

1. Steffane Grouffe. Ibid., p.286.
2. *American Prometheus*. Ibid., p.262.
3. *American Prometheus*. Ibid., p.264.
4. *Jennet Conant*. Ibid., pp.272–3.
5. *Jennet Conant*. Ibid., p.272.
6. Pavel & Anatoli Sudoplatov. Ibid. (Little Brown, Boston, 1994).
7. Spartacus Educational online. Ref. Mikhail Shpiegalglass.
8. *Special Tasks*. Ibid., p.xiii.
9. Spartacus Educational online. https://spartacus-educational.com/Litzi_Friedmann. htm
10. *Sacred Secrets*. Ibid., p.83.
11. *Sacred Secrets*. Ibid., p.84.
12. *Sacred Secrets*. Ibid., p.83.
13. *Sacred Secrets*. Ibid., p.84.
14. *Sacred Secrets*. Ibid., pp.88–9.
15. Nigel West & Oleg Tsarev. *The Crown Jewels* (Harper, London, 1998), p.235.

Chapter 22: The Race for the Atom Bomb

1. *James Kunetka*. Ibid., p.243.
2. Leslie R. Groves, 'Memorandum for Secretary of War Stimson', 23 April 1945, LANL.
3. Henry Stimson., 'Memorandum Discussed with the President', 25 April 1945, GRO.
4. Letter, Robert Oppenheimer to General Groves, 30 June 1945, LANL.
5. *James Kunetka*. Ibid., pp.246–7.
6. Steffane Grouffe. Ibid., pp.388–9.
7. Steffane Grouffe. Ibid., p.389.
8. *Letters & Recollections*. Ibid., pp.290–1.
9. Sherwin. *World Destroyed,* app.L, 'Notes on the Interim Committee, May 31, 1945', p.299.
10. *American Prometheus*. Ibid., p.292.
11. Edward Teller with Judith Shoolery, *Memoirs: A Twentieth Century Journey in Science and Politics* (Perseus, Cambridge, 2001), p.202.
12. *American Prometheus*. Ibid., pp.268–9.
13. *American Prometheus*. Ibid., p.270.
14. *American Prometheus*. Ibid., p.271.

Chapter 23: The Future of the Human Race

1. *American Prometheus*. Ibid., p.272. Victor Weiskopf.
2. *American Prometheus*. Ibid., p.274.
3. *American Prometheus*. Ibid., p.273.
4. *American Prometheus*. Ibid., pp.274–5.
5. Spartacus Educational online.
6. Andrew Boyle. *The Climate of Treason* (Random Hs., London, 1979).
7. *James Kunetka*. Ibid., p.134.

Chapter 24: Soviet Spies Saving the World

1. NKVD Archives.
2. According to Ursula Beurton.
3. *James Kunetka*. Ibid., p.135.
4. Allen Weinstein & Alexander Vasiliev. *The Haunted Wood: Soviet Espionage in America* (Penguin, London, 1998).
5. *Sacred Secrets*. Ibid., p.57.
6. Gold to Samyon Semyonov.
7. Ibid.
8. *Sacred Secrets*. Ibid., p.172.
9. *American Prometheus*. Ibid., p.286.
10. *American Prometheus*. Ibid., p.285.
11. *Sacred Secrets*. Ibid., p.55.
12. Andrew & Gordievsky, *KGB: The Inside Story of its Foreign Operations from Lenin to Gorbachev* (Harper, NY, 1990), p.318.
13. *James Kunetka*. Ibid., p.263.
14. *American Prometheus*. Ibid., pp.287–8.
15. Martin J. Sherwin. *A World Destroyed: The Atomic Bomb and the Grand Alliance* (Knopf, NY, 1975), p.198.
16. *Special Tasks*. Ibid., p.198.

Chapter 25: The Experimental Atomic Test

1. *James Kunetka*. Ibid., p.268.
2. Memorandum, James Tuck to Robert Oppenheimer et al., 30 June 1944, LANL.
3. *James Kunetka*. Ibid., p.271.
4. Hans Bethe & Robert Christy, 'Memorandum on the Immediate Aftereffects of the Gadget', 30 March 1944, LANL files.
5. Letter, Robert Oppenheimer to Leslie Groves, 27 June 1944, LANL.
6. Jennet Conant. Ibid., p.331.

7. Hawkins, Truslow & Smith, 1961, p.266.
8. Richard Tolman to General Groves, 'Report on the First Trinity Test', 13 May 1945, LANL.
9. Eyewitness accounts by *New York Times* reporter William L. Laurence and Brig. General Thomas F. Farrell of General Groves's staff.
10. *Sacred Secrets*. Ibid., pp.295–6.

Chapter 26: A Japanese Target

1. *Jennet Conant*. Ibid., pp.250–1.
2. *Jennet Conant*. Ibid., pp.252–3.
3. *Jennet Conant*. Ibid., p.289.
4. *Jennet Conant*. Ibid., pp.289–90.
5. *American Prometheus*. Ibid., p.299.
6. Russian Archives.
7. *Sacred Secrets*. Ibid., p.50.
8. *Sacred Secrets*. Ibid., pp.51–2.

Chapter 27: Japan

1. *American Prometheus*. Ibid., p.300.
2. *American Prometheus*. Ibid., p.300.
3. *American Prometheus*. Ibid., p.301.
4. Steffane Grouffe. Ibid., p.388.
5. Steffane Grouffe. Ibid., p.400.
6. George Kistiakowsky, 'Trinity – A Reminiscence', *Bulletin of the Atomic Scientific Laboratory*, 11 April 1970.
7. Steffane Grouffe. Ibid., p.392.
8. Steffane Grouffe. Ibid., p.394.
9. *James Kunetka*. Ibid., p.302.
10. William L. Laurence. *Dawn Over Zero: The Story of the Atomic Bomb* (Knopf, NY, 1946), p.234.
11. *James Kunetka*. Ibid., p.319.

Chapter 28: Unconditional Surrender

1. *Jennet Conant*. Ibid., p.322.
2. *Letters & Recollections*. Ibid., p.296.
3. Stimson's diary entry.
4. *Jennet Conant*. Ibid., p.320.
5. Henry L. Stimson. *Harpers Magazine*. 'The Decision to Use the Atomic Bomb'.

6. *American Prometheus*. Ibid., p.321.
7. *Letters & Recollections*. Ibid., p.298.
8. Millikan to Oppenheimer, 31 August 1945 (p.1 dated 1941, p.2 correctly dated 1945), California Institute of Technology: 1941–47 File, Box 230, Oppenheimer papers. Millikan to Tolman, 31 July 1945. Box 28.8, Millikan Papers.
9. *Letters & Recollections*. Ibid., pp.301–2.
10. *Letters & Recollections*. Ibid., p.303.

Chapter 29: Back to Normal

1. Henry Stimson. Diary entry.
2. Jacob Bronowski. *Science and Human Value* (Messner, NY, 1958), p.xiii.
3. *American Prometheus*. Ibid., p.326.
4. *American Prometheus*. Ibid., p.327.
5. *American Prometheus*. Ibid., pp.327–8.
6. *American Prometheus*. Ibid., pp.330–1.
7. *American Prometheus*. Ibid., p.332.

Chapter 30: A World Transformed

1. *Sacred Secrets*. Ibid., p.194.
2. Interview with FBI Agent Robert Lamphere, Green Valley, Arizona, 15 March 1999.
3. *American Prometheus*. Ibid., pp.336–7.
4. *American Prometheus*. Ibid., p.338.
5. *American Prometheus*. Ibid., p.339.
6. *Jennet Conant*. Ibid., p.354.
7. *Jennet Conant*. Ibid., pp.358–9.
8. Millikan to Oppenheimer, 20 February 1946, California Institute of technology: 1941–47 File, Box 230, Oppenheimer apers, Childs, *American Genius,* pp.375–6.
9. *Jennet Conant*. Ibid., p.355.
10. *Jennet Conant*. Ibid., p.356.
11. Birge, 'Physics Department,' vol. 5, chap.17, p.11.
12. *Jennet Conant*. Ibid., p.358.

Chapter 31: American Genius

1. *Sacred Secrets*. Ibid., pp.138–9.
2. Robert J. Lamphere & Tom Schachtman, *THE FBI-KGB War* (Random Hs, NY, 1986), pp.110–125.
3. *Sacred Secrets*. Ibid., p.139.

4. Yuri Modin. *My Five Cambridge Friends* (Hodder, London, 1994), pp.197–8.
5. *Sacred Secrets.* Ibid., p.139.
6. *American Prometheus.* Ibid., p.354.
7. *American Prometheus.* Ibid., p.355.
8. *Special Tasks.* Ibid., p.208.
9. *American Prometheus.* Ibid., p.358.
10. *Sacred Secrets.* Ibid., p.140.

Chapter 32: Enemies in Waiting

1. Jennet Conant. Ibid., p.365.
2. Jennet Conant. Ibid., pp.365–6.
3. Jennet Conant. Ibid., p.366.
4. Jennet Conant. Ibid., p.367.
5. Jennet Conant. Ibid., pp.367–8.
6. Jennet Conant. Ibid., p.368.
7. Jennet Conant. Ibid., p.369.
8. Jennet Conant. Ibid., pp.369–70.
9. *American Prometheus.* Ibid., p.401.

Chapter 33: Soviet Russia's Atom Bomb

1. Jennet Conant. Ibid., p.371.
2. Jennet Conant. Ibid., p.372.
3. Jennet Conant. Ibid., p.373.
4. The *Washington Post,* 10 May 1950.
5. *American Prometheus.* Ibid., pp.438–9.
6. *American Prometheus.* Ibid., p.440.
7. *American Prometheus.* Ibid., p.437.
8. J. Robert Oppenheimer. 'Atomic Weapons and American Policy', *Foreign Affairs,* July 1953, p.529.
9. Professor H. D. Smyth of Princeton University. 'The Smyth Report', Addendum to *The Manhattan Engineering District History* (1940–1945).
10. *American Prometheus.* Ibid., p.442.

Chapter 34: Conspiracy Theories

1. *Special Tasks.* Ibid., pp.207–8.
2. *American Prometheus.* Ibid., p.443.
3. *Special Tasks.* Ibid., p.204.
4. *American Prometheus.* Ibid., pp.443–4.

5. Basil Liddell Hart. *Lawrence of Arabia.* (DeCapo, NY, 1989). And Alex Danchev. *Alchemist of War: The Life of Basil Liddell Hart* (Weidenfeld, London, 1998).
6. Alan Brooke. *The War Diaries: 1939–1945.* Ed. Alex Danchev & Daniel Todman (Weidenfeld, London, 2001).
7. *American Prometheus*. Ibid., p.445.
8. *Special Tasks*. Ibid., p.209.
9. Jennet Conant. Ibid., p.374 and footnote.
10. Jennet Conant. Ibid., p.375.

Chapter 35: The Venona Revelations

1. Yuri Modin. Ibid., p.196.
2. Yuri Modin. Ibid., p.196.
3. *Special Tasks*. Ibid., p.190.
4. Walter Krivitsky. *I Was One of Stalin's Agents* (Enigma, NY, 1985).
5. Yuri Modin. Ibid., p.199.
6. Yuri Modin. Ibid.
7. Yuri Modin. Ibid., p.201.
8. Tom Driberg. Ibid., pp.93–4. Bodleian, MS, England, 6920, p.241.
9. Yuri Modin. Ibid., p.206.
10. Nigel West. *Molehunt* (Weidenfeld, London, 1987), p.137.
11. Yuri Modin. Ibid., p.208.

Chapter 36: The Witch-Hunt

1. *American Prometheus*. Ibid., p.454.
2. *American Prometheus*. Ibid., p.456.
3. *American Prometheus*. Ibid., pp.466–7.
4. *American Prometheus*. Ibid., p.467.

Chapter 37: The Problem of Survival

1. *American Prometheus*. Ibid., p.362.
2. *American Prometheus*. Ibid., p.446,
3. *American Prometheus*. Ibid., p.447.
4. Jennet Conant. Ibid., p.377.
5. James Conant. Private Diary entry.
6. *American Prometheus*. Ibid., p.449.
7. Robert J. Oppenheimer. *The Reith Lectures,* Lecture 6. BBC Home Service. Transmitted 20 December 1953.
8. Jennet Conant. Ibid., p.379.

Chapter 38: The Hidden Struggle for the H-bomb

1. F. A. Hayek. Ibid., p.199.
2. *American Prometheus*. Ibid., pp.467–8.
3. *American Prometheus*. Ibid., p.469.
4. *American Prometheus*. Ibid., p.465.
5. Jennet Conant. Ibid., p.380.
6. Jennet Conant. Ibid., pp.380–1.

Chapter 39: Trial by Hysteria

1. *American Prometheus*. Ibid., p.487.
2. *American Prometheus*. Ibid., p.488.
3. F. A. Hayek. Ibid., p.57.
4. *American Prometheus*. Ibid., p.498.
5. *American Prometheus*. Ibid., p.408.

Chapter 40: A Letter of Indictment

1. *American Prometheus*. Ibid., pp.499–500.
2. Jennet Conant. Ibid., p.382.
3. Source: Wikipedia. https://en.wikipedia.org/wiki/Katherine_Oppenheimer
4. Jennet Conant. Ibid., p.384.
5. Jennet Conant. Ibid., p.387.

Chapter 41: One Thing is Certain

1. *American Prometheus*. Ibid., p.558.
2. *American Prometheus*. Ibid., p.563.
3. *American Prometheus*. Ibid., p.567.
4. *Sacred Secrets*. Ibid., Index, p.388.
5. Igor Damaskin. Translator and Editor Geoffrey Elliott. Ibid.
6. *Sacred Secrets*. Ibid., p.51.
7. *Special Tasks*. Ibid., p.199.
8. Igor Damaskin. Ibid., p.207.
9. Geoffrey Elliott. Ibid., (Little Brown, Boston, 2001). Preface, p.2.
10. Atomic Heritage Foundation online. Ibid. (June 6, 2014).
11. Paul Rose. *Heisenberg and the Nazi Atomic Bomb Project, 1939-1945*. (University of California, 1998). Also David Cassidy. *Beyond Uncertainty; the Life and Science of Werner Heisenberg*. (Bellevue, NY 2009). Boris T. Pash. *The Alsos Mission*. (Ace, NY 1980). Leslie R. Groves. *Now it Can be Told*. (Da Capo, Boston 1983).

Index

A

Acheson, Dean, 147, 153, 189
Acheson-Lilienthal Report, 153
Addis, Dr. Thomas, 49
Adler, Felix, 11
Administration of Special Tasks (AST), 110
Air Force Command, 173
Air supremacy, 68
Alsos Mission, 72
American Civil Liberties Union, 50, 54
American Communist Party (CPUSA), 47, 57, 138, 186, 204
American Ethical Culture Society, 9
Anglo-American collaboration, 68
Anti-Oppenheimer Crusade, 193
Anti-Semitism, 11
Army Corps of Engineers, 73
Atomic bomb, The, 41
Atomic bomb project, 53
Atomic bomb tests, 154
Atomic Energy Commission, 1, 71, 147, 156, 185, 189, 209
Atomic Fission Bombs, 113
Atomic physics, 23
Atomic research, 53

B

Bacher, Robert, 86, 97, 114
Bacterial warfare, 7
Bainbridge, Kenneth, 115, 129, 131, 141
BBC Reith Lectures, 191

"Baker," Dr. Nicholas
Cover–name for Niels Bohr, 88, 125
Barbarossa, Project, 52
Barnett, Shirley, 102–3
Baruch, Bernard, 153–4
Battle of Britain, 6
Beria, Lavrentiy, 5, 111–12, 137, 171
Berkeley, 33–4, 78, 149, 153–4
Bernfeld, Siegfried, 50
Bethe, Hans, 29, 86, 91, 124, 126, 130, 175, 205
Bhagavad-Gita, 36, 113
Black Holes, 35
Blackett, Patrick, 19
Bletchley Park, 68
Blunt, Anthony, 156, 178–82
Bohr, Niels, 8, 91, 116–20
Bockscar, 143
Bolshevik Revolution, 6
Borden, William Liscum, 168–71
Born, Max, 24–5, 27–8, 41
Bridgeman, Percy, 16
British Embassy, Washington, 156, 177–8
British Mission, 93
Brodsky. A.J., 5
Bronowski, Jacob, 102, 146
Brooke, Field Marshal Alan, 173
Browder, Earl, 59, 61, 160, 186
Browder, Felix, 186
"Mr. Brown," 52
Bundy, McGeorge, 189–90, 208

Burgess, Guy, 62, 156, 177–82
Bush, Vannevar, 65–6, 73–4
Byrnes, James, 131, 133

C
Cairncross, John, 68–9, 156
California Institute of Technology (Caltech), 30, 172, 192
Calvinists, 156
Cambridge University, 22
Cambridge Five Spy Ring, 59, 156, 176–7
Capitalism, 37
Cavendish Laboratory, 18, 22, 129
Chadwick, James, 81
Chain reaction, 64
Chamberlain, Neville, 5
CHEKA, 52
Chevalier, Haakon, 47, 54, 76, 101, 158, 159
Chicago Group, The, 65
Chicago reactor, 81
Christ's College, 18, 22
Christy, Robert, 147
Churchill, Winston, 121, 176
CIA, 155
Coal mines, 42
Cohen, Roy, 195
Cold War, The, 146, 162
Combined Policy Committee, 4
Communism, 37, 158
Communist influence, 195
Communist Party, 3, 6, 44, 47, 49, 59, 104, 107, 151, 164
Compton, Arthur, 24, 53, 64–5, 67, 73–4, 80, 124
Conant, James Bryant, 65, 74, 80, 82, 141, 189–90, 192, 205
Contaminated material, 129
Coplon, Judith, 151–2, 155
Creative Destruction, 173
Criminality, 24
Critical assembly, 54
Critical mass, 64, 74, 90

Crouch, Paul, 167–8, 174, 184–5
Cyclotron, 82, 129

D
Dachau concentration camp, 41
Daily Worker, The, 104
Darkness at Noon, 4
Derogatory information, 191
Depression, The, 35–6, 42–3
Dirac, Paul, 23–4, 27
Dobb, Ernest, 6
Dostoevsky, 14, 20–1
DuBridge, Lee, 173, 187, 189, 200
Duffield, Priscilla Greene, 175
Dulles, Allen, 139
Dullet, Joe, 57, 103–105
du Pont de Nemours, 83

E
Eccentricity, 26
Ehrenfest, Paul, 31
Einstein, Albert, 4, 8, 16, 23–4, 27, 200, 204
Eisenhower, President Dwight D., 1, 6, 173, 187, 189, 193–4, 206
Electron, 35
Elliott, John Lovejoy, 12
Eltenton, George, 76, 159
Energy and Mass, 64
Enola Gay, 143
"Enormoz," 78, 125
Ethical culture, 11
Ethical qualms, 127
Ethical studies, 12

F
Falkoff, "Pop", 49, 54
Fascism, 37
Fat Man, 114, 129, 140–1
Father of the Atom Bomb, 157
FBI, 53, 75, 78, 101, 126, 137–8, 151, 155, 157, 159, 162, 177, 183, 185, 198–9, 201
Ferguson, Francis, 12

Fermi, Enrico, 8, 65, 80
Fermi Enrico Award, 8, 209
Feynman, Richard, 24, 90–1, 99
Finletter, Thomas K., 172, 187–8, 192
Fissioning, 67
Fitin, Major Pavel, 125
Florev. George, 5
Foreign Office, 177, 179
Franco, General, 46
Freud, Sigmund, 50
Fuchs, Klaus, 93, 122–7, 162, 205

G

Gadget, The, 114, 131
Gardner, Meredith, 155–6, 170, 176–7
Garrison, William Lloyd, 199–200, 205
General Theory of Relativity, 23
Germany, 36
Gide, André, 26
Gold, Harry, 97, 124, 126
Goodyear Tire and Rubber
    Company, 81
Göttingen, 24
Gray, Gordon, 201
Green, Priscilla, 102
Griggs, David Tressel, 172–3, 187–8
Greenglass, David, 126
Groves, General Leslie, 66, 72, 75, 77,
    80–2, 85–6, 97, 99, 101, 106–7,
    109, 113–21, 127, 130–1, 134,
    141, 153
GRU, 124, 176
Guernica bombing, 46

H

Hahn, Otto, 71
Haigerloch German reactor, 72
Harris, "Bomber", 5
Harris, Kitty, 58, 63, 100, 101,
    103–110, 160, 210, 212
Harrison, Mrs. Kitty, 56–63
Hart, Basil Liddell, 173
Harvard Crimson, 15
Harvard University, 13, 43, 145

Harwell Research Facility, 126
Heisenberg, Werner, 18, 22, 24, 27–8,
    32, 53, 72, 117–18
Hiroshima, 143
Hiss, Alger, 126, 162, 184
Hitler, Adolph, 6, 69, 131
Hitler's secret weapons, 6–7, 69–70
Hobbs, J.C., 95–6
Homer, 156, 176, 179
Hoover, J. Edgar, 151–2, 162, 169, 183
Hopkins, Harry, 64
Houtermans, Fritz, 26, 55
HUAC hearing, 164, 183
H-bomb, 166, 171–2, 186, 189–90,
    192, 194
H-bomb, Soviet Russian, 207

I

Identity crisis, 18
Imperial Chemical Industries (ICI), 53
International Brigade, The, 48

J

Jackson, C.D., 193–4
Japan, 139
Japanese targets, 135
Johnson, President Lyndon B., 210
Jones, Ernest, 50
Jones, Dr. R.V., 70
Jornada del Muerto, 115
Jung, Carl, 45
"Jumbo," 129
Justice Department, 183

K

Kaiser Wilhelm Institute, 65
Kapitza, Peter, 120
Kellex, 95–6
Kennedy, President John F, 209
KGB, 59, 106, 171 176, 179
Kheifetz, Gregori, 52–3, 97, 184, 210
Kierkegaard, 14
King, Admiral, 134
Kistiakowsky, George, 141

Kokura, 143
Korovin, 179–81
Kremlin, 4, 52, 176, 187, 204
Krishna, 36
Khrushchev, Nikita, 111, 172–3, 209
Krivitsky, Walter, 177
Kurchatov, 174
Kursk, Battle of, 68

L
Lamphere, Robert, 155
Lansdale, Colonel, 76, 106–8, 206
Lawrence, E.O., 34, 49, 51, 65, 74, 82,
    85, 133, 141, 145, 149
Lawrence, T.E., 173
Letter of Indictment, 191, 202
Libertarian ethic, 158, 192
Lilienthal, David, 149, 153, 162, 192
Little Boy, 114
Longshoremen, 42
Los Alamos, 74, 85, 87, 100, 113, 117,
    122, 153
Los Pinos, 31
Lutheran conscience, 126, 156

M
Maclean, Donald, 4, 53, 58–9, 62, 156,
    176–82
Maclean, Melinda, 58–9, 179, 181
Manhattan Project, 5, 65–6, 69, 74, 78,
    97, 101, 113, 118, 124, 131, 133,
    138, 146, 162
Marks, Herb, 184–5, 194–5, 199, 206
Malenkov, 172, 207
Marshall, General George C.,
    148, 151
Marshall Plan, The, 157
Marxism, 1
Master Race theory, The, 42
MacArthur, General Douglas,
    134, 144
McCarthy, Senator Joseph, 151, 162,
    164, 183, 195
McKibbin, Dorothy, 87, 96–9, 174, 209

Medal of Merit, 151
Mein Kampf, 42, 45
Menzies, Stewart, 70
Merkulov, Vsevolod, 137–8
Military Strategy (U.S.), 166
Millikan, Robert, 22
MI5, 126, 155, 176–80
MI6, 70, 156
Modin, Yuri, 156, 177–82
Molecules, 28
Morrison, Herbert, 181
Moscow Centre, 4, 53, 58–9, 61, 100,
    106, 110, 122, 132, 155, 158, 171,
    179, 207
Murder Camps, 144
Mussolini, Benito, 46, 146

N
Nagasaki, 143
NATO, 173
Nazi Party, 6, 36
Nazi Germany, 69
Nazis, 12
Nelson, Steve, 57, 78, 104, 152, 183
Neurosis, 24
Neutrons, 130
New Deal, 48, 54
New Mexico, 5, 14, 31, 60, 88,
    145, 175
New York Stock Exchange, 1
Nichols, Kenneth, 191, 198
Nimitz, Admiral, 134
Nixon, Richard, 184, 188
NKVD, 4–5, 52, 58, 63, 78, 110, 124,
    176, 211
Nobel Prize, 8, 16, 18, 23, 32–3, 64–5,
    82, 86, 120, 209
North China Daily News, 52
Nuclear Arms Race, 147, 166
Nuclear bomb, 55
Nuclear chain reaction, 41
Nuclear energy, 67
Nuclear reactor, 7
Nuclear superiority, 166

O

Oak Ridge plant, 115
Office of Scientific Research and
    Development, 67, 73
Oppenheimer. Ella, 9, 36
Oppenheimer, Emil, 9
Oppenheimer, Frank, 13, 30, 33, 37,
    76, 101, 109, 115, 152, 158, 162,
    164, 175
Oppenheimer, Julius, 9, 35, 36, 50
Oppenheimer, Katherine, 76, 86, 95,
    100–102, 106–10, 144, 159–60,
    172, 174, 176–7, 182, 187, 194–5,
    199, 201–4, 210, 212
Oppenheimer, Baby Katherine, 108
Oppenheimer, Peter, 101, 108, 174
Oppemheimer, Robert, 1–240
Oslo Report, The, 70
Ovakimian, G, 111–12

P

Pacific War, 131, 136
Page, Katherine, 31, 175
Pash, Colonel Boris, 74, 76–8, 107,
    160
Pauli, Wolfgang, 27, 32–3
Pearl Harbour, 55
Peenemünde, 71
Peierls, Rudolf, 87, 89, 93, 124
Perro Caliente, 3, 36, 40, 60, 142, 145,
    174–5
Philby, Kim, 62, 156, 176–7
Pilotless aircraft, 7
Planck, Max, 23
Plutonium, 55, 65
Plutonium bomb, 5
Plutonium 239, 73, 81, 92
Political activism, 48, 50, 149
Pontecorvo, Bruno, 97, 127
Positron, 35
Presbyterian, 74, 156,
Princeton University, 24, 145
Problem Number One, 106, 112–13,
    121, 132

Production capacity, 67
Project Vista, 172, 192
Protestant Work Ethic, 95
Proust, Marcel, 21
Psychiatry, 21
Purges, 111

Q

Quantum mechanics, 8, 18, 23,
Quantum physics, 18
Quantum theory, 27

R

Rabi, Isidor, 33, 37, 86, 99–100,
    152–3, 188, 205–6
RAF, 5
Ramseyer, Frank Wells Jnr, 103
Rand, Ayn, 44
Reagan, President Ronald, 210
Red Scare, The, 2, 40
Rocket projectiles, 7
Robb, Roger, 200, 204–5
Roosevelt, President Franklin Delano,
    4, 42, 55, 64, 67, 73, 81,
    96, 113
Rosenberg, Julius & Ethel, 126
Rotblat, Joseph, 121, 127
Russian Embassy, London, 178–9
Russell, Bertrand, 17
Russian Intelligence Archives, 211
Russia's Atomic Bomb, 166
Rutherford, Sir Ernest, 17

S

Sakow, Andrei S., 207
San Fracisco Communist Party, 49
Sangre de Cristo Mountains, 31
Santa Fe, 87, 96, 101, 124,
    172, 175
Schumpeter, Joseph, 173
Scientist X, 183
Scope of Soviet Activity in the United
    States, 61
Second World War, 35

Security clearance, 66, 162
Security and secrecy, 65
Semyonov, Sam, 97, 124
Serber, Robert, 38, 43, 60, 92, 136, 164
Sherr, Pat, 108–9
Shrödinger, Erwin, 22, 24
Skardon, William, 126
Social justice, 10, 46
Somervell, Major General, 66
Soviet Intelligence, 96
Soviet Russia, 6, 54, 76, 101, 151
Spanish Civil War, 46, 57, 104
Spanish Refugee Appeal, 49
Special relativity, 8
SS, The, 42
Stalin, Josef, 5, 52, 110
Stevenson, Adlai, 188–9
Stimson, Henry, 113, 128, 133,
    143, 146
Stone & Weber, 83
Strassmann, Fritz, 71
Strategic Air Command (SAC), 187
Strauss, Lewis, 71, 165, 171, 173,
    185–6, 191–5, 198–200, 208
Student Liberal Club, 16
Sudoplatov, Pavel, 97, 110–11, 171–2,
    174, 211
Szilard, Leo, 4, 65, 116, 131–2,
    135–6

T
Tamm, Igor, 5
Tatlock, Jean, 43–6, 49–50, 56, 77
Teller, Edward, 89, 93, 147, 166,
    171–2, 174, 190, 206
Ten Commandments, The, 37
Tennessee Eastman, 84
Theatre of the Streets, 42
Theoretical physics, 23
Thomson, J.J., 18
Tolman, Edward, 90, 131
Tolstoy, 2
Trade unions, 42,
Trinity College, 177

Trinity, Project, 114, 129
Trinity Test, 114, 131
Trinity tower, 131
Tube Alloys, 53, 68
Trilling, Diana, 202
Trinity College, 6, 37, 156
Truman, President Harry S, 113, 139,
    142–3, 147, 149–50, 153,
    166, 176

U
Ulam, Stanislaw, 171
Ullstein Newspaper Press, 41
Ultra machine, 68
Un-American Activities Committee,
    162, 183, 201
Uncertainty Principle, 22, 33
Unconditional surrender, 139
Union Carbide, 81
Union Miniéres, 83
United Nations Atomic Energy
    Commission, 153
University of Chicago, 53
University of Washington, 208
Uranium, 53
Uranium bomb, 4, 65, 124
Uranium Club, 71
Uranium ore, 72
Uranium 235, 65, 74, 81, 82, 92, 183
Urey, Harold C, 65, 131
U.S. Air Force, 173, 187
U.S. Military Strategy, 192

V
Vandenberg, Hoyt, 188
Venona Cipher, The, 58, 97, 126, 152,
    155–6, 176
Vemork, 5
Verne, Jules, 6
Vista Report, 187
Voice of America, 195
Volpe, Joe, 174, 184–5, 195, 199
von Neumann, John, 94, 99
V2 Rockets, 72

W

Weimar Republic, 24
Weinberg, Joseph, 183–5
Weiskopf, Victor, 28, 93,
   128, 141
Wells, H.G., 6
Whitehead, Albert North, 17
White House, 152
Wigner, Eugene, 65
William James Lectures, 208
Wilson, Robert, 87, 127–8, 148

Winchell, Walter, 203–4
Wire-tapping, 53, 77, 152, 199–200

Y

Yagoda, Genrikh, 110
Yezhov, Nicolai, 110

Z

Zarubin, Elizabeth, 52, 58, 63, 97, 103,
   138, 172, 210
Zarubin, Vasili, 52